Sexual Health
and
Erotic Freedom

Sexual Health
and
Erotic Freedom

Barnaby B. Barratt

Copyright © 2005 by Barnaby B. Barratt.

Email: *Barnaby@BodyPrayerPath.org*
With a Foreword by Vern Bullough
Cover art by Jennifer Everland
Photography by Bryce R. Denison

Library of Congress Number:		2005901579
ISBN:	Hardcover	1-4134-8784-X
	Softcover	1-4134-8783-1

All rights reserved. No part of this book may be reproduced or transmitted in any form or by any means, electronic or mechanical, including photocopying, recording, or by any information storage and retrieval system, without permission in writing from the copyright owner.

This book was printed in the United States of America.

To order additional copies of this book, contact:
Xlibris Corporation
1-888-795-4274
www.Xlibris.com
Orders@Xlibris.com

26821

Contents

Foreword by Vern Bullough 9

Introduction 11

Section One
Crises of Health and Freedom

1: The Rise of Sex Fascism 21
2: The Sexification of America 37
3: A Note on Anti-Sexuality and
 the State of "Normality" 49
4: What would Sexual Health look like? 57

Section Two
Why are we so frightened?

5: The Dynamics of Shame and Guilt 71
6: The Theory of Polysexuality, Traumatization,
 and Incest Taboo 87
7: Suppression, Repression, Inhibition,
 and Compulsivity 119
8: Fear and Aggression 141

Section Three
Choreographies of Pleasure

9: Our Sensual Bodies: Becoming Naked 157
10: Our Sensual Bodies: Touching Tenderly 161

11: Our Sensual Bodies: The Glories of our Genitals 169
12: Playing with Power and Pain 179
13: The Economics of Sexual Service 189

SECTION FOUR
THE FREEDOM TO BE HEALTHY—
VISIONS OF EROTIC LIBERATION

14: Visioning our Birthright 199
15: Five Styles of Sexual Partnering 209
16: The Ten Keys to Successful Sexual Partnering 241
17: Five Ways of Nurturing Sexually
     Healthy Children 281
18: Notes on Surviving America's Sex Wars 297

SECTION FIVE
SEXUALITY IS A (THE) SPIRITUAL MATTER

19: Human Spirit Incarnate 307
20: Notes on Tantric Orgasming (and Prānayāma) 331
21: The Divinity of Human Sexuality 361

Acknowledgements and Appreciations 371
About the Author 373

May all beings be happy and free;
May these writings contribute to the happiness and freedom of all beings.

FOREWORD

Vern Bullough, PhD, DSc, RN.

In this book, Dr. Barnaby B. Barratt, a certified psychoanalyst, sexuality educator, sex therapist, and tantric facilitator, offers us his recipe for sexual health—as he himself has experienced it. He defines sexual health in terms of enjoyable activities which are safe, sane, and consensual. He emphasizes the positive dimension of these criteria as guidepoints—sexual health is not to be defined as a list of things we should not do! In a low key, but deliberately provocative way, he discusses the joys of sexual pleasure in diverse forms, from heterosexual dyadic partnering, to polyamory, playful sadomasochism, self-pleasuring, and same-sex relations.

Barratt can best be described as a missionary whose aim is to liberate us from the shame and guilt which he believes serve to inhibit erotic enjoyment in life. The result is an interesting and challenging book, which compels readers to examine their own belief systems and to realize the erotic potential available to us all. Many will find this book shocking; many will find it enlightening; but few will be able to put it down.

November 2004

Dr. Bullough is Distinguished Professor Emeritus at the State University of New York; Emeritus Professor at California State University (Northridge); and formerly Dean of Natural and Social Science as well as Distinguished Professor at the State University of New York (Buffalo).

INTRODUCTION

I believe passionately that humanity needs a more loving world, and that a more loving world can only be achieved if we humans are free to enjoy the pleasures of our bodies. I believe that, at the heart of our natural being, we humans are a living embodiment of the energies of the divine. So a more loving world *cannot* be achieved if we suppress or repress our natural erotic nature, just as it cannot be achieved by the oppression and persecution of one group by another.

Simply stated, the creation of a more loving world requires sexual health and erotic freedom. We know this because all the evidence in front of us points to the fact that

> *Human malice arises when our natural erotic exuberance is coercively constrained, curbed or curtailed.*

The health and freedom of our erotic enjoyment in life are inherently connected, and they are the wellspring of our human potential for happiness.

In the name of countless religious and political ideologies, many people try to avoid these fundamental truths—for example, by simply denying them, by deliberating over them, or by qualifying them into oblivion. However, as this book will elaborate, both scientific investigation and spiritual "analysis" point to these conclusions. Indeed, they are self-evident. We know that, when we humans are deprived of the sensual and sexual enjoyment of our bodies, we react with spite, vindictiveness, hostility and anger. In sum, we are malicious, and malice arises precisely from sensual and sexual inhibition.

Lovemaking is humanity's saving grace,
and most of the ailments from which the human race suffers could be averted if we allowed ourselves to lovemake more freely.

I know this from over thirty years in which I have been engaged in four kinds of professional experience: as a scholar and university professor, studying psychology, anthropology and philosophy; as a clinician, practicing psychoanalytic healing as well as offering sex therapy; as a sexuality educator, working in many different settings, from lecture halls to neighborhood meetings; and as a tantric facilitator, offering guidance on the sacred path that is delineated by our sexual-spiritual lives. I also know this from my own personal experience—from my own emotional and spiritual journey since childhood.

Life provides humanity with plenty of hardship and adversity. Many of us experience terrifying natural disasters, and we all face the inevitability of disease, decay and death. However, beyond these life experiences of pain and loss, we humans have a remarkable capacity to make life unnecessarily miserable for each other and for ourselves. We exploit, bully and abuse each other. We commit violence and warfare, and we engage in all kinds of prejudicial and hurtful acts against our own human brethren. We institute multiple systems of social domination—institutions whereby the many become impoverished, subjugated, malnourished, ill-housed, and disempowered, so that the few may become richer, more powerful, and more wasteful. We bargain with weapons of mass destruction and we are, as a race, rapidly destroying the planet we inhabit—committing ecological suicide in our own home. Whatever humanity's virtues, it is surely true that we humans are distinctive because, unlike any other living species, we are tragically, and uniquely, capable of hatred. We are distinct in our capacity for malice.

However, although we would seem to have a unique potential to be malicious, we humans also have a remarkable potential for love. Unlike other animals, we are able to engage in self-reflection, to consider the meaningfulness or meaninglessness of our lives, to experience a certain freedom of choice over how we think and feel . . . and we are capable of living life in Love.

So why don't we? Why, when we know what "Love" is, do we so frequently choose to exploit and abuse other humans, to impose our beliefs on others, to destroy the planet, and to make war with each other? What is at the root of our discontent? What lies behind our avarice and our apparent need to dominate others? What activates our judgmentalism and our propensity for hostility and violence?

Obviously, my answer—that human malice arises when our freedom to enjoy the sensuality of life is constrained or curtailed—may be an oversimplification. But the fact that it may be oversimplified must not lead us to avoid its essential truth. Because this is a major truth, a truth that has been systematically avoided through the ages and that is still the best available answer we have to remedy the tragedies of being human.

If we were raised without fear and ignorance of our sensual and sexual selves, if we were accustomed to the enjoyment of our embodiment, if we were erotically free, our capacity for malice would be eradicated. Fearfulness and frustration in relation to our sensual and sexual selves produce our capacity for malice, and the energies of our erotic nature are the spiritual source of our healing.

Somewhere in our imagination, almost all of us hold a vision of life replete with erotic happiness—a life in which our sensual and sexual enjoyment is engaged with freedom, spontaneity and ethicality in a way that is entirely natural. This vision could be realized—except for the fact that, as I will explain, our addiction to the forces of anti-sexuality keeps us locked in our own imprisonment.

This book offers some suggestions as to why this is so, and how we might set ourselves free. It consists of a set of brief essays—"essayettes" one might say—that are intended as a challenge to the preconceived and received ideas that many of us have about "sex." I intend to write in a way that is provocative and unsettling, because I believe we live in such a sexually insane culture that our ideas about sexuality need to be reconsidered radically. In a modest way, this small book is intended to help us rethink our vision of humankind's erotic nature and to realize our spiritual potential for happiness.

I think of these essays as written "from my left-hand"—since it is the hand I use to pleasure myself, rather than the hand I use for writing grocery lists, letters to friends, or professional articles. This imagery means three things to me.

First, I am not writing in the style of a professional publication, nor of a conventional autobiography. This book is written for anyone to read and—hopefully—be provoked or stimulated in relation to his or her vision of human sexuality. So it is neither a comprehensive textbook nor a scientific document. Although I know that there is scientific evidence to support the opinions expressed here, the pages are not filled with cumbersome footnotes and references. Instead, this book is intended as an easily readable—and hopefully enjoyable—statement of advocacy for sexual freedom.

Second, although these essays are largely composed on the basis of my professional and personal experiences and opinions, I hope it will become clear that this book is not an indulgence in religious ideology or political propaganda. Rather, my intention is that you will understand these essays as a coherent effort to free human sexuality from the grip of religion and politics. The intent here is to avoid sermonizing, moralizing, or otherwise engaging in tiresome rhetoric, but nonetheless to make a case for the ethicality of erotic freedom—simply because, contrary to traditional religious and political "wisdom," our potential for sensual and sexual pleasure is humanity's saving grace.

So I think of these essays as running counter to all that is traditionally peddled by church and state. However, my own *spiritual* practice (which does *not* involve an affiliation to any particular religion such as Judaism, Christianity, Islam, or Hinduism) is actually integral to the messages presented in these essays—and I will not fail to indicate this when and where it seems helpful.

So if you are a believer in some version of God, I hope these essays will awaken you to the realization that, when "He" or "She" endowed us with an abundance of sexual energies, it was surely God's intention to empower our spiritual growth and to offer us the most powerful way by which to absolve or eradicate our human egotism—because it is our lovemaking that brings us closest to God and permits us to realize our union with the divine, and it is our egotism that is the malicious aspect of our humanity that keeps us from living life in Love.

And if you are not a believer in God, if you are committed to humanistic thinking and are understandably wary of all notions of "spirituality," please bear with the notion of spirituality that animates these pages. You will find this notion of spirituality relevant to your atheism and, more importantly, you will discover in these essays a radical vision of our collective potential that is truly humanistic.

So this book will be an anathema to priests and politicians of all sorts. However, for anyone who dares to think and to act beyond the rules and regulations imposed on us by religion and politics, it will present passionately the divine potential of being human.

The third way in which these essays are "left-handed" is that they come not only from my extensive experiences as a professional, but are laced with experiences from my "private" life. The evidence for their arguments is derived from my personal journey as an alive and sexually active human being, as well as from my thirty years of practice as a clinician, educator, and scholar. So this book is a publicly "left-handed" challenge to the ways we traditionally treat our sexuality—a challenge made on the grounds of the totality of my professional and personal experience.

I have read several thousand works on human sexuality—books covering every aspect of the topic in writings that are variously scientific, journalistic, political and religious. And I have become weary—and wary—of authors, even so-called "experts," who write in a manner that does not acknowledge openly their own sexual interests and experiences. There is not only a basic dishonesty or hypocrisy in such writings, but also the disguised expression of a fundamental sex-phobia. Why should we listen to any priest, politician, scientist, or so-called "sex expert," who fails to speak freely of his or her own sexual enjoyments?

What credibility has the science of sexuality if it does not include the sexuality of the scientist? What credence should we give to the diatribes of priests and politicians if they speak only to condemn the pleasures of others, and do not candidly admit the pleasures that they themselves enjoy? And what credibility have "sex experts," if they do not acknowledge freely that they love those activities about which they claim expertise? Those who write about sexual matters, and who hope to influence the opinions of others, must expose their own erotic experiences if they are to be worthy of our respect. Otherwise, we perpetuate the very dishonesty and hypocrisy that constantly traps and strangles our sensual and sexual lives.

In these essays, I intend to be worthy of your respect. So both directly and "between the lines," this book gives information about my personal sexual experiences. The motive for these disclosures is not—I believe—some excessive inclination toward exhibitionism. Rather, I write about my own sexual life both because it is the ground from which my views about sexuality have developed, and also because not to do so would—in my opinion—constitute a major breach of integrity.

Our social and cultural organizations have, for too long, made our sexuality a battleground for anxiety and conflict. Despite the hoopla of the public media, which often appears to be sexually stimulating, our personal sexuality has always been shrouded in secrecy, outright falsifications and systematic distortions. For me to write about the necessity of erotic freedom for humanity's health and, at the same time, to maintain some sort of professional facade of non-disclosure would be, at the very least, inconsistent with my beliefs about the sanctity of sexual expression. Indeed, it would surely be a perpetuation of our general tendency to treat sexual expression as if it were a matter to be kept veiled out of some sense of shame and guilt.

So whenever and wherever it would seem to be helpful—and without any apology, shame or guilt—I will straightforwardly disclose my private life, simply because I believe that

The sooner we can all be open with our sexual selves, the happier our planet will be.

It is my hope that, in some modest way, *Sexual Health and Erotic Freedom* will contribute to our liberation, and in this spirit, I offer these essays "from my left-hand."

SECTION ONE

Crises of health and freedom

1

The Rise of Sex Fascism

It is not difficult to believe that America is on the brink of civil war—a war over sexuality. Perhaps this war is already underway. Initially, this is a "culture war" fueled by vicious ideologies, in which some people believe, self-righteously, that they should impose their particular values on the rest of us, that they should coercively obstruct the private pleasures enjoyed by some of us, that they should legislate to control our disposition of our own bodies, and that they should generally enforce their particular version of "morality" on our personal lives.

So actually, this war is already in progress—many injurious battles are currently being fought all around us—and yet, thus far, this is still a cultural war that is partially hidden from public scrutiny.

Consider the following seven events. They all occurred quite recently within a few miles of my neighborhood. They mostly went unreported in the mainstream media—or were subjected to willfully distorted "reporting"—and thus, in some sense, their significance went unnoticed by the vast majority of the public living in the area. I relate them here, because they happened, and because I believe they are indicative of some terrifying developments currently shifting the fabric of American culture. For the sake of the victims, I will omit identifying details.

➢ A neighborhood bookstore maintains an area accessible only to adults over 21 years—an area in which videos and magazines depicting nonviolent sexual acts are rented and sold. The store is quite successful, and evidently enjoyed by the blue-collar citizens who live nearby. One day an out-of-uniform Assistant Sheriff walks in and purchases several magazines and a video, all featuring adults enjoying various forms of heterosexual intercourse. The police subsequently arrive. The store is closed down and padlocked. The owner is charged with multiple counts of obscenity. The local Prosecutor claims that the purchased materials depict "depraved and unnatural acts," violating the community's cultural standards, and without any possible redeeming educational, scientific or artistic merit.

As an expert witness for the defense, I had the opportunity to view all these materials. Without exception, they showed sexual activity that occurs daily in homes across America, so they could not possibly have violated this community's standards (especially since the local community was causing the store to be quite profitable). For the sexually inhibited, these materials certainly might have had an educational value, and they might even be said to be artistic in many respects. It is not insignificant that the video depicted interracial couples and threesomes, and that the bookstore is located in a county that is mostly segregated, for the Prosecutor managed to bring the case to an all-white jury, and was clearly hoping not only to stir their "moral indignity" at these "outrageous obscenities," but also to subtly deploy racist fears to add fuel to the flames of self-righteousness.

That, in this case at least, the Prosecutor failed and the store owner went free is perhaps almost irrelevant—because the store's business was disrupted for many months, and the owner made to shoulder the burden of substantial legal costs.

Moreover the Prosecutor's office did not stop there. A couple of months after the trial, another Assistant Sheriff entered the store, purchased two magazines (one depicting innocuous scenes of heterosexual intercourse, and the other an artsy publication celebrating famous episodes in the history of gay erotica), and the owner was again charged with "obscenity." The owner is likely to be bankrupted by such a pattern of repeated and persistent harassment. The Prosecutor's office evidently has financially deep pockets and a zealous, politically-vested interest in the pursuit of such "cases."

It is perhaps noteworthy that almost nothing about these proceedings appeared in the local newspapers or on local television channels at the time—but at election time, the Sheriff was hailed as the man who stands for "cleaning up the neighborhoods." It is also noteworthy that all this occurred in a county that has potholes in almost every road, a large number of homeless citizens, an even larger population of impoverished and undereducated children, and an infant mortality rate rivaling that of a third-world country. Despite this context, substantial finances are evidently available in order to harass—and make political capital out of harassing—a vendor of unremarkable erotic imagery. Whose interests are being served by these actions of Sheriff and Prosecutor? It would seem that, at the very least, a self-righteous religious crusade is being conducted—guided by religious ideals that are conveniently fashioned to coincide with self-interested political ambitions.

➤ In a local park, a gay man crosses paths with an undercover officer from the local Vice Unit. The Officer does not identify himself, but strikes up a friendly conversation with the citizen. They chat and eventually the Officer suggests, rather seductively, that they go somewhere private for a sexual liaison. The gay man agrees, an apartment is chosen as a suitable location, and the gay man gets into his car to drive to the rendezvous. Two blocks down the road, a police car, with sirens and flashing lights, stops him and he is handcuffed. At the police station, he is told he is being charged with soliciting, as well as "lewd and lascivious conduct." His car is impounded, and money has to be paid before the car will be returned to its owner. The gay man is also told that several other charges can be added, including that of resisting arrest, if he fails to write a confession of his guilt immediately. He is also told that the "no fuss" admission of guilt, and the prompt payment of a severe fine, will result in minimal publicity for the case.

Stories such as this are common—although rarely publicized in the media—and there are several variations and outcomes. In some instances, the Officer will accept oral sex from the gay man, then arrest him, and lie about the events in court. In some instances, the gay man will be so intimidated by the possibility that his family or his workplace could learn about his cruising for homosexual connection—if, indeed, that is what he was doing—that he will plead guilty to any charge and pay any fine in order to hope that the incident might go unnoticed. In some instances, the gay man may spend time locked up. And in some rare instances, the gay man will attempt to fight the charges and will come to find that, in our legal system, when it is the word of a sexual minority against the word of a policeman, the word of the Officer is almost invariably believed.

➢ A small group of women—"lipstick lesbians" and married bisexual women—decide to make money by hiring out their services for bachelor parties. At the request of their customers, two women will come to a party, perform a striptease dance, and then pleasure each other orally or with a double dildo. The performance lasts about thirty minutes, and the charge is several hundred dollars. The women's services are much in demand, and the business is successful—

until a discontented customer, who had apparently imagined that the performers would be available for sexual intercourse, contacts a local law enforcement agency. An undercover operation is initiated, and a large budget is earmarked to ensure its success.

At the denouement of this undercover investigation, eighteen Officers rent a private apartment, and telephone two women to arrange a party. The Officers ask for the striptease, cunnilingus and double dildo act, pay the women handsomely, clap and cheer throughout the performance, and then handcuff and arrest the women as soon as the requested entertainment is over. The local Prosecutor arranges for the home of the principal owner of the business to be padlocked, and all her bank accounts are frozen—some of these accounts are in far away cities where her family live.

This case came to court with charges of solicitation, lewd and lascivious behavior in a public place, and performance of obscene acts. The Judge was a well known member of a religious fraternity, and the Prosecutor was his "fraternity brother." The charge of solicitation was dropped—presumably because there was no solicitation. But the Prosecutor argued that the performance constituted "lewd and lascivious" activity in a public place (despite the fact that the apartment's door was locked, and the drapes of all its windows were closed). He also argued that two women using a double dildo and going down on each other are "inherently obscene acts." The Judge agreed. The defendant was fined heavily and, since she was driven out of business, an appeal could not be afforded.

➢ Another woman—a delightful, witty, intelligent and robust woman in her thirties—decides to offer her services as a dominatrix to comparatively wealthy, professional men in her community. Over a couple of years, she develops a carefully selected clientele that includes corporate CEOs, accountants, doctors, and at least one high-court Judge. She works out of her home, which is equipped with a fantasy dungeon in the basement. Her clients come for appointments individually—most of them come once a week, or at least one or two times each month. Charging a few hundred dollars for each session, she will spend an hour or so playing fantasy games, mock humiliation, spanking, and even lightly whipping her clients. She is quite discreet, and her clients seem well pleased with her services.

One Christmas season, she makes the mistake of inviting several of her business associates to a costume party. As the group gathers for hors d'oeuvres, the home is raided by uniformed police. The front door is broken down. Several of her clients are immediately told to go home; others at the party are held face down on the floor at gunpoint. The hostess is handcuffed and mauled. The party is broken up.

No arrests were made and no charges were ever recorded. Indeed, there seems to be no police record of the event. The woman discontinued her services, and destroyed her book of clients. However, six weeks later, her car happened to stall out in a deserted parking lot in the early hours of the morning, a police car stopped, recorded her license plate, radioed the information, and drove off. After some time, two police cars from a different township arrive, and several Officers get out. They clearly know the identity of the woman, and proceed to throw her to the ground and rough her up. Then they depart, leaving her injured. Subsequently, the woman, probably wisely, made arrangements to sell her home and leave town.

➢ For many years, an elderly gentleman ran a social club for swingers. Once a month the club rented a banquet hall from the local Veterans Association and, by prior arrangement, couples could meet to eat, chat, and dance. It was strictly a "Members-Only" organization. No sexual activity took place on the premises, but it was generally understood that the monthly social event was a private place that couples interested in finding other couples open to swinging could connect and make arrangements for subsequent liaisons.

A few months before the annual Christmas dance, several Officers from the local Vice Squad joined the club using false names and identities. At several parties, they even became a little conspicuous for their "wild" behavior on the dance floor—for example, encouraging others to partially undress. However, towards midnight on the evening of this Christmas dance, these Officers quietly left the dance floor and surreptitiously opened all the emergency exits to the building. At the stroke of midnight, a "Swat Team" invaded the building with guns and bullhorns. The men in the club were made to lie on the ground at gunpoint. Each woman was "strip searched"—literally—several times by the male Officers. All the members of the club were held there for several hours. The money box containing a few thousand dollars that had been collected as entrance fees, and the folder containing the club's membership list, were confiscated. Many of the cars that were legally parked in the street outside the club were impounded—and could only be retrieved days later for fines of several hundred dollars each.

Significantly enough, there was no media coverage of this event, and no charges were ever brought against the elderly club owner. He was, however, driven out of business—the club never operated again—and a few days later he was hospitalized for a stroke.

➢ In the Seniors' Home where they both live, a woman in her early eighties makes friends with a man in his late seventies. The man is terminally ill with cancer. She walks daily from one end of the facility, where her room is located, to the other end, where he resides. She sits by his bedside, holding his hand, and chatting with him for hours. Occasionally, she slips into his bed, hugging, kissing, and snuggling next to his frail body.

We do not know whether they touch genitals or not, whether they have intercourse or not. More importantly, why should this question be of any importance to anyone except these two elderly lovers? We do know, however, that the couple was discovered in bed by one of the staff, and the woman told that she could no longer visit her friend, and that she must confine herself to the women's quarters. When the man complains, and his adult children ask the Director of the facility why their father can no longer see his friend, they are told that, because the woman has a slight dementia, her family could possibly allege that she is being raped and could perhaps take legal action against the facility.

The man died a few weeks later, deprived of the company of his lover. The woman was bereft and a little confused, but some months later she made friends with another resident, a woman in the room next to hers. As this friendship grew, they would spend hours together, sometimes falling asleep cuddling and holding each other. They were discovered, entwined in each other's arms, in the early hours of one morning. The Director summoned the elderly lady to his office, told her that she should be concerned for her "reputation" and warned her that people could think she was a "slut." When the woman protested, her family was contacted and asked to transfer her to a different facility.

➢ A sixteen-year boy in his junior year of high-school starts dating a girl who had recently enrolled as a freshman. They see each other at school gatherings and occasional parties. They talk at recess, and over the telephone. As the weeks go by, they become more affectionate, introduce each other to their families, and go as dates to some family functions. After some discussion and preparation, they decide they want to go beyond kissing, and that they feel ready to experience full intercourse. On the weekend after the boy's seventeenth birthday, they affectionately have sex. Condoms are used, and the experience is considered "sweet" by both of them. The girl is still under sixteen.

Some weeks later, as the summer approaches, they decide to separate and remain friends. They begin dating others. At the beginning of her sophomore year, the girl finds herself pressured into having sex with two other boys, both much older than she. She is upset about these encounters, and cries to her School Counselor that she wishes she were still dating her first lover. She tells her Counselor how she first experienced intercourse. Knowing her to be under sixteen, the Counselor immediately phones the local police and all three boys are arrested. The first lover, thinking that he had done nothing wrong, innocently acknowledges to the police his sexual relationship with the girl.

This seventeen-year-old boy thereby "confesses" that he has committed a felony—statutory rape. His Attorney tells him that, because he has acknowledged the sex act to a police officer, he cannot avoid pleading "guilty" in court, and he is sentenced to three years probation, community service, and a fine. Yet more punitively, wherever he lives, he will—for the next 25 years—have to register himself as a "Sex Offender" with the State Police. His future neighbors will always be able to find his name on the website that publicizes the State Registry of Sex Offenders, and they will know that the decent and considerate man next door is actually a "rapist."

You might think that these seven stories are exceptional. Perhaps they are. But actually, we currently have no way of knowing how widespread these episodes of blatant abuse, persecution, and harassment are—because they are largely hidden from public view, covered up or presented by the media in a vehemently sex-negative manner. There are strong reasons to believe that such events of sexual oppression are actually far more widespread than we might imagine—because, as I will now show, such blatant episodes are the symptomatic extreme of a deeper and more pervasive pattern of anti-sexual "moralizing" and anti-sexual politics that is gaining hold of America. Indeed, there can actually be no doubt that

America is now at war with itself over our own sexualities.

Perhaps we could even wonder whether, in part, America imposes its interests and its values on countries all over the globe, and goes to war so frequently with all sorts of overseas adversaries, who purport to threaten our "way of life," precisely to distract ourselves from the "enemy within"— our own conflicts and frustrations over the sexual impulses that pervade our so-called "way of life." Consider here how conspicuously America is currently at war in the following seven battlefields:

- ❖ A woman's rights over the disposition of her own body, in choosing whether to carry a fetus or not, and in the determination of her own health needs.
- ❖ The civil rights of gay and lesbian citizens to engage in partnerships that are legally binding.
- ❖ The rights of adolescents and young adults to be educated about the methods by which they may choose to embark safely on their partnered sexual lives— rather than having forced upon them a hypocritical message of "abstinence-only" that they will refuse to observe.
- ❖ The rights of younger children to grow in a healthy sexual environment, that allows them the freedom to explore and enjoy their own genital pleasures, that protects them from the abusive interference of adults, and that educates them about sexual and bodily matters in a developmentally appropriate manner.

- The rights of elderly people to sensual and sexual pleasures free from condemnation and restriction by the younger generations.
- The rights of all citizens to have access to erotic education, entertainment, and consensual erotic services.
- The rights of sexual minorities—such as those who enjoy multiple partners, those who choose to live within the "queer" or "kink" communities, or even those who seek to swim and sunbathe naked—to live freely, openly, and with dignity.

The central issue here is the readiness with which some groups are intent on self-righteously imposing their particular values—and projecting their own fearfulness of their own sexuality—onto the lives of others, even when the activity of others does not interfere with their own way of living.

Such activities of sexual oppression are often rationalized as being "for the greater good," or "to protect our children," or "to secure the traditional American way of life." However, such rationalizations are—as we will see—typically bogus. The central issue is fear and ignorance of sexuality, disastrously combined with an alarming readiness, on the part of those who are fearful and ignorant, to impose their values on the lives of others. The central issue is the virulence with which anti-sexual groups are willing to destroy cultural freedoms.

It is well known that, all over the planet, *fundamentalism* in all its varieties—Jewish, Christian, Islamic, and many others—is gaining adherents at an alarming rate. Undoubtedly, this may be understood as a fearful reaction to the socioeconomic and cultural pressures of globalization that comes with the transnational expansion of the capitalist marketplace.

The defining feature of fundamentalist teachings is that there is *one right system* by which to believe, to think, to feel or to act. The logic and rhetoric of fundamentalist doctrines is the condemnation, the persecution, and ultimately the elimination of those who fail to assent to the "one right system." The defining feature of *fascism*—simply stated—is the force that unites those who adhere to the "one right system" in the goal of imposing their values and interests on others. Fundamentalism and fascism are usually well rationalized by the slick maneuvering of human egotism. The "one right system" is imposed on others "for their own good," and so coercion is considered "necessary for the greater good." Missionaries stamp our indigenous peoples in order "to save their souls." Regimes exterminate minorities in order to "clean out the weeds in the garden." Bigots perpetuate prejudice, torture and murder, in order to preserve "law and order."

Fundamentalism and fascism are the apotheosis of our human potential for judgmentalism. Judgmentalism separates and decides that "the one is superior to the other" . . .

. . . "My one right system is different from theirs, better than theirs, and to establish the fact that my system is the right one, theirs must be opposed and condemned."

. . . "For me to feel good and secure in my sexuality, to feel sure that it is the one right mode of sexual expression, any sexuality that is 'other' must be opposed and condemned."

Fundamentalism and fascism are the adversaries of tolerance, freedom and open-mindedness. Indeed, adherents to fundamentalist and fascistic ideals and modes of conduct not only must oppose and condemn all who are "other" than the "one right system," but also are compelled to attack all those whose choice is to respect the values of tolerance, freedom and open-mindedness toward whatever is "other." As a society moves in a fundamentalist and fascistic direction, liberals are forced either to join the radical dissent against the "one right system," or to become complacent and collusive with the illiberal momentum. I believe that we cannot avoid the conclusion that

> *America is in the grip of a fundamentalist momentum*
> *that is antithetical to freedom,*
> *and what we are witnessing is the rise of "sex fascism."*

America is engaged in an escalating internal war between those who politically assert their freedoms, and those who would stamp out these freedoms (and, in this war, liberals will either become radicalized or will acquiesce to the fascistic momentum).

All the examples of persecution and conflict that we have mentioned here are rationalized as "the need to protect" an illusory majority from such "dangers to society" as feminists, gays, those who insist on the freedom to control their own bodies, all manner of nonconformists, individuals who follow alternative lifestyles, and anyone who revels in erotic entertainment. However, these are the rationalizations of those who oppose freedom—a united front fearfully determined to impose its values on others.

American society may be polarizing in other respects as well. There is, for example, an increasing disparity between the expectations and opportunities of the rich and the poor, and this too cannot continue indefinitely without some sort of significant attempt at remedy. One may justifiably fear for the future of American society. However,

> *On a cultural level,*
> *America's next civil war is already underway,*
> *and it is a war over sexual health and erotic freedom.*

Let us examine further the context within which this war is occurring. The United States is unquestionably the wealthiest country in human history. It may not be the best educated, but it could be if its wealth were redirected appropriately. However,

> *In America today, the expression of our sexuality is far from safe, sane and consensual.*

It is well documented that, of all the industrialized nations, the United States has the highest rates of

- Rape
- Abortion
- Unwanted pregnancies, usually with teenagers
- Sexually transmitted infections, including HIV/AIDS
- Child molestation and abuse

And, although scientific data are less available on the following issues, it is unquestionably the case that—of all the so-called "developed" nations—the United States also has the highest incidence of:

- Hate crimes—violence and persecution—against sexual minorities.
- Stigma against individuals on the basis of their sexual orientation or gender.

The citizens of Western Europe are suffering somewhat less from these tragedies, but *not* because they are more sexually abstinent than the citizens of the United States (not a shred of evidence exists to suggest that Americans are being more sexual and, by this means, getting themselves into more trouble). Rather, this is because, as the evidence shows, the Europeans generally have a more relaxed attitude toward sexuality, and they express themselves more openly and frequently. In other words, the difference is that sexuality in "developed countries" other than the United States is more likely to be conducted in a way that is safe, sane, and consensual.

Every one of these tragedies—rape, abortion, unwanted pregnancies, sexually transmitted diseases, the sexual abuse of children, and the persecution of, and prejudice against, sexual minorities—is avoidable. However, they are *not* solvable by an attempt to discourage sexual expression, and to impel our society in a yet more anti-sexual direction.

That is, to suggest that sexuality *per se* is the problem, and that we should all become more abstinent, is profoundly mistaken. Oppression of our sexuality only makes matters worse. For these tragedies are not indicative of "too much sex." Rather, in an important sense, they are indicative of "too little sex." That is, they are indicative of a society that fails appallingly to educate its citizens about sexuality, and thus allows "sex" to fester in fear and ignorance.

We live today in a society that effectively promotes "sex" in a way that is unsafe, insane, and non-consensual. And thus we live in a society that effectively prohibits the natural enjoyment of sexual expression as safe, sane, and consensual.

The scientific study of sexuality—sexological science—has documented clearly how all these tragedies could be avoided. Yet powerful religious and political forces are fundamentally opposed to the notion of freedom, and their tactics not only stomp on our liberties, but effectively ensure that "sex" becomes unsafe, insane, and non-consensual.

For example, notice how, in several of the dramatic stories I reported earlier, there is an almost complete disregard for fairness or for the due process of the law. Rather, there are tactics of infiltration, entrapment, coercion and harassment. Notice how many of the stories involve a manipulation of legal authority or a blatant disregard for such authority and for basic civil rights. Notice how many of them involve not only ignorant and fearful hate-mongering, but also blatant violence. These are the hallmarks of fascist strategies in which adherents of the "one right system" impose their values on anyone who dares to dissent or live differently.

These anti-sexual forces are actually against health, even when they do not explicitly indicate their opposition. Rather, they rationalize their attack on those who do not believe, think, feel, and act according to the "one right system" by falsely claiming that most of the varieties of human sexuality are intrinsically "unhealthy" or "unnatural."

And these forces against freedom claim to care for the welfare of our citizens, but actually they do not. For example, such forces would prefer teenagers to suffer—have unwanted pregnancies, abortions, and a myriad of sexual diseases—under an "educational" system that promotes a policy of "abstinence-only" that they cannot observe, rather than allow them their right to comprehensive sexuality education that would inform our youth, not only about abstinence, but also about the practices of sexual pleasuring in ways that are safe, sane, and consensual.

America is at war, and it is at war over the prerogatives of our bodies. Ultimately, this is a war between those who would claim the right to control other people's enjoyments, and those of us who honor the sacred call of our bodily pleasures. It is a war instigated by those who sincerely believe that they are entitled to impose their personal values on others, and that they should interfere with the bodily functioning of others. Whether of not we realize this, what we are observing is a fundamental attack on sexual health and erotic freedom. What we are observing—with the fascistic and totalitarian burgeoning of fundamentalist dogma in all its varieties—is, at its common core, the rise of sex fascism.

2

The Sexification of America

It is not always easy to grasp just how sexually oppressive and repressive our culture actually is. In fact, although we all suffer from psychological processes of suppression and repression—as well as the processes of either inhibition or compulsivity caused by underlying suppression and repression—we cannot see clearly these processes in ourselves.

Even if we do not experience it consciously, we all suffer anxiety, conflict, shame and guilt about our sexual impulses (and we will discuss this in Chapters Five through Eight). Because we maintain somewhat distorted perceptions and experiences of our own sexuality, it is also difficult for us to assess clearly the extent of the sexual oppression around us.

It is perhaps especially difficult to see the sexual oppression in our society today because, after all, sexuality would seem to be all around us. And yet, in a "sexy" culture such as this, I am still claiming that our sexuality is actually being systematically suppressed, repressed, and oppressed— as much, or perhaps more, than ever.

There is a sociological paradox here, and the paradox is a complex phenomenon that is—I believe—without any exact precedent in the history of human cultures. It is crucial to understand this paradox, which is what I call the "sexification" of America:

*The culture of America today is
both compulsively sex-obsessive and compulsively sex-phobic;
this is the sexification of the American way of life.*

We can examine this paradox more precisely if we consider the following.

On the one side of the paradox, we appear to be a society that is quite obsessed with sex. "Sexuality" of a certain sort appears to be everywhere on the surface of our daily lives. References and allusions to a particular sort of commodified and commercialized "sex" are ever present and very much "in our face." We see "sex" being displayed with almost every magazine, billboard, and television station, as well as on the internet and other media.

However, what we experience through these media are almost always exploitations of the sacredness of our sexual potential as human beings. These are what are sometimes called "reifications"—the social mechanisms by which a sacred, human process is treated as if it were merely a set of objects to be manipulated. "Sex" becomes a commercialized commodity, rather than the powerful and pervasive sensuality of being human. What we experience through these media is mere "sexiness"—a modality of "sexuality" alienated from the spiritual energies of our embodiment.

It is a sexiness that scarcely contributes to—indeed, it often hinders—our ability to realize the sacredness of our sexual potential. That is, for the most part, this sexiness does not empower us . . .

> . . . to talk about our sexual feelings openly with our partners,

... to express our erotic desires in ways that are safe, sane, and consensual,

... or to explore our full range of sensual expression.

I will give just three examples.

- Advertisements for tight jeans, uplifting silk brassieres, machismo toys, cosmetics or surgical "enhancements" do not contribute to our ability to appreciate the sensuality of our body for what it actually is. Rather, they tend to reinforce rather viciously the patterns of our socialization that alienate us from the enjoyment of our bodies as they actually are, instituting within us deep feelings of shame and guilt about our sexuality. They reinforce feelings that our bodies are "not good enough"—and cannot be unless, of course, they are augmented or concealed beneath the latest fashions.

- Presentations of buffed bodies, gyrating on our television and computer screens, swaying to the hefty beat of music in adult clubs, or copulating in the panoramas of "pornography," may be exciting to watch, but they also tend to endorse the pernicious myth that bodies have to be of a particular type in order to be "sexy." Such productions tend to offer us a very narrow and stylized version of what "sexy" is—a version that effectively alienates us from the full range of what our sexuality and sensuality may actually be.

- Soap operas, sitcom dramas, and mainstream movies that frequently depict "hot and heavy" romances, casual sexual liaisons, or the tribulations of monogamous relationships, scarcely educate us about the intimate realities of our own interpersonal connections and the sexuality that sustains them. These media rarely, if ever, show us how to deepen the emotional and spiritual dimension of our own associations. Nor do they even provide sensible examples of casual encounters embracing sexual experiences that are safe, sane, and consensual.

It is not that there is anything necessarily "wrong" with all these productions—and it is certainly not that they should be censored. In and of themselves, there is nothing inherently problematic about much of this sort of "sexiness," and being titillated by such cultural products may simply be fun. The problem is that such productions constitute the bulk of what we see around us as "sex," and that their ubiquity comprises a certain sort of obsessive compulsivity, which actually conditions and constrains our understanding of our own sexual potential. In short, such productions, even while sometimes purporting to widen our options or "open our eyes," often actually limit our sexual expression.

Reified "sexuality" of this sort, the sexuality that pervades the cultural fabric of our everyday existence, typically does not show us how to find joy in the sensuality of our own bodies more freely here-and-now. Even though sometimes such media can facilitate our sexual expression—for example, this is one of the wonderful contributions of the depiction of nonviolent sexual acts in erotic art or quality "adult entertainment"—the most prevalent media presents sexuality in a commodified and commercialized manner that can contribute complexly to our sexual inhibition. That is, it can endorse the notion that our sensual and sexual inclinations do not measure up to the standards explicitly or implicitly presented by magazines, billboards and television stations—and hence it encourages our alienation from our own sexual bodies and promotes the suppression and repression of our own sensual inclinations.

In sum, the alienated view of sexuality that we experience externally in these media portrayals of reified "sex" fails to present us with the naturalness of our own internally generated modes of sexuality expressed in ways that are safe, sane, and consensual. So the problem is not that sexiness of this sort is necessarily negative. Rather, the problem is that it rarely makes more than a minimal contribution to our positive understanding of how to enjoy our sexual lives, and that it often serves to constrain and constrict our own sexual expression.

What this culture promotes and peddles is "sexiness" as a marketable commodity. That is, titillating, sensationalistic, and exciting-but-banal. With this form of "sexuality" flooding our daily lives, we actually become more conditioned, constrained and constricted in our own sensual and sexual expressiveness.

Thus, for example, we may be surrounded with references and allusions to, or even images of genital intercourse; yet, in our high-school curricula, we cannot discuss the structure of the clitoris, nor do we teach our youth how to sustain greater pleasure from their erections.

Again, it is not that we should be against genital intercourse—or the availability of its depiction—far from it. Rather, it is that, if its distorted depiction is part of the staple diet our culture offers, our experience of our own sexuality becomes constrained and constricted. Thus, for example, we watch "sexiness" on billboards, in magazines, and across our screens, but we cannot talk with our friends about the sensuality with which our bodies may be touched, or about the deeper longings of our hearts.

The ubiquitous cultural images that surround us present a "sexuality" that has almost entirely been appropriated for another, ultimately anti-sexual, purpose. This is why I call it compulsively "obsessive." Because the compulsivity of an obsession—as every psychotherapist knows—is not a relaxed, natural enjoyment of our human potential for pleasure.

When something is distorted obsessively, it is driven by anxiety and conflict, indicating the operation of underlying shame and guilt. In fact, the compulsive obsessive quality of our culture's preoccupation with "sex" is indeed largely driven by, and shares its roots in common with, the other aspect of the paradox of sexification—namely, the fact that we live in a culture that is also compulsively sex-phobic.

On the other side of the paradox, we find vehement adversaries of this culture's sexiness. We live in a society that is not only "sex-obsessive" but also compulsively "sex-phobic." We have already discussed the rise of a viciously illiberal rightwing with escalating economic and political power. This rightwing represents forces that speak in the name of religious self-righteousness—forces that are bigoted and dogmatic, fundamentalist and fascistic. I will give just three examples.

- These anti-sexual forces would abuse our children and adolescents by subjecting them to the ideology of abstinence-only "education." The purpose and the effect of this ideology is to terrify our youth away from enjoyment of the natural sensuality of their bodies, and to refuse to teach them how to celebrate their sexuality in ways that are safe, sane, and consensual. Moreover, since there is virtually no evidence that dictating a coercive doctrine of abstinence has ever actually succeeded in squashing adolescent interest in "fucking," this ideology ensures that "fucking" will probably be all that adolescents do.

That is, alienated and frightened away from the natural sensuality of their bodies, adolescents pummeled by the ideology that "abstinence is the only right way" will usually proceed to have intercourse in a way that is basically anti-sexual, anti-sensual and ill-prepared.

Without comprehensive sexuality education, children will more often embark on sexual explorations in ways that are not safe, not sanely discussed, not undertaken with appropriate preparations, and sometimes not even fully consensual.

In sum, the ideology that peddles "abstinence is the only right way" fosters the current situation in which our young people cannot talk about sex, cannot prepare themselves for the emotional and physical responsibilities of sex, and hence will continue to suffer diseases, unwanted pregnancies, abortions—and an initiation into their partnered sexual lives that is often tragically less than satisfactory.

- These anti-sexual forces would promote the ill-conceived notion that sexuality is dangerously addictive, and can only be responsibly enjoyed under very restricted conditions. Along with the ideology of abstinence-only comes the absurd proposition that, "if you are not abstinent, you may be addicted."

This notion touches on complicated scientific and ethical issues because, for many people in this culture, sexual activity can become, and often is, horribly and painfully compulsive. Such people suffer greatly. Indeed, in this society, it can be argued that sexual expression is either avoided or paradigmatically compulsive. Typically, we are not free to cultivate and nurture our sexual potential in a way that is natural, and so we suffer its becoming compulsive—compulsively obsessive or compulsively phobic. In this sense, compulsivity is the psychological outcome of our socialization—a socialization that dictates the suppression and repression of our sensuality and sexuality. That is, compulsivity in both directions is evidence of suppressive and repressive processes that are culturally normative (and we will discuss this further in Chapter Seven).

The label of "sex-addiction" readily serves ideological purposes, suggesting that the solution to compulsivity is not sexual emancipation and enhancement—by which we retrieve the naturalness of our sensuality in ways that are safe, sane, and consensual—but sexual extinction. That is, the addiction label too easily serves an anti-sexual mandate, suggesting that obsessive conduct should be coercively replaced by phobic behaviors.

Instead of seeing compulsivity as the result of our sexual suppression or repression, and accordingly healing it by celebrating the natural sacredness of our sensual embodiment, "sex" is being treated as an inherently dangerous and frightening power to be kept under lock and key.

- These anti-sexual forces would "clean-up" our neighborhoods, and even the privacy of our bedrooms. The doctrines of abstinence-only and of sex-addiction conjoin with the traditional conservative ideology that some types of sexual activity are "right" and the rest are "wrong." In this context, "wrong" has little to do with the criteria of health—the criteria of what is safe, sane, and consensual. Rather, it has everything to do with the hegemonic ideology of "normal" versus "abnormal"—a distinction that is often justified in terms of theological deliberations about what God allegedly wants, and what "he" condemns.

Today the anti-sexual forces are gaining ground. And they promote a pernicious judgmentalism that advances the proposition that there is "one right system" of sexual expression—or, at least, if not just one, then perhaps just one or two—and that whatever is outside this system should be censored. The central mandate of these forces is the elimination of all that is sexually "other" than this "one right system." That is, the elimination of all those who enjoy the diversity of human sensuality—all those who assert the freedom of human sexuality.

As was indicated earlier, this program of censorship is hypocritically rationalized as "the need to protect" an illusory majority from such "dangers to society" as feminists, gays, those who insist on the freedom to control their own bodies, all manner of nonconformists, individuals who follow alternative lifestyles, and anyone who revels in erotic entertainment. In the implementation of this mandate, the "sexiness" that pervades our culture's media would also be "cleaned-up."

This program of censorship throws us back toward a puritanical tradition in which the only "right" way to be sexual is penile-vaginal intercourse, in the context of a legalized marriage, undertaken in the missionary position, not more than about once a week and preferably with minimal orgasmic satisfaction. Everything else—from expansive erotic touching, solo pleasuring, oral sex, anal sex, gay sex, lesbian sex, multiply partnered sex, to all manner of erotic performances and adventurous lifestyles—is to be eradicated. With this agenda, the sex-obsessive quality of our society is to be purified through tactics that are profoundly sex-phobic.

The rightwing that represents these anti-sexual forces is motivated by ignorance and fearfulness toward the miraculous and powerful nature of our sexuality. And their tactics in the religious and political arena promote and exacerbate ignorance and fearfulness. However, in a less malicious and censorious way, the sex-obsessive compulsivity that is pervasive throughout our culture also arises out of the suppression and repression of our natural sexual and sensual inclinations.

It is crucially important to understand this paradox.

Sex-obsessive compulsivity and sex-phobic compulsivity react to each other, and against each other.
They build on each other and against each other.
But at their source, both arise from an ignorance and fearfulness toward the wonders of our sensual and sexual potential as human beings.
That is, in differing ways and to different extents, both are compulsive reactions against the powerful wellspring of our erotic potential.

One reaction reifies our erotic nature as if indulgently, yet in such a way as to alienate us from its fullest enjoyment. The other reaction combats our erotic nature, censoring its multitude of manifestations, in such a way as to alienate us decisively and self-righteously from our entitlement to its enjoyment. *I believe this sexification of America is intensifying, and it is symptomatic of a deepening rift within the fabric of our culture.* If a concrete example would be helpful, consider the following comparatively minor incident: the brouhaha around Janet Jackson's nipple.

As is well known (since it was the talk of all the news media), Ms. Jackson is a popular celebrity whose right nipple was briefly exposed on national and international television as part of her half-time performance at the "Superbowl" in January 2004. The exposure was very quick, and the television cameras that sent the image around the world were at a considerable distance from her—such that, in fact, the nipple itself was scarcely visible. However, in the ensuing days and weeks, the media pounced on the event in a typical and symptomatically double-edged manner.

On the one side, the exposure was shown again and again—in endless television reruns and magazine photos—but now with the breast seen *in close-up* and with the nipple pixilated into blurriness. And on the other side, the media also gave extensive air-space and column-space to an outpouring of shock and horror over the incident. A wide range of outcries about "indecency" were given publicity, repeatedly—outcries about the importance of protecting young people from such "appalling" scenes, and about the need for more strenuous censorship in the media.

Surely, this is insanity. It seems almost no one asked: Why shouldn't nipples be shown freely on television?

Nipples are, in most respects, rather unremarkable; in fact, almost every American citizen, old and young, has a couple of them. They may be very beautiful, and they may be a source of great pleasures when caressed to arousal. And some nipples also perform the natural and sacred function of feeding infants—a practice which is also, in the United States, almost entirely banned from public view.

Paradoxically, the erotic potential of Ms. Jackson's nipple is precisely what goes missing under the hoopla of sexification. With all the brouhaha, *both* of the obsessive voyeurism *and* of the phobic cries of outrage, the beauty of this breast with its protuberant nipple, as well as the erotic pleasures that if may afford Ms. Jackson and her partners, go entirely missing in action.

This then is one measure of our society's sexual sickness. It is the tragically anti-sexual impact shared by both sides of the paradox of our culture's sexification.

In a sense that is crucial for us to comprehend, fundamentalist and fascistic opposition to the phenomena of sexification pursues the same goal as the mechanisms of sexification itself, namely that of depriving us of our sexual-spiritual energies. The hostile and self-righteous conservative opposition merely advocates a different mechanism of compulsivity.

Phobic compulsivity, in which suppression and repression lead to censorship and inhibition, seems distinct from the more liberalizing compulsivity of sexification, in which suppression and repression tend to lead less to inhibition and more to obsessive reifications.

However, beneath the surface appearance of antagonism, these adversarial tendencies in the sociocultural arena are both terrified and somewhat united in their suppression and repression of the authenticity of our erotic potential.

3

A Note on Anti-Sexuality and the State of "Normality"

What is called "normal" in our society would seem to be a quite dismal state of affairs. So many of us live out our lives sexually worried. We curb our sensuality, guard our erotic impulses, censor our fantasies, and diligently focus our energies on all sorts of non-sexual or anti-sexual aspirations. Sexual inhibition becomes automatic—fostered as either obsessive or phobic compulsivity—yet our anxieties and conflicts persist.

In my professional practice of healing, I see daily the tragedies of being human in a culture that is so deeply conflicted about the erotic nature of being human. Individuals who suffer from psychotic processes, from various forms of what are called "character problems," from crippling neuroses, and from all sorts of psychosomatic disabilities, all bear witness to the torment that is caused when we grow up alienated from our erotic sourcing.

However, just as dramatic is the way in which those who appear thoroughly "well adjusted" are also alienated from their sexual and sensual grounding. This alienation is manifested in countless forms of personality structure, as mental and somatic blocks, obstructions, and hindrances to the flow of erotic energy through the course of life.

We grow up erotically numbed. What passes as "normal" and "well adjusted" in this culture are individuals suffering extensively and intensively from sensual and sexual alienation. That is, individuals who are alienated from the pleasures of their own erotic embodiment. This erotic numbing is both emotional and somatic.

Emotionally, the "well adjusted" individual has to be somewhat "closed down"—relatively unresponsive and unempathic. Sexual activity is often undertaken without the *joie de vivre* that is its essence.

Somatically, the "well adjusted" individual has to be somewhat "uptight" and insensitive—relatively unresponsive and rigidified. This "closed down" condition of reduced somatic sensitivity occurs in top athletes as much as in those who are physically challenged. Such persons are "out of touch" with the lifeforce that flows within them. Chronic anxiety about sexual arousal instigates psychosomatic defenses in which parts of the body literally become anaesthetized. Such reactions often cause reduced genital sensitivity and difficulties with orgasming. Unconscious fearfulness over sexuality—for example, as a result of childhood traumatizations—often leads to tension and rigidity psychosomatically. Inflexibility of the pelvis and spinal column, as well as thoracic tightness—that is, a "closing down" of the structures associated with breathing and with orgasmic release—are also common longterm reactions to erotic fear and inhibition.

In these ways, the sensual and sexual alienation of the "normal" individual manifests both in emotional defensiveness and in the "body armoring" of the connective tissues and the general muscular-skeletal system. Although this rarely comes to light, because of the fear and ignorance—as well as privacy and secrecy—surrounding our personal erotic lives, the strongest evidence of this emotional defensiveness and armoring is found in the restricted orgasmic functioning of the "normal" or "well adjusted" individual. To put it simply

> *In this culture, well-adjusted "normality" entails an attenuated or distorted capacity for sexual arousal and orgasm . . . In this culture, to pass as "normal," one must be erotically numbed.*

In this culture, normality requires that we condition and curtail our sensual and sexual pleasures.

Many of us tell ourselves that "sex is not all that important to me," and then we immerse ourselves in substitutive activities. We plunge into all manner of heartless addictions, or we become preoccupied with policing the sex lives of others. We even lose our awareness of how disconnected we have become from our sensuality. We no longer recognize our own inhibition, nor do we see its roots in our unconscious shame and guilt.

So many of us also tyrannize ourselves with worries about the "appropriateness" of our behavior, about our social "respectability," about how we "fit in," and about ensuring that we do not get "out of line." We worry about what others think about us, and especially about what they would think about us if we were to allow our erotic natures free rein. With the collaboration of the media that are all around us, our educational systems, the medical establishment, and all the apparatuses of church and state, we forget the sacred call of our innermost nature.

We become empty shells, alienated from the wellspring of our inherently erotic impulses. Focused on conformity, we worry about our social standing and thus we readily dishonor our sexual and spiritual selves. We are committed to finding our particular role in the cultural nexus—we are committed to sacrificing our desires for the sake of our social acceptance. But we remain worried, frustrated, and addicted to substances, as well as to wealth, to power, and to fame— or at the very least addicted to the hope that these qualities might somehow characterize our future. Meanwhile, most of us just "do our work," like faithful cogs in a rickety machine. Beneath the surface of our social presentations—beneath all our social masks—we remain unbearably lonely. We become alienated from ourselves, but well adapted to society's machinery. Not many of us, if any, live authentically—in this society, it is next to impossible.

Aside from exceptional circumstances, to become sensually and sexually deadened is prerequisite to our social success. Succumbing to such alienation, we become one of the worried "well"—frightened by much of life, sensually deprived, our energies devoted to our acquisition of material advantages, to the synthetic pleasures of titillating media, to our religious preoccupations, and to our ambitions for familial or political power. This society actually requires that we be sensually frustrated and sexually conflicted—and the ideologies that are presented continuously by the media, by educational systems, by the medical establishment, and by all the apparatuses of church and state, ensure that we participate psychologically in the perpetuation of our own sensual frustrations and sexual conflicts.

Consequently, in this sick society, those few individuals who live authentically in the honoring of their erotic nature do not usually survive or thrive. And perhaps in this respect, all societies are more or less sick. To greater or lesser degree, they require conformity. They require us to become sexually inexpressive, for they compel the phobic censorship of our erotic inclinations. Since no censorship of our erotic nature can be total, they require that sexual expression be limited to reified and obsessive modes of indulgence.

It may be simplistic to argue that *all* our social and psychological ailments stem from the conflicts of sensual deprivation and sexual anxiety—although many remarkable thinkers, from Sigmund Freud (in his earlier writings) and Wilhelm Reich, to a number of more contemporary writers and poets, have been accused of precisely such a theoretical over-simplification. But the fact remains that the plethora of those dubious theories (in psychology, sociology, and anthropology, as well as in all the natural sciences), which have tried to discount or diminish the role of sexuality as *the prime motivator* in human affairs, have proven distinctively unimpressive.

This is not surprising. After all, our sexuality encompasses everything about our embodiment. It is our sensual and erotic connectedness with all that is around us. It is the medium of our alignment or misalignment with the universe, the grounding of our being-in-the-world. Other factors that appear to motivate humans can all be understood in terms of the energies of our sexual and sensual embodiment.

For example, consider here our preoccupations with the gain or loss of material possessions, and of interpersonal relationships, our preoccupations with the power that accrues from fame or disgrace, and praise or blame, and our preoccupations with comfort or discomfort on both physical and emotional levels. Consider also our propensity for malice—for judgmentalism, hostility and violence. In one way or another, all such matters derive from the energies of our erotic embodiment. That is, they arise because such energies have been perverted—subjected to suppression, repression, inhibition and compulsivity.

Can it be doubted that our capacity to abuse and exploit each other, our proclivity for prejudice, discrimination, and warfare, are all manifestations of our underlying disconnectedness from our erotic bodies and our spiritual selves? That is, from the fact that we do not grow up knowing how to live safely, sanely and consensually—how to live ethically and healthily in natural harmony with ourselves, with the human community, and with our planet. We might well ask ourselves . . .

. . . Would the world's robber barons be so preoccupied with dominating and exploiting the poor and the weak, if they were living spiritually grounded and sexually gratifying lives?

... Would ethnic and religious communities be at each other's throats, if their members were living spiritually grounded and sexually gratifying lives?

... Would adults abuse children, would partners hurt and violate each other, would gangsters engage in seemingly senseless violence, if they were living spiritually grounded and sexually gratifying lives?

... Would we be trashing the precious planet that we inhabit, if we were living spiritually grounded and sexually gratifying lives?

... Would we be so preoccupied with our malicious thoughts, feelings and actions—our capacity for hostility, prejudice, intolerance and judgmentalism—if we were living spiritually grounded and sexually gratifying lives?

In a profound way, all our human challenges stem from, or are associated with the frustration of our sensuality. All such matters are problematic to us precisely because they represent our *alienation* from the here-and-now of our bodily pleasures. In this society, our innermost alienation is the prerequisite of our adjustment to the external circumstances of our environment. If one undertakes a careful psychological analysis of the world's problems, the following profound truth becomes clearer and clearer.

Sexual anxiety and conflict, inhibition and frustration, are always the cause, the catalyst, and the consequence of human malice.

Moreover, in a culture of sexual anxiety, conflict, inhibition and frustration, not only does malice fester and flourish, but our capacity for genuinely erotic arousal becomes concomitantly limited—often to the extent that either our sexual stimulation has to be engaged compulsively, or we are unable to be aroused at all. And our capacity for orgasm becomes yet more limited (unless, as I will later discuss, our "climaxes" become inflected with aggressive force).

The vast majority of "well adjusted" women in our culture have serious difficulties attaining the pleasures of full orgasmic release. They are emotionally defended and bodily armored. Either they are stranded in a "pre-orgasmic" state of arousal, or they experience an orgasmic releasing that is minimal—relative to their potential—and that requires an aggressively forceful amount of stimulation. If they were not inhibited in this way, their orgasmic capacity would be more easily engaged, they would be readily able to become multi-orgasmic, and they would experience a far deeper and more satisfying mode of orgasmic releasing.

The situation with men is less obvious, but perhaps even more serious—because, contrary to popular belief, men suffer from orgasmic difficulties even more frequently than women—for they are often even more emotionally defended and bodily armored. To express it bluntly, the majority of men may know how to "fuck and cum," but have lost most of their potential for lovemaking and for the fullness of orgasmic releasing. It is, of course, a fact that a large majority of men can ejaculate (although comparatively few of them are able to bring the timing of their ejaculation under the relaxed and natural functioning of their orgasming). But male ejaculation is not equivalent to full orgasmic releasing.

In fact, the vast majority of men do not experience the full-bodied involvement of orgasm when they ejaculate. They "come" but the experience is more or less limited to a genital reaction. If they were to experience the fullness of orgasm, their entire bodymind would be engaged, and they would experience wave after wave of a more total psychosomatic releasing. They would also not have to wait through the refractory period that occurs between ejaculations, but rather they too would become multi-orgasmic.

For both men and women in this culture, our erotic numbing stifles and truncates our orgasmic enjoyment. Although there is often a compulsive, and regrettable, preoccupation with "sexual performance" (which may or may not succeed in giving us "bigger bangs"), this preoccupation is always propelled by underlying anxieties, and is therefore limited in its helpfulness or its healing possibilities. The anxieties usually go unacknowledged and unaddressed. Consequently, a preoccupation with "sexual performance" never brings an individual closer to the natural processes involved in fulfilling their erotic potential, and becoming authentically multi-orgasmic. Most of us live out our lives never knowing the ecstasy of which we are capable—if we were liberated from our conflicts and anxieties. Most of us never know the fullness of a free-flowing passage of energies connecting our hearts, our genitals and our entire bodymind. This is not a matter of "performance," this is—as we will discuss—a spiritual happening.

In our society, to be "normal," one must grow up erotically deprived and inhibited. To be "normal," we are socialized to restrain our sensual and sexual capacity. Indeed, to be "normal" means that we cannot realize our erotic potential. Our erotic and our emotional lives are constrained and constricted. This is the requirement of our "successful" socialization and acculturation. We live less than our potential—spiritually, emotionally, and erotically. We live terrified of our own erotic exuberance. We live not only preoccupied with fears of death, of craziness, and of being socially outcast, but also with all the preoccupations of "getting ahead." Our spiritual depletion is part-and-parcel of our failure to honor our erotic potential. And this is what passes for a successful social and cultural "adjustment."

Endnote: If you would enjoy a scholarly exposition of the way in which our mental life is produced by suppression and repression of what psychoanalysts call the libidinality of our desire, please consult my *Psychoanalysis and the Postmodern Impulse* (Baltimore, MD, Johns Hopkins University Press, 1993). For a discussion of these ideas in relation to the notion of the sexuality of our spirituality, please consult my *The Way of the BodyPrayerPath* (Philadelphia, PA, Xlibris, 2004).

4

What would Sexual Health look like?

Living in this culture, it is not easy for us to appreciate the notion of sexual health, or even to define it. As we have discussed, what our society designates as "normal sex" is the result of massive forces of prohibition and inhibition that we encounter in the course of our socialization.

Growing up in our culture compels each individual to become ignorant and fearful of his or her own erotic potential. The outlets that our culture provides for sexual expression (outlets that are ubiquitously sex-phobic or sex-obsessive) do not enable us to realize our potential for sexual joy, and do not provide us with avenues for the healthy cultivation of our erotic natures.

To the extent that our erotic nature is subjected to suppression, repression and oppression, it becomes difficult for us to know what it might be like to live sexually healthy lives in a sexually healthy society. In fact, sexual "unhealth"—so to speak—is so ingrained within us and all around us that it appears normative.

Obviously, we witness unhealth not only in the prevalence of rape, abortion, unwanted pregnancies, sexually transmitted diseases, and the sexual abuse of children. We also witness unhealth in the malice of those who persecute, and are prejudiced against, sexual minorities—and this is an unhealthiness that, especially when adorned with clever but spurious rationalizations, appears almost normative, and is perpetuated by our mainstream media. We also witness unhealth in all those who suffer sexual dysfunctions and disorders—as well as in the distress of those whose modes of sexual expression run them into social difficulties or psychological distress.

However, in suggesting that, in our society, sexual unhealthiness appears normative, I am not only suggesting that all these phenomena may be considered examples of unhealth, because I also wish to suggest that what our society has traditionally endorsed as the epitome of "sexual health"

> ... a singular partnership, focused on penile-vaginal intercourse, with other modes of sexual expression omitted or at least subordinated to this focus, undertaken mostly in the missionary position, not more than about once a week unless in the "honeymoon" phase of the relationship, and usually undertaken with minimal, if any, orgasmic satisfaction ...

is, when it actually occurs, symptomatic of a pervasively normative pattern of the suppression and repression of our erotic potential.

Because erotic prohibition and inhibition—along with distress, anxiety and conflict—seem normative to us, it is difficult for us even to imagine or envisage what sexual health might look like.

Consequently, institutional definitions of sexual health labor to delineate the character of our unhealthy sexuality—so as to begin to specify how something otherwise than "unhealthy" might look to us. The vision of what might be "sex-positive" is perennially circumscribed by the extent of our awareness of our deep-rooted tendencies to be "sex-negative."

We shall return to this discussion in several later chapters. But at this juncture, it seems useful to note a couple of relevant issues, and in particular to discuss briefly a rather controversial point that is foundational to every discussion of human sexuality. Namely that

*There is an inherent connection
between
sexual health and erotic freedom.*

In the context of the anti-sexual forces of our socialization (given the compulsivity of our both sex-obsessive and sex-phobic culture), it has become far from obvious to us that health requires freedom, and that freedom is intrinsically healthy.

Indeed, it is evident that this society encourages us to subordinate the truthfulness of our erotic nature to the pernicious forces of judgmentalism.

Again and again, we see how powerful anti-sexual forces promote a notion of "health" that involves the selective eradication of erotic expression, and the abolition of our freedom to be fully erotic. That is, vicious anti-sexual forces would attempt to define our "sexual health" precisely in terms of the negation of erotic freedom.

Sexual health could be defined in terms of the emotional and somatic freedom of our orgasmic potential. However, given the numbed and anti-orgasmic condition of what passes as "normality" in this culture, such a definition would be utopian, despite its validity. Rather than proceed in this direction, I have thus far—in my critique of the ideologies promoted by these anti-sexual forces—offered a minimalist definition of sexual health. I have implicitly and explicitly

suggested that "health" would mean that our sexual expressions are
   . . . Safe,
   . . . Sane,
   . . . Consensual.

As we will see, I believe there is virtue in this minimalism, and not just because it opens the way to a "sex-positive" assertion of our entitlement to erotic freedom. At this juncture, let us briefly elaborate this tripartite definition.

➤ *Safe* would certainly mean that sexual activities are conducted in a manner without undue risk of physical or psychological harm. The notion of "undue" risk is important here, since there is no activity in life that is without a certain amount of risk. So for any sexual activity, as in every other sphere of our daily lives, we have to assess the probability of risks involved; and we are advised to engage in the activity only with whatever measures reduce risk to an acceptable level. That is, we are advised to engage in the activities having adopted whatever risk-reductive procedures are available and appropriate. Concretely and specifically, this would imply that sexual activity does not involve the transfer of bodily fluids that can transmit diseases, unless participants know their disease-free status.

➤ *Sane* would also mean that sexual activities are conducted in a manner that honors and protects not only the physical wellbeing but also the psychological or emotional wellbeing and integrity of all participants. It means that whatever sexuality we engage, whether by ourselves or with partners, the connections it involves will be enjoyable and life-enhancing. For example, the notion of sane sex implies that we enjoy our sexual pleasures under conditions of clear awareness, and usually not when inebriated or otherwise cognitively impaired.

Keeping sexuality sane is typically a matter that involves only the participants in the particular act, so long as the individuals concerned are capable of exercising responsibility for their own sanity. However, there is one situation in which a possible third-party must be taken into consideration, for under no circumstances is it sane to produce a child that is not wanted. Those who enjoy penile-vaginal intercourse can only do so sanely if they attend to contraception, and are mindful of the risks of unwanted pregnancy.

Finally, this notion of sanity also implies that "sex acts" undertaken in a manner that psychotherapists might designate "defensive" are not representative of sexual health. For example, healthy sex is not engaged as a power play, or for reasons of gaining some sort of advantage over another person. Acts undertaken compulsively—that is, in a psychological effort to alleviate ignorance, fear, anxiety and conflict—are reactions to psychological stress and distress that are not examples of health. Compulsivity is neither healthy nor free, whatever its appearances.

➢ *Consensual* additionally not only means that sexual activities are to be safe and sane for *all* participants, but also specifies clearly that healthy sexual activity can only occur between partners who have an equal ability to offer their consent. Safety and sanity cannot be the prerogative of the strong. Safety and sanity are also the entitlement of the weak.

Foremost, this means concretely that sanity depends on the diligent observance of the incest taboo, and it also requires the health-protecting extension of this taboo to all homologous situations—for example, in the protection of children's right to enjoy their own modes of sensual and sexual expression free from interference by adults, and in the protection of everyone from situations in which the differential power of participants implies that sexual interaction cannot be genuinely consensual.

The issue of the incest taboo, and its homologous extensions, is critical to any understanding of sexual health, and to any understanding of the reasons why we humans are so terrified of our own erotic potential. So this will be discussed further in Chapter Six.

At this juncture, let us merely offer a few preliminary considerations as to what this notion of the *consensual* quality of sexuality might mean for our definition of health. Unfortunately, here again, we need to mention some examples of "unhealth" so as to arrive at our understanding of health.

I believe we well know that it is not healthy for caretakers, or other adults, to inveigle a minor into their own sexual activities or fantasies, and that this applies even when the minor appears to want this sort of participation.

This sounds simple, but it is a more complicated matter than it appears—because it is actually essential for emotional health that there be certain erotic currents between children and their caretakers. So we will postpone to later chapters the discussion of these complexities, and of all the issues of the healthiness of "boundaries." But here we do need to mention how the question of what is consensual needs to be extended.

For example, it cannot be sexually healthy to engage in a "sex" act if the motive for this engagement is other than erotic enjoyment (and we already mentioned compulsivity as an example of sex acts motivated by forces other than erotic enjoyment).

If the motive for a particular act is basically an *assertion* of unequal social, political, or even psychological power, then it cannot be genuinely consensual, and thus is not authentically or healthily sexual. It cannot be healthy for the "master" to have sex with the "slave" (unless they are two individuals who are not master and slave, but merely playing at these roles). For in such a situation, the motive of enjoyment is eclipsed by the power differential and it cannot be a truly consensual encounter—even when the "slave" appears to want this sort of attention.

I use the example of "master" and "slave" figuratively here, in order to express a relationship with an inherent and unsurpassable power differential. Consider the extrapolations of the master/slave situation to encounters involving boss/worker, teacher/student, counselor/client, doctor/patient, and so forth.

In all these situations, there is an unavoidable power differential that obfuscates and appropriates the erotic impulse. We know—from our preliminary discussion of the prevalence of compulsivity in this society—how often "sexual" activities can be recruited to anti-sexual motives, and this is always what is at issue in these situations.

Similarly, it cannot be healthy to engage in a "sex" act if the motive for this engagement is basically a nonconsensual *submission* to unequal social, political, or even psychological power. It cannot be healthy to say "Yes," if we feel "No." And it cannot be healthy sex if you assent to the act for motives other than erotic enjoyment—for example, if we feel we are compelled to perform an act in order not to be punished, or to be rewarded with an increment of social or political power.

And we may think here of all the traditional marriages in which wives feel compelled to perform acts with their husbands—and *vice versa*—because of their economic or psychological dependence. Sadly, marriage is often an institution in which, on a basic level, sexuality can never be fully consensual—and we will return to this point in Chapter Fifteen.

We might notice here how the three criteria—safe, sane, and consensual—are mostly about how we conduct ourselves. They are mostly about behavior, but they are also about the way in which external behaviors bear on our internal sense of emotional integrity and wellbeing.

There are important distinctions here—between behavior and feelings or fantasies—which we will elaborate in later chapters.

Here let us mention just one example where such a distinction is critically operative. To play out a nonconsensual act, in the context of a fully consensual partnership, might actually be a very sane way for individuals to express and render harmless certain feelings they experience in their fantasies. However, to perform a nonconsensual act in a nonconsensual manner would always be unhealthy, and a tragic way to express what misleadingly purports to be a "sexual" impulse.

In a certain sense, feelings and fantasies are crucially different from behavioral conduct, and this has to be understood in any discussion of the parameters of sanity and consensuality.

Some important implications emerge from our consideration of sexual health thus far. The centerpoint of our discussion is that, in a sexually healthy society, we would all conduct ourselves according to the following truth.

Sexual health means that our erotic conduct is safe, sane, and consensual.

If we grew up sexually healthy, we would know deep in are hearts that

If it's not safe, sane, and consensual, it's neither sexy nor sexual!

But sadly, in this society, we are far from experiencing this truth. Instead, what we experience as sexiness is typically compulsive—in a phobic or obsessive manner—and hence is, at its heart, neither fully sane nor fully consensual. To counter all the sex-negative messages with which our culture surrounds us, and to add a sex-positive spin to this definition, we may take the matter further in the following way.

Because our erotic potential as humans is, at its source, a magnificent blessing, we may even assert that

Sexual Health and Erotic Freedom

Sexual activities, which are safe, sane and consensual, are healthy and to be encouraged!

But we are immediately confronted with how tragically far the world we inhabit is from embracing such an approach to our sensual and sexual potential.

However, the minimalist character of our definition of sexual health advances an approach to health that is comparatively unencumbered by the moralizing typically promoted by religious and political authorities. For "safe, sane, and consensual" is a workable definition implying that sexual health does *not* necessarily have anything to do with

- How many partners a person has...
- What gender the partners are...
- How long the partnership lasts...
- What zones or parts of the body are pleasured...
- How the body is pleasured...

In fact, all sorts of sensual and sexual pleasures—from expansive erotic touching, solo pleasuring, oral sex, anal sex, gay sex, lesbian sex, multiply partnered sex, to all manner of erotic performances and adventurous lifestyles—can be engaged in ways that are safe, sane, and consensual.

This differentiates our understanding of "sexual health" from all the moralizing rhetoric, as well as all the rules and regulations, with which it has traditionally been encumbered, and brings us to the following conclusion:

Sexual health is never a matter of prohibition and restriction.

All the moralizing ideologies to which our erotic potential has been subjected are basically concerned with making us into "normal" and "well adjusted" citizens. However, whenever it is preached that sexual "health" means

...not solo pleasuring, and not having more than one partner,

...not having a partner of similar gender,

...not having a partnership that is unauthorized,

...not pleasuring certain forbidden zones or parts of the body,

...not pleasuring the body in certain forbidden ways,

we can be sure that "health" is not what is actually concerning the preacher. Indeed, what is being preached is the moral probity of erotic attenuation.

In our society, anti-sexual ideology is usually peddled as if it were a concern for "health."

For example, we now have a society in which sexual variation—from expansive erotic touching, solo pleasuring, oral sex, anal sex, gay sex, lesbian sex, multiply partnered sex, to all manner of erotic performances and adventurous lifestyles—still tends to be viewed as if it were like a cancerous tumor. It is still preached that society would be healthier if such behaviors were eradicated. Yet, as I said before, all such activities can be undertaken safe, sanely, consensually—and pleasurably! So why would anyone want to prohibit or restrict them?

We must note here that, in a thoroughly misleading sense, the ideologies of prohibition and restriction do appear to operate appropriately and successfully in relation to matters of physical health. For example, "health" means *not* ingesting toxins, and so forth. And the idea of combating some things in order to preserve others also seems to apply to matters of physical health. For example, we do indeed eradicate the cancerous tumor in order to maintain the body that houses it.

But to analogize from these sorts of ailments to matters of sexual health is entirely misguided.

Yet more importantly, when it comes to human behavior, it must be emphasized that, without exception

> *Ideologies of prohibition and restriction*
> *always lead us away from sexual health.*

If anyone continues to doubt this, let us return to the issues of sanity and consensuality. If our sexual expression is to be sane and consensual, it must be freely chosen and freely engaged. It must be chosen out of awareness and enjoyment, and not out of ignorance and fearfulness. Although people may sometimes choose to act insanely, and although they may sometimes feel free to abuse the freedom of others by engaging in conduct that is not consensual, there is no such thing as enforced sanity or coerced consensuality.

In short, sanity and consensuality require the freedom of the individual to act accordingly. And, despite all the moralizing ideologies that surround us, the fact is that

> *When it comes to sexuality,*
> *humans cannot be healthy unless they are free,*
> *and,*
> *if an individual's conduct is not freely engaged,*
> *it cannot be healthy.*

Given that the ideology of freedom purports to be the hallmark of American culture, we might expect that this inherent connection between health and freedom would be readily acknowledged. However, quite the contrary is the case. We live in a society where it is customary to define sexual health in terms of prohibitions and restrictions. We live in a culture that equates "sexual health" with lack of erotic freedom.

Sooner or later, lack of erotic freedom promotes sexual unhealth—simply because safety, sanity, and consensuality in our sexual conduct require that we have the freedom to engage in such conduct. Our sexual expression cannot be healthy unless it is free and, unless it is freely engaged, no activity can be truly healthy. We can conclude here that

Sexuality cannot be healthy except when it is freely engaged, and erotic freedom is essential for sexual health.

Health means freedom and freedom means health. It is yet another measure of our society's sexual sickness that we appear to have long since forgotten this inherent connection. We have forgotten it simply because we operate in such a sexually ignorant and fearful culture. We grow up in a sexually oppressive culture, we internalize anxiety and conflict over our erotic impulses as we become victims of our own capacity for suppression and repression, and we have difficulty imagining what a sexually healthy community might be like. Tragically, our erotic capacities have become emotionally and somatically attenuated by our social conditioning.

We no longer know the exuberances of sexual health as they might be! But we do know that if we hold to the criteria of safety, sanity, and consensuality, which are—at the very least—needed for sexual health, then we will require our freedom of erotic expression.

SECTION TWO

Why are we so frightened?

5

The Dynamics of Shame and Guilt

We grow up deeply terrified of our own erotic potential. We have been so socially conditioned that not only have we internalized the inhibitions and prohibitions of our culture, but we have done so by psychological processes of suppression and repression such that we are mostly unaware of the extent to which our own sexuality frightens us.

We are frightened of the call of our body's sensuality, yet we do not consciously know that we are frightened. Such is the psychological power of the unconscious that we are profoundly ashamed and guilt-ridded in relation to our erotic potential, yet our shame and guilt remains largely beyond the purview of our conscious self-reflections.

Perhaps one of the most valuable lessons that psychoanalysis teaches comes from its descriptions as to how pervasively human behavior is governed by the psychological forces of shame and guilt—even when appearances do not allow us to see that this is the case. In fact, a major lesson of psychoanalysis is that we are unaware of the extent to which shame and guilt motivates our conduct, because most of our shame and guilt is unconscious, and we are only consciously aware of "the tip of this iceberg."

As we will see in the next chapter, this lesson is an aspect of a greater contribution to the understanding of our humanity that psychoanalysis offers concerning the essential role of the incest taboo in the development of our sexuality.

The power of shame and guilt over us is enormously enhanced because not only do these forces govern many of our actions, but this influence occurs even while our sense of shame and guilt remain sequestered beyond our conscious self-reflections. So we often act out of shame and guilt, even while telling ourselves that we are neither ashamed nor guilty.

In the clinical practice of psychotherapy, these insights are tragically illustrated in every session. However, if you have no experience with psychoanalytic inquiry, the idea that our consciousness often deceives us, and that our actions are extensively governed by unconscious forces, may not be immediately evident. So I will sketch briefly a few particularly vivid examples from my psychotherapeutic practice.

➢ A young man in his twenties, who is sexually active with a regular girlfriend, has the opportunity for a sexual encounter with a female coworker. The evening after their liaison, he feels thoroughly satisfied with the encounter and decides to celebrate with several drinks at a bar. Although he is usually a cautious man and a skilled driver, he manages to skid his car out of the parking lot, crashing it into another parked car, and causing himself the inconvenience of having to pay several hundred dollars for the repair of both vehicles.

➢ An educated woman in her thirties, with a highly successful professional career, feels confident that she has transcended her strict religious upbringing, in which sex was supposed to be reserved for marriage. She feels herself to be "liberated," and embarks on a lifestyle involving a succession of risky encounters with a variety of men. She views condoms as "too much of a bother," and professes to feel that her many brief liaisons are "totally cool." Eventually, she contracts a sexually transmitted infection, at which point she feels mortified and withdraws from partnered sexual relations for the next several years.

➢ A married man comes to therapy because his wife is complaining that he never wants sex with her. He does not understand why he appears to lack sexual interest in her. He loves her greatly, finds her very attractive, and is not having sex with anyone else. He seems to like sex, however, and masturbates furtively and frequently without his wife knowing. In therapy, he speaks glowingly of his admiration and affection for her, especially emphasizing what a "great mother" she is with their child, who is now entering kindergarten. He then tells the therapist that he and his wife had a "very hot" sex life when they met, and indeed for a year or two after they married. His interest in sex with her "mysteriously disappeared," about the time she became the mother of his child. He is utterly baffled by this "coincidence."

➢ A woman in her twenties really wants to be able to orgasm with her female partner. However, she only orgasms when pleasuring herself by rubbing her own vulva. With her partner, she finds herself more inhibited. She greatly enjoys receiving cunnilingus, which her partner very much likes to offer her. She becomes very aroused by the caresses of her partner's tongue, but then quickly becomes anxious. She is flooded with thoughts that she is "taking too long," that her partner "might become tired or impatient," or that she "might be dirty down there." With the eruption of these worries, she loses her arousal and cannot climax in the presence of her partner.

➢ A young boy secretly defies his parents, hiding sexually explicit magazines under his mattress, and masturbating vigorously at every opportunity. At the religious academy he attends, he has witnessed other boys being severely humiliated and punished when caught pleasuring themselves. He is sure that his parents would be shocked and angry were his secret pleasures discovered. He feels alone and frightened. He begins to have fantasies of jamming his penis into a light socket, and he masturbates so frequently and so frantically that his penis becomes raw.

Examples such as these are actually commonplace. With the privilege of being a psychotherapist and listening to patients who come for sexuality counseling or for sex therapy, I have come to realize that *everyone* has some form of psychological conflict over their sensual and sexual impulses—even if the conflict is not clear to their own reflections.

What is important to learn from these abbreviated vignettes is not only that these individuals are wracked with sexual conflict, but that they are consciously unaware of the extent of their own shame and guilt:

The young man in his twenties does not see any connection between his sexual escapade and his car accident.

The professional woman in her thirties does not understand how she orchestrated a miserable punishment for her own efforts at self-liberation.

The married man does not see that he has an unconscious inhibition about having sex with his wife precisely because she has become a mother.

The woman in her twenties would consciously deny feeling ashamed of her vulva or of her delight in her lesbian lover, yet she preempts her own orgasmic satisfaction with an eruption of anxiety.

The young boy does not realize that he is himself making his masturbation compulsive and painful, not only because he is trying to avoid punishment by those in authority, but also because he feels a need to punish himself. His compulsivity is a compromise between his erotic impulses and the prohibition that he has internalized. The psychological formation of the compromise is like a bargain struck between different forces within his mind—he continues to masturbate but he now punishes himself for doing so. He is mostly unaware of the operation of this formation within him.

On the basis of more than thirty years of psychoanalytic inquiry, I have come to believe that

*It is almost impossible to overestimate
the pernicious power of shame and guilt over the human psyche.*

Deep dynamics of shame and guilt preoccupy our mental functioning—our judgments, our emotional dynamics, as well as our daily conduct—and, more often than not, these phenomena operate unconsciously. Indeed, as I have indicated, the forces of shame and guilt exercise even greater impact over our minds precisely because they operate outside reflective awareness, and what we experience consciously are only the residues of the powerful anxieties they cause—the product of compromises we unconsciously form between conflicting forces within our mental functioning. Moreover,

*The dynamics of shame and guilt
not only operate outside our conscious awareness,
they are also always, directly or indirectly,
about our sexual impulses, our sensual body, and our erotic potential.*

Let us discuss these matters further. Shame is defined here as a fundamental and usually unconscious sense that

    ... "I am not really loveable,"
    ... "I am not deserving of happiness,"
    ... "I am somehow defective or unworthy,"

... "I do not belong on this planet,"
... "I am, deep-down, without value or significance,"
... "I am ill at ease or filled with my "primordial envy" and destructiveness.

In a certain sense, it is true that, beyond all our representations of our selves and our world, we are all ultimately empty and insufficient—and I have written about this elsewhere. But this is not the issue at the level we are discussing.

Psychoanalysis, as a spiritual-existential discipline, as well as other lines of spiritual inquiry, teaches us that "deathfulness" pervades the life of the human subject, and that "emptiness" is the inherent condition of all phenomena—that each human being is merely a transient package of energy, a conduit for the divine. Moreover, we are all insufficient or inadequate—in psychoanalytic terminology, we are all "castrated"—for we are not the author of our own lives, not the creator of our own thoughts, and we do not have access to the locus of authority by which the meaningfulness of our lives is governed. Although these propositions may seem morbid or pessimistic, they can actually be, at the level of spiritual insight, joyful revelations.

However, our propensity for shame operates at a different level of the human psyche. It operates within the realm of our mind's convictions about our realities and about the substantiality of our selves.

Shame is neither spiritually grounded, nor joyful. Rather, it is a pernicious mode of thinking and feeling that prevents us from undertaking the very spiritual journey which would bring us the realization that joy is to be found in the very emptiness and insufficiency that characterize our lives.

Shame operates within the realm of our representational reality. It operates on the level of our deepest images of self and other. That is, shame is a sense that pertains between "me" and others in the world, mediated by what psychoanalysts call the "ego ideal." This "ego ideal" is not in our awareness, and is rather like an internalized set of ideas or beliefs, the general content of which is that "*if* I were loveable, I *should* be this or that, which I am *not*."

Shame—unlike feelings of embarrassment and humiliation, which are often the consciously accessible symptoms of deeper representations of shame—operates in a manner that often cannot be verbalized. It influences us pervasively and unconsciously, expressing itself as innumerable conscious and unconscious feelings of wretchedness or as a pervasive avoidant anxiety in the face of our spiritual potential for magnificence. Shame attaches to the most fundamental representations of our selves in relation to others. It is ultimately a fundamental sense that we cannot *enjoy* just *being* whoever it is that we are.

Shame's influence is most obvious with individuals who blatantly maintain a masochistic relation to the world (and note that masochistic people rarely see their own masochism, instead disguising and rationalizing it to themselves). However, those who more ostensibly maintain a sadistic relation to the world are also found—on psychoanalytic scrutiny—to be enacting patterns of hostility and aggression that are derived from a deep sense of shame about their own *being*.

When there are masochistic trends in someone's personality, the hostility that always arises from shame is indulgently directed against the self; when these trends are more blatantly sadistic, the hostility is redirected against others. The difference is perhaps not as significant as the fact that both proclivities arise from the dynamics of shame. In a slightly simplistic formulation, we can say that both trends illustrate an individual's psychological effort to "feel good" about being themselves.

We should not be misled by the fact that, in the psychological development of the human being, things often appear consciously opposite to the way they are in the powerful operation of the unconscious. For example, an individual who appears self-infatuated, "puffed up" and egocentrically conceited, is not someone who is free of a deep sense of shame. Rather, from psychoanalytic inquiry, we know that those who make a religion of adoring themselves are suffering as much from a deep sense of shame about being themselves, as those who make a religion out of loathing themselves or being blatantly self-abnegating.

Where does shame come from, and in what way is it always about our sexual impulses, our sensual body, and our erotic potential?

From our earliest encounters with the world—from our preverbal babyhood—shame and fear domesticate themselves within our bodies, inscribed as contractions and the tightness of blockages in the flow of our energies, and thence in our most foundational representations of our self.

The stories and the feelings that express our shame always begin with bodily experience, a loss of innocence in which we come to be ashamed of our body's forms and functions. Shame arises from the prohibition of our sensuality, and comes to characterize our deepest representations of our self in relation to the world. It originates in a dyadically structured or one-on-one encounter with a social world that does not support our natural bodily pleasures and our natural exuberance—that is, a world that does not allow us to cultivate a basic sense of our selves as the magnificent and divine creatures that we are.

Shame arises in the earliest experiences of dyadic mirroring in which the mother, father, or other primary caretaker appear to respond to the child, and the child develops a "self" in response to this formative pattern of interaction. This interaction is not primarily verbal, since linguistic abilities are not yet developed. Rather, it is primarily sensual or bodily—initiated both by the infant's own physical expressions and by the caretaker's involvement with the infant's bodily expressiveness and general functioning.

It is thus important to understand how shame, at its deepest roots, is always generated in relation to bodily experience—and how it later manifests most blatantly in our failure to appreciate and enjoy the sensuality of our bodies, our capacities to breathe, to move, to mobilize our inner energies, and to feel the expansiveness of our sensual pleasures.

Shame effectively prevents the enjoyment of life, instead miring us in feelings of hollow worthlessness.

Shame can be distinguished from guilt, although in the psychological composition of most individuals, the two operate in tandem, fueling each other in what might be characterized as a "feedback loop." The earliest foundations of our sense of shame prepare us for the later development of our sense of guilt, and the operation of our sense of guilt reinforces our shame. Guilt is defined here as a basic and usually unconscious sense that

> ... "I am not deserving of happiness *because*...
> I have somehow thought, felt or done something for which I should be punished."

Interestingly enough, whereas shame concerns the fundamental representations of our *being*, guilt is more concerned with propositional representations about our *doing*.

It is as if our sense of guilt always originates from some dim intimation of distant "crimes" we committed in early childhood, even though we have long since forgotten—our memories shrouded by repression—what they were or why we should have developed guilt around them.

Thus, on the occasions we are consciously aware of feeling guilty to some degree, this guilt is rarely if ever about the "infractions" that actually established our capacity to feel guilty. As we develop through childhood, our guilt usually builds on shame as our minds accumulate stories, ideas and beliefs.

The influence of guilt is most obvious in individuals who are blatantly self-punitive. Note that individuals who are always getting themselves punished are usually not aware how they are themselves bringing punishments into their lives. Even when they have some awareness of this pattern, they are almost never able to articulate why they unconsciously believe they deserve punishment.

For example, the woman who repeatedly devotes herself to a succession of rather cold and indifferent lovers is often unaware that her devotions may be serving a self-punitive mandate, let alone that the unconscious guilt driving this pattern comes from her experience of forbidden childhood wishes—such as secretly erotic feelings toward a caretaker.

The influence of guilt can also be observed in individuals who may not appear to be unduly self-punitive, but whose lives are constrained and constricted by their obsessive preoccupation with the observance of every rule and regulation.

For example, the man who expends much of his life "dotting every *i* and crossing every *t*" is usually unaware that his dedication may be serving a self-punitive mandate (keeping him from wild and spontaneous experiences of pleasure), let alone that his fear of "letting loose" is a pattern associated with unconscious guilt coming from his experience of forbidden childhood wishes—such as forbidden erotic feelings that at the time seemed utterly uncontrollable.

However, we should not be misled by individuals who disregard social norms—such as those who break societal conventions or standards—and appear to do so without guilt. On psychoanalytic scrutiny, we often find that "anti-social activity" comprises the individual's effort to prove that he or she "has nothing to feel guilty about." Moreover, often such individuals eventually allow themselves to get caught and punished. Again, in the psychological development of the human being, things often appear consciously opposite to the way they really are in the powerful operation of the unconscious.

While shame starts with our earliest encounters in the social world, and its origins lie in preverbal experiences, the origins of guilt are concurrent with the first verbal experiences of early childhood.

Consider here a simplistic illustration. Our hand was removed from our genitals as our diapers were changed, instituting an inner sense of shame about who we are. Later, we imagine our mother's body as our hand caresses our genitals, and we somehow know that this is a *"No!"* experience, which institutes an inner sense of guilt about what we are doing, have done or imagined doing.

Thus, although it also operates mostly outside the purview of our reflective consciousness, guilt is sometimes more verbally graspable than shame—merely because the operation of our guilt was only established mentally during or after our acquisition of language.

Whereas shame appears to simply exist unconsciously without an attribution as to "why" (I just *am* unlovable or bad, undeserving, ugly, and so forth), guilt is effectively structured in terms of unconscious propositions that imply a causal attribution (I am unlovable or bad *because* I did something, such as wishing, fantasizing, imagining or actually enacting this or that).

Guilt is initiated by the transgression, or imagined transgression, of a prohibition, and is thus mediated by what psychoanalysts call the "superego." This "superego" is not in our awareness, and is rather like an internalized set of rules and regulations—prohibitions by which thoughts, feelings and actions may be judged—as well as a force that demands self-punishment for any transgression of these rules and regulations.

Thus, in our unconscious representations, guilt is formulated in propositions such as "I am not loveable for doing *x*, for doing something to *y*, or for imagining doing *z*, and *because* of this, I *should* suffer punitive consequences." Typically, at least one, and often all of the components of such a proposition are outside the purview of reflective consciousness. Yet the hidden proposition influences our conscious sense of who we are, what choices we make, and our ideas about what we deserve from our lives.

Where does guilt come from, and in what way is it always about our sexual impulses, our sensual body, and our erotic potential?

From our encounters with the world as toddlers—as we become verbal in early childhood—guilt and fear domesticate themselves within our bodies. As with shame, guilt is inscribed as contractions and the tightness of blockages in the flow of our energies.

It may be easier to comprehend how the stories and the feelings that express our shame always originate with bodily experience, for shame arises in a direct encounter between our sensuality and a coldly prohibitive or non-responsive world. It is more difficult to grasp how guilt—for example, our guilt over an act of theft, exploitation or violence—is connected to sexual inhibition and prohibition, to the suppression and repression of our sensual inclinations. This is because with guilt the connection is often, but not always, indirect.

Guilt originates from the social conditioning of our erotic potential, but unlike shame, it originates in a triadically structured encounter between our self, the other that arouses our sensual impulses, and the representation of taboo.

Consider here the simplistic example just given. In the delirious and delightful fantasies of early childhood, our hand caresses our genitals pleasurably as we imagine our mother's body, while at the same time we somehow know that this is a *"No!"* experience. Indeed, this is the primordial *"No!"* experience, the prototype of all prohibitions and restrictions. We will discuss the nature of taboo in later chapters. For now it is only important to recognize that this triadic encounter—

"me" feeling genital pleasure, the representation of my mother's body, and the representation of taboo—has the most profound effect both on the child and on our personality thereafter.

Guilt manifests most blatantly in our—mostly unconscious—judgmental evaluation of our own behavior, resulting in our inability to appreciate and enjoy the sensuality of our bodies, our capacities to breathe, to move, to mobilize our inner energies, and to feel the expansiveness of our sensual pleasures.

Guilt effectively prevents the enjoyment of life,
instead strangulating it in a myriad of rules and regulations,
which we may either follow guiltily,
or condemn ourselves to guilt and punishment for not following.

Guilt originates in the encounter between bodily experience and the representation of taboo. It is always derived from the impulses of bodily experience in relation to the law and order of the forbidden, and in the aggressively forbidding quality of this encounter.

Initially, the law and order of the forbidden is represented as the primordial *"No!"* that always incites aggression—at least to some degree—and so, in this respect, the psychological formation that generates our feelings of guilt is founded in aggression. However, the primordial *"No!"* is deeply encoded in the representational system, by which we come to understand our selves and our world. The very structures of our cognition have the boundariness of taboo deeply inscribed within their law and order.

As this representational system is brought to bear on the regulation of our bodily impulses, the notion of the forbidden—the operation of taboo—comes to be extrapolated to all sorts of other societal rules and regulations that are not directly concerned with bodily functioning. So we become guilty not just over our sexuality, but also over a myriad of other prohibitions. Moreover, as our lives become increasingly enclosed by prohibitions and inhibitions, the aggressive quality of our mental productions inevitably increases.

Additionally, because the capacity for guilt is founded in an aggressive triadic encounter (in which impulses conflict with prohibitions that are both externalized and internalized dialectically), this capacity is usually involved in our propensity for violence. Hostility and violence—as well as our general human propensity to be malicious—are expressions of the frustration of our sensual impulses. As such, they often emerge from unconscious guilt as ways of attempting to assuage, appease, or protest and bluff against the conscious experience of guilt.

All this will be discussed further in Chapter Eight, for there are complexities here that need to be understood. For now, perhaps we need only consider the following. Would humans be malicious, if they were not sensually and sexually frustrated, and to what extent is this frustration the result of prohibition—prohibition that is usually internalized in an unconscious sense of guilt?

In the psychology of our everyday lives, shame and guilt operate like mythical monsters behind closed doors. We are not aware how extensively our daily conduct is influenced by the forces of shame and guilt, nor are we aware how extensively our daily conduct is shaped by our fear and anxiety over the possibility of acknowledging to ourselves how deeply we feel shame and guilt about ourselves.

Much human behavior—and certainly many of our compulsively sexual and anti-sexual thoughts, feelings and actions—can only be explained dynamically as a direct expression of our shame and guilt, or as an expression of our need to find some way to deny and to counteract our unconscious shame and guilt. The significance of these dynamics cannot be overestimated.

In the study of human behavior, it is often said that the ideologies of religion and politics, presented in the course of child-rearing practices, are what alienate us from our sexuality and our erotic potential. Such an explanation emphasizes how we are sexually oppressed by means of our socialization and acculturation. The explanation is correct, but inadequate. The psychodynamic processes are somewhat more complex.

More perniciously and powerfully than the direct oppression of our sensual proclivities—and all the fear that this engenders within us—is the way in which we come to suppress and repress our own erotic inclinations. In a sense, every child has no choice but to collude with his or her own sexual alienation because, to a greater or lesser degree, every child develops shame and guilt about their sexual bodies.

Thus, it is not merely that religion and politics inhibit our sexual expression, it is—far more perniciously and powerfully—our unconscious internalization of the ideologies of anti-sexuality as the psychological forces of shame and guilt that ensures our vicious alienation from our own enjoyment.

Shame and guilt—as well as the fear of experiencing our shame and guilt—domesticate themselves within our bodies as constrictions in the spiritual flow of our lifeforce, and are expressed not only in the visionless self-hatred of our stories and feelings about ourselves, but also in our failure to realize our potential for erotic enjoyment.

As complex as this is to grasp, we need to comprehend how double-edged these dynamics can be. Shame and guilt cause us to participate in our own alienation by leading us to be compulsively sex-phobic, but they also cause us to participate in our own alienation by leading us to be compulsively sex-obsessed. To give some examples:

Severely inhibited persons, for whom sexuality seems to be "just not that important," have long since closed themselves down, due to early experiences of shame and guilt that are largely unconscious.

Prudish and judgmental individuals, who are preoccupied with policing the sexual activities of others, act in this manner precisely to ward off the conscious experience of shame and guilt over their own sexual impulses and fantasies.

Prurient people, who frantically or aggressively pursue their "sexual" activities in a manner that is not safe, sane or consensual, and that eventually causes harm to themselves or others, conduct themselves in this manner precisely as if to prove to themselves that they experience neither shame nor guilt over their sexual inclinations—which, of course, implies that shame and guilt are indeed unconsciously operative.

Our erotic lives are thus wrecked by psychological conflict in one or other direction—precisely because the pernicious and powerful forces of shame and guilt within us render us inherently conflicted over the realization of our own erotic potential—and the operation of these forces within us is not within our conscious awareness, making our liberation all the more complexly challenging. Sadly, although our socialization and acculturation are vehemently anti-sexual, we also have inscribed within ourselves our own tendencies to thwart ourselves erotically, to be frustrated or aggressive, and to perpetuate our own misery.

Endnote: If you would like to read a more detailed discussion of psychoanalytic insights about the "deathfulness" and the "castratedness" of the human subject, consult my essay, "Desire and Death in the Constitution of I-ness" in *Way Beyond Freud: Postmodern Psychoanalysis Observed,* edited by Joseph Reppen, Martin A. Schulman, and Jane Tucker; London, UK, Open Gate Press, 2004, pages 264-279.

6

The Theory of Polysexuality, Traumatization, and Incest Taboo

Our survey of some of the dynamics of shame and guilt prepares us for a more general exploration of some of the complex dynamic processes of sensual and sexual growth from the cradle to the grave.

I will now present a theory of human erotic development that is not entirely new, since it draws on some of Sigmund Freud's discoveries. However, my articulation of these discoveries frees them from the sex-negative ideologies with which their theorization has traditionally been infused. In this sense, the theory to be presented here is—to the best of my knowledge—comparatively innovative. The three coordinates of this theory are:

- That we are all born with a "polysexual" potential for erotic pleasure;

- That the traumatic experiences of our early development cause the loss of this potential, and the constraint or curtailment of our erotic desire;

- That the necessity of the incest taboo is the unique source of our fear of sexuality, which becomes unnecessarily extrapolated to a multitude of anti-sensual and anti-sexual rules and regulations, inhibitions and prohibitions.

This theory serves to demonstrate to us how, in any culture, externalized oppressive forces against sexual expression and the internalized suppressive and repressive forces of shame and guilt are in a continual dialectical development. This interaction of externalized and internalized representations—or forces that operate against sensual and sexual freedom—involves a nonlinear dynamic of interdependence.

This implies that the processes of our erotic emancipation—if it is to be a genuine liberation from the forces of oppression, suppression and repression—will need to be sexually and spiritually profound, complex and challenging.

We need to emancipate ourselves from anti-sexual forces that are internalized in our thoughts and feelings, as well as from the oppressiveness of external forces.

On Polysexuality:

A central axiom of this theory is that we are *not* born into this world alienated from the pleasures of our body.

We are not born wracked by the conscious and unconscious forces of shame and guilt—such that our erotic repertoire is severely conditioned, constrained, constricted and curtailed not only by oppressive social norms, but also by our own inner processes of suppression, repression, inhibition and compulsivity.

We are not born condemned to suffer for our erotic nature. Our infantile potential for bodily pleasure is not inherently associated with anxiety—yet invariably, by adulthood, our sexuality is characterized, to greater or lesser degree, by its association with psychological conflicts. Indeed,

Sexual Health and Erotic Freedom

We are born into this world exquisitely designed for pleasure and for the enjoyment of life.

We are born with a powerful and wide-ranging potential for sensual and sexual joy. Through the processes of our socialization and acculturation, this potential is repeatedly stifled and truncated by successive experiences of traumatization.

We start life with an enormous and magnificent erotic potential, which becomes a source of conflict, and is successively attenuated and anxiety-ridden. We start life living fully within our embodiment, and we come to live increasingly "in our heads"—alienated from the sensuality of our erotic energies and our sensual embodiment.

We start life with an open potential for erotic enjoyment
—we are polysexual—
and then, through repeated processes of traumatization,
our repertoire of sensual and sexual pleasures
becomes much stifled and truncated,
marked by anxiety, and increasingly compulsive.

The infant—that proverbial "bundle of joy"—is, in fact, a packaging of neurons engineered with a wondrous potential for an abundance of joyous pleasuring. Moreover, this potential is open, in the sense that it permits all sorts of developmental possibilities. It can be reductively shaped in any number of ways.

So, for example, we are not born with a gene for shame and guilt, nor are we born preprogrammed to suppress and repress our natural erotic exuberance.

Rather, we are born "polysexual," which means that, at birth, we have the potential to manifest, in adulthood, any and every pattern of sexual inclination—or erotic "lovemap" as these patterns are sometimes called—that has ever been experienced by an adult human being.

We are born fully open to all the human possibilities of pleasure, and—through a succession of traumatizations—we become selectively closed to these possibilities.

Freud rightly argued that we are each born with a wellspring of "libidinality"—which was his term for the exuberance of erotic energies flowing within our embodiment. And he further argued that the patterns, by which this libidinal polypotentiality eventually finds emotional and behavioral expression in adulthood, are the result of reductive shaping, "channelization," or conditioning of this inherently free-form and free-flowing energy throughout the course of our childhood and subsequent experiences.

Putting a rather sex-negative spin on this notion, Freud suggested that the infant is "polymorphous perverse" and that only by passage through successive childhood experiences of conflict over sexual impulses would he or she emerge as a sexually structured—that is, sexually limited—adult human being. A "sexually structured" adult is one whose sensual inclinations are stable and more or less focused on a single variation of erotic activity—that is, an adult whose erotic energies are decidedly not open, spontaneous, free-form, or free-flowing. Aside from the sex-negative connotations of his use of the notion of "perversity," some of Freud's ideas are both important and valid.

Our erotic energies start open,
spontaneous, free-form and free-flowing.
Through our early development,
they become compulsively repetitive and positioned
—fixated in tightly circumscribed patterns of sexual expression.

Of course, Freud made the ideological assumption that it is somehow beneficial for adults to emerge from their childhood experiences with a stifled and truncated, but seemingly stable, repertoire of erotic interests. He assumed this, despite the fact that, as he demonstrated, this reductive stabilization of our sexual expression is achieved in reaction to psychological conflict and the inner management of anxieties.

It has seemed to some commentators that Freud's assumption amounts to the notion that heterosexual intercourse in the missionary position constitutes the best, the "most natural," or even the "one right system" by which to express libidinal energies in the arena of adult activities—and for this, Freud has been lampooned by several of his radical critics.

But Freud's theory must not be discarded merely because of the ideological trappings with which he articulated it. For the central axiom of this theory is well demonstrated by psychoanalytic inquiry, and it must be emphasized that

From birth, we bring into this world an abundance of spontaneous, open, free-form and free-flowing libidinal energies, and our psychological development, through socialization and acculturation, forces the constriction and curtailment of these energies in reaction to a sequence of traumatizations.

Modifying and elaborating this psychoanalytic theory, I am renaming the notion of "polymorphous perversity," as the theory of "polysexuality." Again,

Polysexuality is our inherent nature and our birthright; it is, for all of us, our erotic potential. We are all born with a polysexual potential for erotic pleasure.

That is, we are born with an abundance of open, spontaneous, free-form and free-flowing libidinal energy. This notion must be combined with an understanding of the processes by which our developmental experiences actually involve a series of traumatic reductions in this potential. Thus, our erotic pleasures become increasingly stifled and truncated, less and less free, and more and more compulsively repetitious.

At birth, our erotic nature is such that
we have the potential to grow into adults
who might experience every type of sensual and sexual pleasure
that has ever been experienced by an adult human being.

Yet the experiences of our socialization and acculturation do not cultivate this erotic potential. Rather, it is treated as a threat. Our "maturation" involves the forceful diminution of this potential, and makes it the cause of our anxieties and our self-alienation. This is what is called "sexual development." Our sexual traumatizations amount to a series of experiences in which we are progressively robbed of our potential for erotic pleasure.

One challenging implication of these insights is that we are not born to a particular sexual orientation, nor to a specific psychological experience of our gender. Rather, we are born with a potential to experience all manner of pleasures from within our selves, and with partners of every gender, orientation, lifestyle and preference.

So it might be added that an individual who claims to be exclusively heterosexual or exclusively homosexual—or exclusively interested in any other sexual variation of adulthood—is actually an individual who is announcing how traumatically circumscribed his or her capacity for sensual pleasure has become.

Those who are still able to experience the bisexuality— or better *polysexuality*—of their sexual repertoire have, in a certain sense, retained more of their original erotic potential than those who experience their sexual interests as more limited.

I believe that psychoanalytic inquiry and other modes of scientific study bear out this conclusion.

Sexual Health and Erotic Freedom

*Those who proclaim that they are exclusively heterosexual
are merely announcing that they have tragically lost sight
of their capacity to enjoy homosexual pleasures due to their own
unconscious processes of suppression and repression.
And those who proclaim that they are exclusively homosexual
are simply announcing that they have tragically lost sight
of their capacity to enjoy heterosexual pleasures
due to their own unconscious processes of
suppression and repression.
We are innately polysexual at birth,
and through our socialization and acculturation,
we steadily become less than we might have been.*

Among those who profess to be exclusively homosexual (gay or lesbian) in their fantasies and activities, one commonly finds a greater fearfulness toward the erotic bodies of the other gender—usually this fear is almost entirely suppressed or repressed out of awareness. This is *not* to suggest that homosexual impulses are a "defensive reaction," because the enjoyment of the sexual bodies of one's own gender is natural.

Rather, what occurs with such gay and lesbian individuals are traumatizations in which the sensuality of the other gender becomes frightening, and these individuals' potential to take pleasure in this sensuality has dropped out of their erotic repertoire and has effectively been erased from their awareness.

In sum, homosexual feelings and behaviors are entirely natural, whereas a phobic reaction toward heterosexual feelings and behaviors is the regrettable result of traumatic experiences.

Correspondingly, among those who profess to be exclusively heterosexual in their fantasies and activities, one commonly finds greater fearfulness toward partnered sexual encounters with the erotic bodies of their own gender— even if solo pleasuring is thoroughly enjoyed—and often this fear is almost entirely suppressed or repressed out of awareness. This is *not* to suggest that heterosexual impulses are a "defensive reaction," because the enjoyment of the sexual bodies of the other gender is natural.

Rather, what occurs with "straight" individuals are traumatizations in which the sensuality of their own gender has become frightening—at least, in the context of erotic partnering—and these individuals' potential to take pleasure in this sensuality has dropped out of their erotic repertoire and has effectively been erased from their awareness.

In sum, heterosexual feelings and behaviors are entirely natural, whereas a phobic relation toward homosexual feelings and behaviors is the regrettable result of traumatic experiences.

These conclusions may be unpopular to those who are committed to the judgmental "politics of identity," with its double-edged effort *either* to establish what appear to be minority sexual interests as legitimate positions within the range of human sexual variation *or* to assert that the majority sexual position constitutes the exclusively legitimate mode of human sexual expression.

If our sexuality is ever to be truly free,
we have to move beyond these politics of identity
into a context of sexual liberation in which we are all able to
embrace every aspect of our erotic potential.

If it were generally accepted that we are all inherently polysexual, why would any of us feel the need to identify as *either* this *or* that? The problems of human sexuality mostly arise because of the vicious effects of those impulses that we deny, suppress and repress, within ourselves.

It must be emphasized, however, that this theory of polysexual potentiality—in which homosexuality is understood as a post-traumatic erasure of heterosexual impulses, and heterosexuality is understood as a post-traumatic erasure of homosexual impulses—does *not* imply that sexual orientation is a matter of choice, nor that it can become a matter of choice. The erasure of certain aspects of our erotic potential typically occurs very early in life.

The traumatizations that are critical in setting the course of our individually distinct patterns of suppression and repression occur most frequently, most decisively, and most stringently, when we are infants and toddlers. As was indicated in our discussion of the origins of shame and guilt, these traumatizations begin earlier than, or concurrent with, the child's emerging capacity for linguistic speech.

As with the establishment of the "mother tongue," matters of our sexual patterning are inscribed in us so early that they are effectively "hard-wired"—even though they are still a matter of experience, and not a matter that is genetically predetermined.

Infants are born with many biological variations—chromosomal, endocrinological, and anatomical. But the content and quality of their adult sexual patterning is not written in their genes. Rather, critical early experiences—much of them prelinguistic and unconscious—set in motion the "deeply-wired" establishment of patterns of erotic interest and arousal that will be steadily reinforced as childhood development progresses.

Homosexuals can be coerced to experiment with heterosexually partnered encounters, and heterosexuals can be coerced to experiment with homosexually partnered encounters, but the basic orientation of their sexual patterning cannot be changed once it is established in early life. Again, sexual orientation is *not* a matter of choice, but this does *not* imply that it is therefore a matter of genetics.

There is no such thing as a gay baby, a lesbian baby, or a straight baby. There are only babies with a polysexual potential for erotic pleasure—whose very early development will set in motion the establishment of sexual patterns and orientations that cannot later be experienced as a matter of mere preference or "choice."

On Traumatization:

Erotic desire is quite mysterious. It comes to us from deep within the wellsprings of our being, and we can neither choose it, nor explain it. If you doubt this, I invite you to perform the following experiment.

> . . . Close your eyes for a moment and recall the most recent occasion in which you spontaneously felt sexually aroused. Perhaps it was the feel of a warm breeze on your skin. Perhaps it was the shapeliness of her legs and the smile on her face. Perhaps it was the slope of his shoulders and the warmth of his chest.
>
> . . . Whatever it was, hold it in your imagination for a minute. Then ask yourself: "Why is *this* experience arousing? Why this particular sensation on my skin? Or why these particular shapely legs and this smile? Why this particular sloping shoulder and this warm chest?"
>
> . . . You will rapidly realize that whatever "explanations" come into your mind, they are entirely inadequate. Typically, if pressed for an "explanation" of the desire that has just arisen in your awareness, you will resort to insisting that the particular experience just *is* arousing—even while, on reflection, you know that others would not necessarily have found it so. This sensation, these legs, this smile, these shoulders, this chest . . . they just are *"hot"!* That's all that can be said.
>
> . . . It is even puzzling that others don't immediately see how *"hot"* this is—we are

rarely able to understand, with genuine empathy, how another individual does not desire what we find desirable. Moreover, if someone else suggests that we may not find these experiences so *"hot"* at some later time, in the moment of our desire, this prediction feels almost absurd to us!

So desire is quite individual and mysterious. We do not choose it. We cannot explain it. Moreover, it naturally shifts within us in so that, *within limits*, what is exciting today may not be tomorrow, and what is not exciting today may become erotically charged tomorrow.

Once our sexual patterning begins to be inscribed within us, it can perhaps be opened up a little—through healing practices that facilitate our sexual growth and that, to some limited extent, can undo some of the constrictive and restrictive consequences of our personal history of traumatizations.

Through psychotherapy, many individuals find that their repertoire of erotic enjoyment opens and expands as fears and anxieties are addressed and healed.

For example, I personally found that once I healed the fear of homoerotic feelings that I had developed in childhood, I not only came to enjoy an erotic connection with certain men, but the quality of my sexual relations with women improved significantly.

Healing homophobia—and opening to the enjoyment of homosexual pleasures—did not diminish my erotic enthusiasm for women in the slightest. In fact, the intensity of my enjoyment when engaging in sexual sharing with women increased, and my ability to be a "good lover" with women improved dramatically.

Evidently, my previous conflict over homosexual impulses, my inner struggle to suppress or repress homosexual feelings, had been negatively affecting my ability to lovemake with a woman. Previously, my heterosexual expression had been somewhat marred by my anxiety-ridden need to ward-off homosexual impulses.

Under conditions of inner "conflict management," *all* sexual expression becomes less that what it might otherwise be. The very wonderful fact about healing practices—when ethically undertaken—is that we can only become more sexually free, open and expansive.

> *Traumatization robs us of our erotically polysexual potential,*
> *whereas genuine, ethically conducted, healing practices*
> *enable us to reappropriate our sexual freedom,*
> *and to have restored to us*
> *the open and expansive nature of our erotic energies.*

To return to the analogy with our induction into a "mother tongue," note that we all start life with the potential to adopt any language as our "first language." Similarly, at birth, our erotic potential is virtually unlimited. However, again like the acquisition of a "mother tongue," once the basic priorities of the patterning of our sexual desire are established, their fundaments cannot be changed.

The development of a particular sexual patterning begins very early in life, and its installation is enormously complex— far too complex for it ever to be controlled by human intentionality. Healing practices sometimes succeed in freeing, opening and expanding our erotic potential, but *not* because we can "decide"—on the level of conscious intentionality—to modify our sexual desire. Rather, all we can do is work and play to understand our desires in all their fullness—and perhaps to allow the dissolution of some of those inner anxieties fueling the suppression and repression of those erotic desires that may appear to have long since dropped out of our repertoire.

Our sexual development is indeed a prime example of the way in which nonlinear, interdependent complexity governs all natural phenomena. The basic patterning of the ways in which we do and do not express our—initially polysexual—erotic desire is established as early as, or earlier than, language itself. This is the force of our unconscious erotic patterning and its development through traumatizations that damage and deteriorate our capacity for sensual and sexual desire.

Central to this theory of the establishment of our sexual patterning is the notion of traumatic experience, and how it reductively shapes our erotic repertoire by eroding and eviscerating our natural polysexuality. The central insight here is that

Traumatization produces psychological conflict, resulting in the establishment of individually characteristic patterns by which anxieties over sexual expression are managed.

So we now arrive at a specific notion of traumatization, and of how traumatic experience triggers the suppression and repression of our erotic potential and our sexual desires.

A traumatization—whether for children or adults—is any event that overwhelms the individual's psychological capacity to process the experience cognitively and emotionally. What this implies is that the traumatic event has compelled or coerced the subject across a boundary—or threshold of stimulation—that previously seemed to have been reliably established.

In psychoanalytic terminology, the experience of being overwhelmed in this way comprises an encounter with our inherent deathfulness—and "castratedness"—as was mentioned in the previous chapter. However, for the purposes of our discussion, we may simply think of being overwhelmed as an experience not only of the abrupt loss of our established sense of self, but also of the abrupt loss of our world as we have represented it. In this sense, a trauma is psychologically like an encounter with annihilation.

Traumatization is, by definition, an experience that threatens our mental organization by causing a rupture in our ability to equilibrate (which, in the terminology of cognitive psychology, means both to assimilate and to accommodate) the "new" event within the system of our established representations of our selves and of the world in which we have been living. Colloquially, this "new" event is "too much for us to handle." It dramatically ruptures our capacity to make sense of our selves and the world we live in—so it is terrifying.

Overstimulation, understimulation, and conflictive stimulation—which, as we will discuss, means any stimulation that crosses a significant boundary that the individual believed to be required and reliable—can all have traumatic consequences for an individual.

Thus, what is "traumatic" will always be relative to each individual's pre-existing mental representations, and will differ at each phase of the individual's psychological maturation. For example, a father who wipes his daughter's vulva when bathing her in infancy is unlikely to traumatize her; whereas a father who insists on doing so when his daughter is older is likely to damage the girl's sense of her own sexuality.

In psychoanalytic terms, when the stimulation constituted by an event disrupts the capacity of an individual's mental organization to process, or "make sense of," the experience, the entire organization "faces," in some way, an intimation of its own annihilation. It "faces" this glimpse of its own annihilation, as if in a concrete experience of the "deathbound" or "castrated" condition of its own subjectivity.

Emotionally and spiritually, a traumatic experience always provides us with an intimation of the abyss that is within each of us and within all other phenomena—a metaphysical encounter of the "void within," and an "unthinkable" experience of our own inherent "deathfulness."

Even this brief discussion indicates the enormous complexity of our sexual development. This is why I stated that the diminution of our erotic potential by our history of successive traumatizations is indeed a prime example of how the transformation and transmutation of all natural phenomena is governed by processes that are characterized by their nonlinear and interdependent complexity.

This brief discussion also suggests how individually specific are the criteria for what will or will not be experienced as traumatic, but that

An experience of traumatization always involves a compulsory or coerced crossing of a boundary or threshold.

Whether the boundary or threshold involves overstimulation, understimulation or conflictive stimulation, there is always a sense in which the individual has significantly relied on it, such that the traumatic event now signals that the world "makes no sense."

This is profoundly frightening, because a world that "makes no sense" jeopardizes the very existence of a coherent "self" within it. The traumatic event thus "shakes" the individual at his or her psychological foundations. Whether on a subtle or a dramatic scale, traumatization is the experience when "things fall apart," and our very being-in-the-world might seem on the brink of extinction.

This is perhaps the most important aspect of our discussion of traumatic experience, especially as it pertains to the development of our sexual patterning and the progressive loss of our erotic potential. So we will now examine briefly the importance of thresholds or boundariness in human functioning.

On Incest Taboo:

Our entire psychological lives and the realities of the world we live in are composed of thresholds or boundaries. Consider here seven of the major ones with which we labor daily and throughout our lives:

... between what is pleasurable and what is not,

... between what is "me" and what is other or "not-me,"

... between what is past and what is future,

... between what is literally or verifiably "real" and what is figuratively or imaginatively "real,"

... between what we are aware of and what is beyond, or suppressed and repressed from our awareness (that is, between what is reflectively conscious and what is dynamically unconscious, or between whatever comes from the knower and whatever comes from the unknowable or the knowable unknown),

... between whatever constitutes "law and order" and whatever does not,

... between what is "good" and what is "bad" (or between whatever is "Right, Proper, True and Effective" and whatever is not).

As we begin to study thresholds or boundaries—especially in the context of psychoanalytic inquiry—we come to understand how essentially paradoxical many of the issues actually are.

The conclusions that we can draw from this study may seem somewhat philosophical, but all of them are confirmed by anthropological and psychoanalytic research. Without digressing into too much detail, I will indicate what I believe to be the main conclusions of these studies.

Our experience of thresholds or boundaries is absolutely necessary for the establishment of our capacity to think, feel, and act in the world. Although their operation is almost entirely relative, and ultimately arbitrary, our essential human capacity to experience boundariness always eventually refers back to the primordial boundary of incest taboo.

If you doubt the relative and arbitrary nature of boundariness, consider carefully any of the major thresholds or boundaries listed above.

In terms of their relativity, note how these boundaries always avoid definition except in relation to other boundaries. For example, if you challenge someone who believes that public nudity is "immoral" and should be illegal, they will sooner or later claim that nudity inevitably leads to fornication or sexual abuse.

In relation to the arbitrariness of boundaries, note how any of these thresholds could have been drawn somewhere other than wherever they are currently experienced as being drawn. For example, no expert in child development can tell you at precisely what age, in months and years, a father must cease bathing his young daughter—at what exact point does a pleasurable and caring mode of interaction become an instance of sexual abuse, and why.

For the most part, the specification of any particular boundary or threshold can never be absolutely ascertained, and we can never comprehend why it could not have been a little more one way or the other. Nor can we articulate, in anything more than an inchoate fashion, why it is there at all, even when we strongly sense that it somehow has to be there.

Yet, despite this relativity and arbitrariness, the functional operation of boundariness is absolutely necessary for the very possibility of our experiencing a self that lives in its representational world. Without our capacity to sense the existence of boundaries, to experience their transgression, and to formulate our selves in relation to them, there would be neither sanity nor civilization.

This is especially evident when we come to consider the boundaries or thresholds that are functionally operative in the development of our sexual patterning. But, in general, it may be said that our capacities to think, feel, and act, all depend crucially on our ability to constitute our selves in relation to a multitude of thresholds or boundaries.

In considering the necessity of boundariness, and the manner of their formation, we tend mistakenly to believe *either* that boundaries exist "out there" in reality *or* that they come from "in here" and are authored by human intentionality, as products of our creative consciousness.

However, in a critically significant sense, it may be that neither belief is correct—for there is a crucial sense in which the realm of symbolic language, the representational or sign systems within which we live, are both "outside" and "inside." We do not author the representational system within which we think, and in this sense it comes from "outside" us. Moreover, the "reality" that we think to exist "out there" is only able to be experienced—effectively only exists—when it is represented in a significatory system. In this sense everything occurs "inside" the languages of our representationality.

Without delving into the philosophy of all this, let us consider briefly its application to our sexual development, from our libidinal polypotentiality to our "maturation" into erotic self-alienation.

Scientific research suggests that there is just one special boundary or threshold that, although somewhat arbitrary in the details or specifics of its operation, does not appear to be relative to the constitution of others. That is, one particular boundary which is difficult to define in terms of our other experiences of boundariness. This is the "primordial boundary" of incest prohibition, the incest taboo.

What this means is that there is a crucially important sense in which, at the deepest levels of their genesis and their operation, all psychological boundaries and thresholds—and indeed the very notion and experience of boundariness itself—can be referred to a "point of origination," which I call the "boundary-imperative of incest taboo."

The "boundary-imperative of incest taboo" is necessary for us to be able to experience all other modes of boundariness. In this sense, the operation of the prohibition against incest is what ensures our psychological health because it ultimately safeguards our ability to think, feel, and act in the world with any degree of sanity.

All the identities, positions and stories by which we make our way through our representational world—what I have elsewhere called the "narratological imperative"—depend on the operation of the incest taboo.

In this sense, our psychological existence depends on the prohibition against incest.

Yet, despite this privileged and primordial status, this taboo is like all other boundaries in that it is not absolutely fixed in time and space. Rather, its operation is also somewhat relative and arbitrary. However, it is only relative and arbitrary in the sense that the specifics of its enactment may vary somewhat from one culture to another, from one family to another, and perhaps even from one individual to another. It is *not* relative and arbitrary—but very much an absolute of our humanity—in the double sense that every culture, family and individual, has an incest taboo, and that it is *the* privileged boundary, from which our capacity to experience all other modes of boundariness is derived.

The incest taboo is *neither* "out there" in reality *nor* is it authored by our conscious intentionality, "in here." In a sense, it is given to us and required by us, and we constitute "who I am" in relation to it. Nowhere does it appear to be encoded in the material world, even though it is not something any of us authored creatively. Thus, our inquiry into the nature of the incest taboo teaches us something about all boundary phenomena, because the incest taboo is unquestionably a feature of the way in which all humans represent their reality.

> *The incest taboo is "deeply-wired" within us,*
> *because it inheres to the very structure of the languages*
> *by which our realities are represented.*
> *It is neither encoded in the material world,*
> *nor is it consciously created by us.*
> *Rather, it is an unavoidable boundary at the very foundation*
> *of our ability to think, feel, or act.*

There is no physical or material reason why incest cannot be committed. Contrary to some mythology, genitals do not wither and rot if incest is committed; and whatever genetic consequences there may be to inbreeding, such effects only emerge after several generations and so are unlikely to be known about, yet alone directly experienced, by the participants in an incestuous liaison. So, evidently, this taboo is extraordinarily and enigmatically powerful, for it is not reinforced, so to speak, by external consequences.

Moreover, this taboo did not—and could not possibly have—come into existence because some human subject deliberated over the matter and said something like: "By God, look at all these (incestuous) acts and wishes; for the sake of our sanity, we better have a taboo against them!" Thus the taboo against incest is not the conscious creation of human intentionality.

In contradistinction to these two, rather absurd, accounts of the genesis of the incest taboo, it is almost certain that this taboo came into existence concurrent with, and inherent to, the origination of symbolic language systems at the very beginnings of human culture with the emergence of reflective consciousness in the Late Pliocene and Early Pleistocene Eras. So, despite the fact that its specific interpretation may vary between cultures and other groupings, its existence is universal and is profoundly necessary for our health. This is why, across all cultures, anyone involved in a direct transgression of this taboo almost always suffers horribly.

All this teaches us something further about boundariness. That is, since our experience of boundaries ultimately refers back to the incest taboo, it becomes evident that

> *Ultimately, human subjectivity does do not create boundaries, but rather is created by them.*

In this sense, the examination of boundary functioning eventually demonstrates the derivative character and constitution of human intentionality. Boundaries foundationally create and define human subjectivity—the way humans think, feel and act.

To be more specific, our personality and our subjectivity is created and defined through our passage within the symbolic languages—or representational systems—to which the incest taboo inheres.

In a certain sense, our individuality and our sexual development only evolve within a system of boundaries. Moreover, in the course of our individual development, we only come to know where a boundary occurs when—so to speak—we bump up against it, cross it or transgress it. Boundaries are only known by means of their performative repetition by human subjects.

In this sense, as consciously reflective subjects, we only know boundaries because they are performed and re-performed (in their observance or in their transgression) by human subjects, in what psychoanalysts call the "repetition compulsion."

As subjects, we establish ourselves—who we are, how we think and feel, and how we judge matters in the world—by this ongoing relation to matters of boundary. As the sole primordial boundary, the incest taboo ultimately defines the boundary between our awareness and what we suppress or repress from our awareness.

As complex as this may seem, it is crucial to our understanding of human sexuality, for

> *The boundary-imperative of incest taboo*
> *establishes the possibility of all human discourse,*
> *and, directly or indirectly, it defines and determines*
> *the way in which we are erotically traumatized.*

This boundary-imperative operates immaterially and in a sense transpersonally, like a "point of origination" for all the boundaries which make possible a world that might "make sense."

> *All boundaries are derived from the boundary-imperative of incest*
> *taboo, and this taboo defines and determines the possibility of*
> *every condition and operation of human self-consciousness.*
> *The incest taboo also defines our sexual development,*
> *because its various performances define and determine*
> *what the individual will and will not experience as traumatic,*
> *and therefore defines and determines what aspects of our erotic*
> *potential will be suppressed and repressed.*

It is most important for us to keep in mind that, because the specific performance of the incest taboo—its interpretation and enactment—varies widely in the myriad of experiences that an individual undergoes in the course of his or her socialization and acculturation, individual histories of traumatization are highly variable and the patterns of adult sexuality are correspondingly multitudinous.

As I see it, the discovery of the significance of the incest taboo for all aspects of human functioning is the most profound and powerful of all psychoanalytic contributions to the understanding of our humanity.

As complex as the discovery of the—unconscious—significance of the incest taboo indeed is, it explains both how our erotic potential becomes eroded or eviscerated in the course of our personal history of traumatizations, and concomitantly how our mental functioning becomes fractionated with the formation of a consciousness committed to the suppression and repression of our sensual and sexual impulses.

For these reasons, some psychoanalysts have referred to the incest taboo as *"The Law"* of laws, by which it is meant that our encounters with the incest taboo represent the primordial encounter with the experience of *"No!"* And it is this encounter that sets the frame for all the subsequent ways in which prohibitive and restrictive rules and regulations will be established.

For example, extrapolating beyond the *"No!"* that we experience—when, to return to our earlier example, we imagine our mother's body as our hand caresses our genitals—we become ready and willing to assimilate all the extensive rules and regulations against erotic pleasure that our socialization imposes upon us. Thus,

> *The problematic consequence of "The Law" of laws*
> *is not that it forbids incest*
> *—a sacrifice that is utterly necessary for our sanity—*
> *but that it also renders us vulnerable*
> *to the observance of countless other laws*
> *that effectively constrain or curtail our sensual and sexual*
> *enjoyment of life, and that have little or nothing to do with the*
> *dangers of incestuous indulgence.*

This is why the boundary-imperative of incest is "The Law" from which all other laws gain their authority over us, even though many of these extrapolations or appropriations of authority are entirely unnecessary. Indeed, they would seem to serve only to damage or deplete our enjoyment of life—to deprive us of our capacity to realize our erotic potential.

This extrapolative or elaborative power of the incest taboo over us is able to occur as a sort of "over-extension," precisely because the taboo against incest itself is so "deeply-wired" into our psychological constitution. What psychoanalysis demonstrates is that incest itself—with the deathfulness or "castratedness" of our consciousness—always confronts us as the abyss of metaphysical horror, in a way that we can never fully articulate.

Incest is, ultimately, a horror toward which all our thinking, feeling or acting is, in a certain sense, a "defensive" response. The character of these "defenses" will be discussed in Chapter Seven.

For our health, it is absolutely necessary that the incest taboo be observed, but the surplus extension of this taboo to innumerable other rules and regulations that prohibit our sensual and sexual enjoyment of life, and that traumatically alienate us from our erotic potential, is absolutely unnecessary.

The vitally important power of the incest taboo is the ultimate reason why we are so frightened of our sensuality and sexuality. Yet there is no valid reason for us to be afraid of any non-incestuous expression of our potential for erotic pleasure.

Our erotic liberation can only be achieved if we confront and counteract the fearfulness that has been traumatically inscribed within us in the course of our socialization. It can only be achieved if we reappropriate the joys of all those modalities of pleasure—of which we have been robbed precisely because they somehow became associated with *the* taboo that truly matters.

By way of conclusion, let us survey some of the crucial implications of these arguments.

Foremost, it must be emphasized that the individual's lifelong struggle with the incest taboo is inestimably magnified by the fact our earliest and most formative erotic experiences always occur in the context of our incestuous relationships.

As will be described later, it is vital for our health and happiness as infants, toddlers and children—as well as thereafter—that we are touched, cuddled and caressed. Our neurological development as well as our psychological development—our physical and emotional health—depends on our receiving adequate stimulation of this sort. This is a vitally significant issue. We cannot do without the stroking, the warm embrace, and the kisses—in sum, the arousing stimulation of our libidinal energies—by those who first care for us. Yet these very same caretakers are later found to be, and designated as, forbidden to us as sexual partners. Typically, this means that our development is characterized by the following threefold psychological struggle.

➤ For our physical and emotional health throughout the remainder of our lives, we need to receive, in our infancy and early childhood, the sensual and sexual attention of our mother, our father, our siblings, or other caretakers.

➤ As we come into language, we then later discover that to go beyond this early stimulation and arousal of our libidinal energies and to engage in further sensual and sexual activity with these very same people, either in our imagination or in our actions, is forbidden to us by the incest taboo.

➤ So we spend much of the rest of our lives disguising and attempting to shift our erotic desire over towards fantasies, activities, and relationships that are non-incestuous. If we are to succeed in not losing our erotic potential in the most drastic and damaging manner, we have to succeed in making a series of overwhelmingly complicated transitions in this direction.

The significance of this struggle—not only for each of us as individuals, but also for the entire wellbeing of humanity—cannot be overestimated.

Our sensual and sexual impulses are initiated in a relational context that is later found to be, and designated, incestuous.

As Freud and others correctly emphasized—and as is amply confirmed by every subsequent psychoanalytic inquiry—our earliest erotic bonds with our caretakers constitute "the prototype of all subsequent love relations."

Moreover, as we have already indicated, the "problem" of incest is a symbolic one—for the child discovers the incest taboo, and the prohibition of the primordial *"No!"* is designated, as soon as he or she enters into the representational world. That is, as soon as he or she is formed psychologically as an individual. In this sense, incest is not experienced as an abstract issue of genetic connection. Rather, *whoever* the earliest caretakers may be, these members of the "family of origin" become the progenitors of incestuous desire.

Again, the "problem" of incest operates psychologically in terms of our positioning within the symbolic order of the sociocultural nexus, rather than on the level of biological inheritance.

So the "problem" is not avoided by adopting the baby to a non-biological parent, nor is it avoided by raising the baby with some form of substitutive mode of caretaking. In fact, such "solutions" bring additional complications.

And the "problem" is certainly not to be avoided by offering the infant only minimal erotic attention, for this merely compromises the infant's chances of subsequent health and happiness. Indeed, such a strategy ensures the individual's loss of his or her erotic potential.

So the developmental process of shifting erotic desire cannot be evaded.

> *The almost impossible task of individual maturation*
> *is how to make the transition*
> *to non-incestuous sensual and sexual interests*
> *with minimal traumatic loss of one's erotic potential.*

How can the child, the adolescent and the adult succeed in suppressing and repressing their natural inclination toward erotic fantasies and erotic activities that are manifestly connected to their early incestuous experiences, and yet retain as much as possible of their exuberant erotic potential?

The burden of this challenge occurs within each individual's psychological development. However, different cultures contextualize this challenge in different ways—with varyingly benign but generally adverse consequences.

For example, in most cultures, a mother may wash her infant son's penis. In some cultures, she may even caress it to give pleasure or to soothe the infant. And in a very few cultures, she is even allowed to take the infant's penis into her mouth. In most cultures, this contact is gradually or abruptly terminated as the son ages into childhood, but other sorts of non-genital caressing, such as hugging, may continue. In some cultures, the mother may cease any physical contact with her son as soon as seems feasible.

At what age of the child these various forms of touch "should" be phased out varies greatly from one culture to the next. But in every culture, a mother's touching her son's penis involves complicated rules and regulations that variously permit or prohibit this contact depending on the child's age and circumstances.

However, in no culture is it acceptable that the mother rub her son's penis against her vulva or take it into her vagina; and indeed, if the son is an adult, there is no culture that finds it acceptable for a mother to caress her adult son's penis with her mouth.

There is an additional complication to the challenges of development—namely, that caretakers have erotic feelings for the children whose growth and maturation they oversee. Moreover, just as it is essential for young children that they experience sensual and sexual feelings for their earliest caretakers, it is also essential for the health of the child that caretakers have erotic feelings for the child. This is absolutely imperative for the child's ability to experience the benefits of his or her early experience. Yet, in almost all cultures, even a discussion of such a topic is highly charged and more or less forbidden.

So our sensual and sexual development is a complex passage involving both the child's erotic feelings for his or her various caretakers and family of origin, as well as the latter's erotic feelings for the child, and the fact that these vital experiences will sooner or later become taboo. The feelings will eventually be suppressed and repressed both by the child, and by the caretakers.

As children encounter the various ways in which the boundaries of this taboo are culturally interpreted and represented, such encounters have traumatic effects, and this is how our erotic potential is eroded and eviscerated as it falls prey to our successive traumatizations.

Such is the crucible of our sensual and sexual development, the foundation of all our shame and guilt, our fear of our own erotic potential.

The crucial and unavoidable role of the incest taboo in human functioning explains fully why we are so frightened of our erotic potential.

Again, it is not that the incest taboo can be avoided, since it is essential to our safety and sanity. Rather, it is the manner in which it is negotiated that is critically important.

So to a certain extent, some loss of our erotic potential is inevitable, since we cannot avoid the incest prohibition. However, the quality of our early incestuous experiences, and the way in which we transition away from erotic arousal in incestuous relations to the experience of such arousal in non-incestuous situations, will crucially affect how much of our erotic potential we will lose in the course of our development, and what sort of sensual and sexual patterning we will experience throughout our life's course. These dimensions of our development are crucial for our sexual health and happiness throughout adulthood.

Not only does the exact interpretation of the incest taboo—or more precisely, the set of incest taboos—vary from culture to culture, but the way in which it is extended beyond the family of origin is also various. In our society, there would seem to be some elaborations or extrapolations of the incest taboo, to what I have called "homologous" relations and situations, which are also crucial to our health and happiness.

For example—as we discussed earlier—because we know that the consequences of the following liaisons are always damaging to the participants, we know that, in our culture, the incest taboo extends to the following circumstances.

➢ It is harmful for an adult to interfere in a child's right to enjoy his or her own modes of sensual and sexual expression, and especially harmful for adults to inveigle or recruit a minor into their own sexual activities or fantasies. This applies even when the minor appears to want this sort of participation. (And obviously the issue of boundaries here is particularly complex because, as we have just described, it is essential for the physical and emotional health of a child that there be an erotic current running back and forth between the child and his or her caretakers.)

➢ It is harmful for "masters" to inveigle or recruit their "slaves" into their sexual activities or fantasies—even when the latter appear to want this sort of participation. The connotations of this sort of liaison are always incestuous, and the conduct of such affairs cannot be other than aggressive. As extreme examples of this, we might note how frequently the abuse of prisoners, especially prisoners of war, appears to have a "sexual" current.

➢ There are also several types of relationship that, in this culture, stir unconscious incestuous feelings to the point where sexual liaison can be—in many cases—both very enticing and seriously harmful. The connotations of these relationships would seem to contain elements of both caretaker/child and master/slave. These typically harmful relations and situations include sexual liaisons such as boss/worker, teacher/student, counselor/client, doctor/patient, and so forth.

In sum, wherever there is a differential of real social power, healthy sexual partnering cannot occur. This is because the psychological weight of anti-sexual forces that cater to our egotism—notably, issues of overt or covert hostility and aggression—always eclipses the erotic possibility of the liaison, even when it does not appear to do so.

As will be further described in Chapter Twelve, our fascination with power differentials can only be made safe, sane and truly consensual if a "real" power differential is not involved. When such differentials are entertained merely in fantasy or in playful fantasy enactments—such as roleplaying between fully consensual adults of equal sociocultural stature—healing may occur, as well as erotic pleasure.

However, although I am suggesting that the above circumstances represent extensions of the incest taboo that need to be observed, it is perhaps more salient to argue that, in our society, there are "one-thousand-and-one" prohibitions that may have originated as extensions of the incest taboo, but are, more accurately, merely reflections of our fearfulness of sexuality that is derived from our encounter with this taboo. These "one-thousand-and-one" prohibitions are not only utterly unnecessary, they are damaging to us. They represent ways in which our erotic potential has been stifled and truncated by moralizing ideologies that purport to be as serious as matters of the incest taboo.

Although both incestuous nurturing in infancy
and the prohibition of the incest taboo with its essential extensions
are necessary for our sanity and our survival
(and thus the traumatization of our erotic life is
somewhat inevitable), in our culture,

our fears and prohibitions of sensual and sexual expression have become elaborated into a multitude of restrictive rules and regulations against erotic pleasure.
These moralizing ideologies have only a spurious connection with the ethicality of the incest prohibition,
yet they gain the force of their harmful authority over us because of our need to avoid incest.
We thus become fragmented and alienated shells of the magnificent sensual and sexual creatures that we naturally might have been.

In sum, we grow up absurd. The forces of anti-sexuality are all around us, as "The Law" of incest taboo becomes fearfully extended into one-thousand-and-one rules and regulations that operate against our erotic potential. Consider all the rules and regulations about

... How many partners *should* we have—usually only one at a time, and preferably not just one's own self.
... What gender partner *should* we have. We *should* be straight if we can be and, if we can't be, we *should* model our lifestyle on the exclusive heterosexual ideal.
... How long, how emotionally involved, how legal, *should* our partnerships be. Our sexual expression *should not* be too recreational, *should* preferably be in the context of a "serious" emotional attachment, *should* preferably be legalized, and so on.
... Which zones or parts of the body *should* be pleasured, and which *should not* be pleasured. We *should* be careful to touch here rather than there, with this person rather than that, and so forth.
... How and where the body *should* be pleasured, or not. We *should* only expose our body in private; we *should* engage in intercourse only under restrictive circumstances and in restrictive ways; we *should* lovemake this way but not that; etc.

Such rules and regulations with which we encumber our
erotic lives are merely manifestations
of how frightening our polysexual potential becomes to us
as we encounter the incest taboo,
collide with boundaries,
and experience a sequence of traumatizations
of our sensual and sexual nature.

Although the incest taboo needs to be observed, the "one-thousand-and-one" rules and regulations do not. Indeed, they are harmful to our emotional and spiritual life, and their observance renders us sensually frustrated and sexually conflicted. We are mired in shame and guilt. Although born exuberantly sensual and sexual creatures, we become fragmented and alienated shells of our own magnificence, and we inevitably participate psychologically in this tragedy.

7

Suppression, Repression, Inhibition, and Compulsivity

Our erotic emancipation requires that we heal our sensual and sexual self. Although we must confront the external mechanisms by which we are politically oppressed—such as the forces of sex fascism described in the first section of this book—such confrontations are necessary but insufficient.

Our erotic emancipation also requires the healing of our own internalized forces of anti-sexuality, the psychological forces of suppression and repression. It requires that we understand and address the processes by which we participate in our own alienation from our natural enjoyment of our erotic embodiment. We need to confront some of the psychological processes by which this alienation is instigated and maintained.

Our sensual and sexual liberation is not only a political task, it is an emotional and spiritual challenge.

As we have discussed, our sexuality is an exuberant, flowing energy within us. It is, essentially, the lifeforce that runs within and through us from the cradle to the grave. Although it births us with an almost infinite capacity for sensual and sexual pleasures, the realization of this erotic polypotentiality is, in the course of our "normal" development, serially constricted and conflicted by our experience of traumatizations. That is, given a "normal" development, our capacity for bodily pleasure and the range of our enjoyment of erotic expression typically "matures" to become narrower and shallower.

In this chapter, we will examine some of the ways in which our psychological processes participate in our own alienation from our erotic potential. We will examine how the forces of anti-sexuality function within us, how we internalize shame and guilt, and how we anxiously manage the conflict between our natural impulses and these internalizations.

In order to illuminate this discussion, let us begin with a description of a major taboo—the restrictions and prohibitions around the pleasuring of our genitals.

The taboos against looking at our genitals, knowing about our genitals, and touching or playing with our genitals, operate on many levels. Instead of engaging the natural rhythms of genital self-pleasuring, we activate a range of defensive maneuvers such as

> ➢ Abstaining from feeling the pleasures of our genitals and becoming sensually inhibited or repressed in general (in which case our enjoyment with partners, as well as our solo sexual life will become severely restricted).
> ➢ Redirecting our self-pleasuring impulses into some other "substitute" activity that may be pleasurable, such as stroking some other area of the body or engaging some other physical, or even mental, activity.
> ➢ Attacking—criticizing, vilifying and persecuting—others who do allow themselves the very pleasures that we are blocking within ourselves.
> ➢ Indulging a "substitute" activity that is self-hostile rather than self-loving, such as developing habits that hurt our own body.

> Masturbating frantically and compulsively so that the activity is no longer pleasurable, but rather it becomes an urgent anxiety-driven attempt to exorcize our conflicts about self-pleasure.

Motivated by our unconscious shame and guilt, most of us are engaged, much of the time, in some combination or permutation of these sorts of activities—all of which are attempts to obstruct the full expression of our erotic desires.

On the one side, as we have already discussed, taboos against sexual expression seem to come from somewhere external to each of us as individuals. For example, we know that powerful social forces will arraign us if we expose our genitals in public. We may hear clergy and politicians of all persuasions inveighing against sexual pleasuring outside of the procreative purposes of legal marriage. Or we may remember—from some early inscription—how during our youngest years, our caretakers might remove our hands from our genitals, perhaps scolding us, or perhaps simply telling us in seemingly gentle words that the area is "dirty," and thus giving us a strong injunction against the pleasures of self-exploration.

On the other side, we are aware that these taboos also come from somewhere within each of our individual minds. To some degree, they have long since been deeply internalized as a fundamental condition of what is called our socialization or acculturation—we have, so to speak, "made them our own." We are all deeply imbued with shame and guilt, and construct much of our lives in terms of reactive efforts to manage these anxiety-driven forces within us.

For example, we are aware that, under most circumstances, no powerful social agency is going to arrest us if we privately invite our lovers to examine our genitals, yet many of us experience some inhibition or anxiety about issuing such an invitation.

Moreover, information about the healthy care and functioning of our sexual bodies may be somewhat difficult to acquire for many people, especially in a culture that is erotically phobic. In our society, such information, which is greatly needed in childhood, is more readily available to adults (when it is almost too late for it to be useful). Even then, it is more available than it is utilized. By adulthood, many of us are already conditioned to prefer to continue our lives in denial and worried ignorance.

Some of us might admit that we wish for enriched experiences with our genitals, yet few of us implement this intention. Between wishing for bliss and translating this intention into practice, inner conflicts around shame and guilt frequently deter or derail us.

We will now briefly survey some of the subtle yet powerful ways in which we cognitively, emotionally and behaviorally manage our conflicts between our erotic desires and the anti-sexual forces that we have internalized.

We will list five major "strategies" by which our everyday mental functioning thwarts the flow of our sensual and sexual pleasures and energies.

This list, which draws from the discoveries made by psychoanalytic inquiry, is somewhat arbitrary and seriously simplistic in several ways. It might be condensed to fewer than five, but it could easily be elaborated and expanded to many more. My discussion of these strategies will convey a general sense of their operation rather than an accurate assessment of their psychodynamic complexity. I will try to present these mental strategies without jargon—that is, in a way that makes them accessible to a reader unfamiliar with the relevant scientific literatures. Finally, my descriptions will be somewhat artificial because, for any particular individual, these mental maneuverings never operate in isolation but always in constellations.

➤ Strategy #1: *Repression/Inhibition*. We exist as what I have called our "bodymind"—meaning that our "body" and our "mind" are not separable, but aspects of a holistic system.

This implies that, as persons, we are a set of anatomical and physiological structures, which are the conduit for myriad subtle energies, feelings and sensations; and somehow, housed most evidently in our nervous system, we also have mental faculties that construct our representational world as the identities, positions, and stories by which we conduct our life's narrative.

What we commonly call our "mind" is a system of representations, and our mental functioning consists of transformations of these representations. We have representations of our self, of "objects" other than our self (things, persons, abstractions), and of all the events or actions that can occur between these entities. Our mental functioning is a repetitive and compulsive enterprise that incessantly *re*-presents these entities in configurations of thought, feeling, and action.

Whereas life is a continually flowing reality of erotic exuberance (that intimates our insufficiency and deathfulness), our mind repetitiously and compulsively represents matters, as if to assert an illusory constancy of our self and our world—as if to assert the validity of identities, as the apparent certainty or permanence of static repetitiousness. This repetitious compulsion to represent matters, which I have called the "narratological imperative" (and thus to make sense of self and world, as a set of identities, positions, and stories), causes the mind to chatter incessantly. This chattering mind— consider here the chattering condition of the unimpeded stream of ordinary or conventional consciousness—forms the fabric of our egotism.

Without discussing these notions any further at this juncture, it is very obvious that this mind treats itself as if it were not merely a set of events within the holistic universe of our bodymind and its ecosystem. Rather, we tend to operate as if "mind" is entirely distinct from our physicality, and even from our emotionality and from our spirituality. Western philosophy has been trenchantly dualistic; with our egotistic "mind" treating itself as if it were master of the organism, and the "body" its slave or servant.

In our cultural tradition, we view the mind as if it were a sort of executive agency that might enable us to exist "in our heads." This—deluded—"executive agency" then treats the body as if it were merely an instrument or machine at its command, and our bodily energies as if they were merely supplies to be commandeered and exploited at the behest of the executive.

What is of central importance for us to understand is that our egotistic mind—or representational system—treats itself in this manner precisely because the maintenance of its illusory and delusional sense of its own identity depends on the suppression and repression of the sensual and sexual energies of our erotic lifeforce.

Suppression means that our chattering mind pushes an impulse out of its immediate consciousness. Repression then means that our mind attempts to keep our erotic desires not only out of our reflective awareness, but unacknowledged and locked away somewhere in the unconscious dimension of our bodymind. Suppression usually precedes repression, and the latter brings about the absence or inhibition of sensual and sexual desire.

For many of us—indeed, for all of us to greater or lesser degree—our history of both implicit and explicit traumatizations has resulted in some closing-down or shutting-off of our erotic desires.

Our mind instead preoccupies itself with its "important" investment in maintaining our egotistic identities, positions and stories. This repetitious and compulsive labor includes "important" matters, such as damage control (how to avoid risk, humiliation, punishment), human resource management (how to control the behaviors of those around us), asset accumulation (how to make more money and acquire more property), public relations (how to have others think well of us), self-aggrandizement (how to have ourselves think well of us), and so forth.

The erotic potential of our bodymind, as a conduit for the energies of pleasure, almost disappears, sometimes seeming to leave nothing more of its sensual and sexual momentum than the scantiest trace. Our "mental executive" tends to treat us as if we were an automaton, running on empty, and forgetting our erotic sourcing.

With the repression of erotic desire, our sensual and sexual energies seem to disappear, but they do not merely dissipate and cease to exist. Rather, they become locked in our anatomical structures causing blockages in the flow of subtle energies. Often their repression causes the body to break down physiologically and we become ill.

In this respect, we can see how misleading is the distinction between "body" and "mind" that has preoccupied western philosophies (which is why I use the more holistic notion of the "bodymind"). When we understand how our anatomical structures and physiological functions participate in our "mental defenses" against the free-flow of erotic energies, we realize that the "body" *is* unconscious mind.

The mind's repressive activity results in what psychoanalysts and therapeutic body-workers understand as symptom-formations and character-formations that are physically manifested in our anatomy and physiology. Some common examples would include: stiffness along the spinal column, immobility of the hips and pelvis, constrictions of our capacity to breathe fully and evenly from the depths of the abdominal cavity, specific configurations of tightening in the ligaments and other connective tissues, addictive behaviors, dermatological eruptions, patterns of chronic pain, and all manner of psychosomatic illnesses.

Although our society is reluctant to address this issue, the truth is that sensual and sexual repression is physically— as well as emotionally and spiritually—dangerous.

The psychology of repression manifests as the inhibition of sensual and sexual expression. Inhibition is ubiquitous and subtle, but it is also often dramatic. We see all around us: people who have never danced naked in the sunlight; people who allow themselves to become severely deprived of touch; people who have never explored the genitals of their own gender, as well as the other gender, with the tenderness of their mouth; people who have never laughed or cried with erotic exhilaration; people whose capacity to fantasize exultantly has long since died as they become sensually self-deprived and sexually blank.

Repressed and inhibited, we soldier on, like the walking wounded, famished but allowing ourselves little more than the slightest glance at the menu card, never allowing ourselves to partake of the feast. For many of us, it is a menu that we have almost forgotten how to read.

When we are devoid of our sexual-spiritual energies, through the repressive constitution of the chattering mind, death becomes terrifying (even when it is apparently welcomed as a relief), and "love" deteriorates into a trite routine of benevolent transactions. As our chattering mind depletes our erotic energies with its incessantly compulsive repetition of identities, stories, and positions, our understanding of "love" and "death" degenerates into the platitudes sold in greeting cards.

➢ Strategy #2: *Channelization/Segregation*. Whatever the extent of our traumatization, the repression and inhibition of our erotic energies is never, and can never be, total. Despite our mental effort to keep our sensual and sexual energies in exile, our erotic impulses surface somewhere and our mind attempts to regulate the manner of their expression. In addition to "pure" suppression, repression and inhibition, additional strategies by which our mind attempts to contain the exuberance of our erotic energy are deployed.

The most evident strategy—to which we have already alluded frequently—is to allow a certain amount of highly controlled and modified erotic expression, and to limit this expression to certain contexts and occasions.

Although there are various processes involved in this—processes that are well described in the psychoanalytic lexicon—I will refer to it here as the "channelization" or "segregation" of sensual and sexual desires. With this strategy, the expression of "sex" is rule-governed, and in a profound sense anti-sexual.

In our culture, channelization or segregation is widespread and commonplace. Erotic expression is allowed "there" but not "here," or "then" but not "now." This implies that we must live with substantial repression and inhibition of our sensual and sexual inclinations, alleviated only by this limited and delineated channelization or segregation of erotic expression.

All the cultural maneuvers involved in the "sexification" of America (which we discussed in Chapter Two) are closely analogous to the psychological processes involved in this strategy.

Erotic expression is encouraged provided that it is "commodity-sex," salacious, titillating and comparatively banal: "Get turned on by tight jeans, uplifting silk brassieres, machismo toys, or cosmetics and surgical 'enhancements,' but do not fully appreciate the sensuality of your erotic body for what it actually is; groove to buffed bodies, gyrating on our television and computer screens, swaying to the hefty beat of music in adult clubs, or copulating in the panoramas of 'pornography,' but do not enjoy the sheer sensuality of the erotic body in which you actually live; model your conduct on soap operas, sitcom dramas, mainstream movies that frequently depict 'hot and heavy' romances, or even the 'fucking' displayed in X-rated videos, but do not actually feel free to follow the call of your heart and your genitals."

Another example occurs in the way our society traditionally idealizes a stylized mode of erotic expression: Sex is "okay" if it involves penile-vaginal intercourse between a man and a woman who are legally married—although, since the alleged "purpose" of this event is mostly procreative, it is not acceptable to enjoy it too much. Society tries to command that its youth should wait for the privilege and responsibility of coitus; but, having waited, the couple will receive little or no useful information about how to increase the potential pleasure they may receive from it.

In a sense, our society tolerates genital heterosexual intercourse, but refuses to condone or support its orgasmic pleasures. Moreover, sensual and sexual expression involving other configurations is variously subjected to prohibition, anxiety, shame and guilt.

Although its geography varies from individual to individual, this segregation of our erotic expression is routinized and substantially reinforced by public opinions, medical mythologies, religious doctrines, and legal politics. Almost all of us can recognize our own attitudes in at least some of the following:

> . . . "It's okay to touch myself here, in this way, but not there, in that way (even if it feels good)."

> . . . "It's fine to kiss someone you have just met, but genital touching is for later."

> . . . "Genital intercourse is wonderful, but only if is in the context of a serious committed relationship."

> . . . "Sexual love between consenting partners is beautiful, but only if the partners are of different gender."

... "It's normal for couples in their twenties or thirties, but it's disgusting even to think of older people doing it."

... "Adults need to know some stuff about sex, but children should not be told much, even if they are curious about it."

... "Sex between two people is normal, but with more people it becomes kinky, and the participants must have psychopathological difficulties with true intimacy."

... "If I were to fantasize about something that I would never actually do, then I will be more likely to do it, and that would be unacceptable, so I try only to fantasize about sex that is okay."

... "Partners who act out their fantasies consensually are just demonstrating that they are unable to be content with normal sex."

... "If I allow my pet to lick my arms, that is just affection, if my pet were to lick my genitals, that would be perversion."

As we have discussed, our sensual and sexual expression becomes surrounded by innumerable rules and regulations. Some of these we can fully articulate. Some we recognize ourselves as believing, although we could not necessarily have stated them clearly, even if asked to do so. Some we endorse automatically without recognition of the way they affect us. And some are so subtle that they appear only as the ripples of shame and guilt surfacing around a topic that is somewhat displaced away from the relevant conflict or "issue." As has been wisely written, we are rarely upset for the reason we think we are upset.

Our socialization and acculturation offer us "values" by which we choose to limit our erotic expression within a constricted range of activities that are "acceptable." Some activities are acceptable only on the condition that they are not fully enjoyed. For example, every sex therapist has interviewed couples who engage in genital intercourse because they believe they are "supposed" to do so, despite the fact that one or both of the partners experiences it as less satisfying than self-pleasuring or some other activity.

When our desires are segregated into "acceptable" channels, our conventional mind is always acting as the judge of what is acceptable. Rather than being enjoyed as a response to our bodymind's yearnings for pleasuring, our "sex" life is now governed by values and ideologies.

However, "sex" that does not arise spontaneously from the erotic pleasure of our sensual body—but rather that is orchestrated and administered by our mind's assimilation of cultural values and ideologies—can never be authentically sexual.

Under this strategy, erotic expression becomes more and more constricted, routinized, and emptied of its passion. Our sensual and sexual life easily becomes enmeshed in, and usually strangulated by, a weave of *"shoulds"* and *"should-nots."* When we start even to think about sensual and sexual possibilities, our mind immediately spits out judgments about what would be inappropriate, abnormal, perverted, wrong, sick, immoral, weird, sinful, and so forth.

Because the mind that has assimilated all sorts of prohibitions and restrictions is fearful of the erotic potential of our bodymind, judgments are applied in order to constrict, segregate and channelize, our own sensual and sexual activities. Then, in yet another strategy that reinforces our suppression and repression, we apply these judgments to others.

➤ Strategy #3: *Manipulating the "Other."* When our mind does, so to speak, decide to permit some form of controlled and rule-bound erotic expression—constricting the activities it allows and constraining the pleasures that may be experienced—it is evident that a "secondary gain" of an egotistic sense of self-righteousness is often also accrued.

For example, if a person believes that it is acceptable to take pleasure from finger-massaging the temples, but not from fingering the anus—which might evoke significant feelings of shame or guilt—then abstinence from the latter activity is likely to be accompanied by a self-congratulatory sense of being a "better" person.

And the implicit or explicit meaning of "better" is "better than" someone else who does enjoy such activity.

From condemning an impulse within ourselves, our anti-sexual mind jumps quickly into a preoccupation with condemning it in others. Because our traumatizing socialization is transmitted to us by others and by the culture in which we develop, we are inclined, almost without hesitation, to use our thinking about "others" to reinforce our defenses against our own erotic expression.

Our chattering mind is very comfortable in the role of an arrogant and obnoxious missionary.

Here is the structure of this strategy. Suppose I think about the possibility of a sexual act that is forbidden, and that would stir shame or guilt within me if I were either to do it—or even to acknowledge my excitement in thinking about it. By implication, whenever I consider the possibility of this act, I am acknowledging that the act could be performed, and probably is being performed, by someone else, an "other" person or group. I am actually having a fantasy about "them" doing "it," but I rarely label it as such.

Now whenever I consider this act but abstain from it, I can easily reinforce this suppression and repression of my inclination by preoccupying myself with judging those who engage in, and perhaps even enjoy, this particular act. My judgmentalism may be articulated to myself in private, but also to the public. It may take the form of a mild feeling of being superior to the other, such as "I am right, and they are wrong." It may involve my active formulation of further criticisms and condemnations of the other. And it may lead me to make it my mission to persecute and punish the other.

Three aspects of this strategy are noteworthy. First, that I attribute my own desires to the other. Given my egotism's inner need to be judgmental, it scarcely matters whether the other is actually engaging in or enjoying the act from which I am abstaining. If the other is indeed doing the activity, then they are obligingly providing me with an "externalization" of my own desire. If the other is actually only doing the deed in my imagination, then I am "projecting."

Second, while using or abusing the other in this way, I may be aware that I would secretly enjoy doing what the other is doing. In this case, I have suppressed the impulse within myself and am instead busying myself with judging the other. Or I may no longer be aware that I could enjoy doing what the other is doing. In this case, I have repressed the impulse, am no longer conscious of its attraction to me, and am instead busying myself with judging the other.

Third, this strategy is inherently hostile, aggressive, and often violent. Consider how something that was once erotic has somehow been transformed into critical judgmental activity. Also consider how self-hostility, as the refusal to accept one's own erotic desire, is here replaced by hostility toward the other. Moreover, it is accompanied by an aggrandized sense of self-righteousness.

An additional aspect of this strategy is implied here, which is highly significant (and will soon be discussed in more detail). In a way that is perhaps remarkable and complex, exercising our judgmentalism is itself charged erotically. Its "erotic charge" involves a transmutation of its sensual quality into an aggressive quality.

Let us illustrate how we manipulate the "other" by looking into the rather obvious example of the homophobia of heterosexual men.

Consider a "straight" man who enjoys having his "cock" licked and sucked by his female partner, and is delighted that she seems to enjoy this activity. In his fantasies, he knows he has thoughts about what it would be like if he were himself to suck a penis, but he has suppressed these thoughts, deciding that it would not be something he would ever do. Or maybe he has forgotten ever having had such thoughts and has repressed them. He then starts thinking about "those" men, the ones who do suck penises, and he becomes "disgusted" with these "cocksuckers," who, in his mind, are obviously inferior to the man he is.

In another scenario, this "straight" man may harbor suppressed or repressed fantasies about what it would be like to receive anally from a partner, to be entered and stimulated by a penis or dildo. And, since he, like many misinformed heterosexuals, is convinced that gay men are constantly "taking it up the arse," his preoccupations now focus on these "sins" of the gay community with their "dirty" habits and their feminized "faggot" lifestyle.

These are the basic psychodynamics of all the hatefulness that separates what our chattering mind designates as "me" and "not-me"—or "self" and "other"—illustrated in terms of the raw hatefulness that is homophobia.

At its heart, dislike of something in oneself initiates dislike of this quality in the other; and, if enough anxiety is involved, dislike readily grows into hate.

Hatred is always what motivates attitudinal mindsets such as homophobia, even when it is dressed with a scientifically absurd rationale about the exclusive "naturalness" of heterosexuality, or with pious stupidities about the alleged "immorality" of oral sex, anal sex, same-gender lesbian sex (not to mention expansive erotic touching, solo pleasuring, multiply partnered sex, and all manner of erotic performances and adventurous lifestyles).

In terms of understanding this hatefulness, notice here how it starts with self-hatred as an underlying, deeply troubled lack of self-acceptance, which is replaced by hostility toward the other.

Notice too how homophobia is always linked with misogyny—the man viciously judges himself or any other man who might wish to give the very same pleasure that he receives with delight from his female partner. Beneath the prevalent hatred of gay men lies the heterosexual's fear of women as well as his fear of his own erotic potential.

This sort of strategy is so powerful that, even when it starts with what might be considered "mild criticism" or polite condemnation, it eventually leads to outright hatred and violence.

I personally know of a young man, not yet twenty, who enlisted in the military some years ago. Although he was not "out" and had scarcely ever practiced his homosexuality, the "straight" men in his unit correctly inferred that he was gay. Late one night, these men became somewhat intoxicated and, while the officer on duty "turned a blind eye," they anally gang-raped the young homosexual man—who committed suicide before daybreak. The authorities, of course, hushed up this "incident"—and the only reason I know of it is because that man was my first cousin.

We all manipulate our perceptions of others, and our actions toward others, in order to control and constrain the expression of our own sexual inclinations. Thus, we manage our own inner conflicts and anxieties over the polysexuality of our erotic potential. As I previously stated, we are accustomed to enmesh our sensual and sexual life, and to strangulate it, in a weave of *"shoulds"* and *"should-nots."* Our chattering mind is enormously productive in churning out judgments about what erotic expressions would be inappropriate, abnormal, perverted, wrong, sick, immoral, weird, sinful, and so forth.

To preserve the illusory and deluded stability of our anti-sexual mind, this judgmentalism must be exercised repetitively. Since we are abstaining from these modes of erotic expression, we preoccupy ourselves with those "others" whose activities are not so abstinent. Fear of our own sexuality is the source of human malice, our considerable proclivity for cruelty toward each other.

➤ Strategy #4: *Turning Sexuality into Something Else*. The psychodynamics of the strategies we have discussed so far begin to suggest the cleverness of our anti-sexual mind, not only in blocking or redirecting our erotic potential, but also in transmuting sensual or sexual energies into something else. There are two major and interconnected ways that this occurs within all of us.

First, our mind manages to redirect or channelize erotic energies into the force of its own judgmentalism. Although the judgmentalism of our chattering mind combats, hinders or obstructs, the free-flow of our spiritual and sexual nature, it also requires this energy for its own functioning. So, in the course of our psychological development, our mind "scores"—that is, appropriates and exploits—the bodymind's erotic energies for the fueling of its own activities.

Second, as our mind redirects or channelizes our erotic energies to fuel its own functioning, it not only obstructs their natural free-flow, but it also transmutes them into a force that appears somewhat "desexualized." The force of our judgmentalism is both compulsive and "aggressivized." Thus, in the operation of our chattering mind, it is as if the bodymind's sexual energies are transmuted into their own nemesis: malice, hostility and violence.

This is why the more our mind chatters the less genuinely sensual and sexual—or loving—we will be. And this is why the more we are judgmental, the less genuinely sensual or sexual—and the more hateful—we will be.

Erotic energy cannot be rendered entirely non-erotic, so this also explains, at least in part, why we are so attached to our egotism—because the exercise of our judgmentalism always remains tinged with the perverted residues of something erotic.

There is much more to be said about the inherent meanness of our judgmentalism, and about the invariably aggressive consequences of sexual suppression and repression. And there is much more to be said about the way in which our egotistic mind's preoccupation with power readily turns "sex" into something other than the sacred sharing of erotic energies. But we will postpone some of this discussion to our next chapter.

➢ Strategy #5: *Compulsivities.* It attests to the cleverness and the deludedness of our mental functioning that we can believe we are having "sex" when engaged in manifestly "sexual" activities that are latently engineered as the avoidance of sexuality or its transmutation into something else.

"Sexual" abuse, as epitomizing the anti-sexual, is only one extreme example. As mentioned in the first section of this book, the "sexification" of our culture turns all manner of erotic impulses into compulsivities that are anti-sexual.

Beneath the vile anti-sexuality of the abuser or the rapist—and the person who commits incest, or anyone who betrays a sacred trust by coercively "crossing a boundary"—whether the coldly contemptuous or the heatedly enraged variety, is always a yearning for genuine connectedness. However, genuine connectedness, which we may well call "love," is terrifying to the abuser or the rapist. Consequently, what is most desired is ultimately destroyed even in its possibilities.

In a certain sense, the psychodynamics of rape, incestuous "boundary crossing" and abuse are the same dynamics of the chattering mind's fear of its own bodymind's sexual-spiritual energy. Rape, incestuous boundary violations, and abuse present the logic and rhetoric of our judgmental egotism, now enacted in a disastrously extreme manner.

Judgmentalism is the primordial act of "rape." Our egotism seems to yearn for "love" but knows only how to dominate, control, possess and violate, and, in so doing, destroys the very essence of our own erotic desire.

Even when the enactment of "sex" is not as violently extreme, the same dynamic operates. That is, whenever "sex" is conducted under the aegis of our egotistic judgmentalism, its erotic nature is either avoided in a phobic manner, or indulged anti-sexually in an obsessive manner. In both cases, the driving force of the activity is inevitably compulsive.

For example, when the purpose of abstinence is to prove that one is "morally superior" to those who are not, then the choice to refrain from sexual expression will become compulsive—because one's moral superiority will have to be proved again and again in order to satisfy one's egotism.

Likewise, when the purpose of "fucking" is to prove that one is powerful in the marketplace of social transactions, the bliss of erotic pleasuring will have been drained from the activity—and again the activity will have to be repetitious, because one's powerfulness will have to be proved again and again in order to satisfy one's egotism.

Repetition is never "successful" and so our anti-sexual mind is always imprisoned in repetition-compulsivity. In this culture with its intensifying paradox of sexification, almost all the "sex" we see around us has this compulsive and repetitious quality.

Compulsive activities may appear manifestly to be about "sex," but latently they are always governed by anti-sexual purposes, and ultimately they are never erotically pleasurable, let alone orgasmically uplifting.

Compulsive activities are the prototypical constructions of our anti-sexual mind. Whether phobic or obsessive, they are always anxiety-driven, and the anxiety is always about our erotic potential.

On the phobic side, there is a strong tendency to manipulate the other—to condemn in the other the very desires that one unconsciously experiences within oneself.

On the obsessive side, it is often as if our mind is trying to prove something to itself, as if it were saying "See! I *am* king! I am *not* frightened, I am doing this or that *sex* act again and again and again!" But, the act is always undertaken in a manner that is inherently anti-sexual.

Compulsive activities are the mind's attempt to manage its unconscious anxieties by engaging in frenetic—and futile—actions. These are constructed as what psychoanalysts sometimes call "reaction formations."

If these formations are phobic, individuals compulsively assert to themselves that they have mastered their sexual anxiety, and that this is "proven" by their abstinent avoidance.

If these formations are obsessive, individuals compulsively engage in "sex" in order to prove to themselves that they have mastered their sexual anxiety, and this is "proven" by the sheer obviousness of all their counter-phobic activity.

In these ways, compulsivity is always a frantic and desperate means of dealing, by phobic or counter-phobic performance, with the terror of our erotic potential. Such performances are evidence of the very anxieties they are intended to assuage or disprove.

In sum, these five strategies by which we avert the realization of our erotic potential are actively engaged in all of us, moment-by-moment and day-by-day. We cannot entirely forego these processes, but we can come to understand them—to witness them compassionately, and thus to loosen their grip on us. We can, at least to a certain extent, become aware of their operation within us, and thus weaken the force by which they imprison us. With awareness we can call them into question:

- ➤ *Where, somatically and emotionally, am I blocked? Where has my passion and my erotic exuberance disappeared to?*

- ➤ *If I am allowing myself certain modes of sexual expression, why am I not allowing myself and experimenting with the enjoyment of other modes of sexual expression—activities not previously in my repertoire?*

- ➤ *How are my judgments about others really a reflection of my anxiety about aspects of my own self that I am trying to repudiate?*

- ➤ *Where are the energies of my life being diverted to, and what are the seemingly "non-erotic" activities that are so preoccupying to me?*

- ➤ *How erotically free am I, or how much are my chosen modes of sensual and sexual expression engaged compulsively, whether in a phobic or an obsessive manner? And is my erotic life truly orgasmic, such that it propels me on a spiritual and emotional journey of joy, bliss and ecstasy?*

We indeed need to oppose the oppressiveness of our society, to work and play toward a culture in which we can truly enjoy the freedom of sensual and sexual expression. But we also need to challenge our own thoughts, feelings or actions that characterize the erotic patterning of our lives. We need to call our selves into question in the manner of these inquiries. This is vital for our sexual and sensual emancipation, as well as for our emotional and spiritual liberation.

8

Fear and Aggression

We urgently need to free ourselves from our fearful imprisonment in the judgmentalism of "one-thousand-and-one" prohibitions and restrictions that deprive us of the fullness of our erotic enjoyment. We need to do this not least because this deprivation is the root cause of our human capacity for malice. In this chapter, we will review why this is so.

Why are we so frightened of our erotic nature? Ultimately, we are frightened because our polysexual potential is confronted by the primordial law of incest, which is "The Law" of all other laws. This fear founds our judgmentalism, which engineers and extrapolates our human capacity for malice.

The incest taboo needs to be respected.
All other anti-sexual rules and regulations do not.

The incest taboo is the primordial boundary or threshold, the paradigm or prototype for all other experiences of boundariness. Deeply encoded within us, it is psychologically "The Boundary" of all boundaries—"The Law" of all laws. Without it (which means if we appear to fall outside it), the universe of our psychological reality falls apart. "The Law" of incest taboo does not come from the world outside us, yet nor was it originally authored by the intentionality of human consciousness.

Rather, it is foundationally inscribed in the deepest structures of our capacity for symbolic language. It is "The Law" that permits the representational universe of all mental functioning—our "psychic reality"—and it emerged with the very beginnings of human culture, as well as our earliest capacity for reflective consciousness. These developments occurred somewhere in the Late Pliocene and Early Pleistocene Eras. For all of us, the incest taboo is thus experienced as the primordial *"No!"* and is the paradigm or prototype for all subsequent *"No"* experiences.

We begin life in a condition of erotic bliss, submerged in the mother's womb to be born as a highly sensual and sensitive infant, a conduit for the orgasmic flow of sexual energies, erotically bonded to the bodies of our caretakers. At some point in our development, we have to come to terms with the primordial *"No!"* This *"No!"* inscribes the unsurpassable fact of life—that the bodies of our caretakers are most forbidden to us, and that we must observe this taboo if we are to mature into the world of humanity.

This primordial *"No!"* thus institutes what we might call "The Trauma" of all traumas, the collision of our erotic desire with the necessity of incest prohibition and restriction. This is the collision that founds our capacity for *reflective* awareness, instituting the dynamic boundary between our consciousness and whatever is repressed from consciousness.

Notice here that the operation of the incest taboo requires a judgment: *this* is *"No!"* but *that* is not. So the operation of the primordial taboo both founds a primordial act of self-estrangement, in which we lose some of our access to the flow of erotic energies within our embodiment, while it also founds our capacity for judgment. This estrangement is necessary for in itself the incest taboo is not malignant, despite the fact that it is "The Trauma" from which judgmentalism arises.

What is malignant, however, is the expansion of this taboo into one-thousand-and-one unnecessary rules and regulations. This is what I call the "surplus extension" of "The Trauma" into one-thousand-and-one traumatizations— the elaboration or extrapolation of this judgment into the egotistic judgmentalism of our "chattering mind."

This "extension" takes us beyond a dynamic estrangement between our erotic energies and our reflective awareness. It is the cause of our frozen alienation from the joys of our embodiment. Thus, it is the source of our human tragedy.

With these developments that are cultivated by the processes of our socialization and acculturation, a warm dynamic of estrangement from the flow of our erotic energies becomes the almost complete and frozen alienation of our mind from the flow of our erotic enjoyment.

The benign blessing of mind is perverted into the curse of an imperialistic, chattering and judgmental, egotistic mind.

> *We come to live "in our heads"*
> *alienated from the flow of our hearts,*
> *our genitals and our erotic body.*
> *In terms of our spirituality,*
> *we "mature" from enlightenment into egotism.*

The logic and rhetoric of judgment involve a dual momentum of separation and subjugation. There is some sort of decision, that *this* is to be discriminated from *that*, and there is some sort of categorization, in which *this* is condemned and *that* is not. The force that fuels any act of judgment is, in a certain sense, appropriated from the exuberance of erotic energies that flow through our bodymind. Judgmentalism steals from the sourcing of our sensual and sexual embodiment.

As I articulated this earlier, our judgmental or chattering mind "scores"—appropriates and exploits—the bodymind's sensual and sexual energies for the fueling of its own activities. The founding of the judgmental consciousness of our egotistic or chattering mind is the primordial act of rape. Judgmentalism is the procedure by which we come to live "in our heads" rather than in our hearts, our genitals, and all the energies of our erotic bodymind.

Observance of the incest taboo is absolutely necessary for our health and the possibility of sanity. The judgment involved in this prohibition is required for our psychological survival. However, this judgment rapidly festers into the cult of judgmentalism. Our wholesome fear of incest renders us vulnerable to the ravages of our socialization and acculturation, in which "The Law" is expanded into one-thousand-and-one unwholesome rules and regulations prohibiting and restricting the sensuality and sexuality of our embodiment.

The single necessary traumatization, "The Traumatization," blisters into one-thousand-and-one unnecessary and malignant procedures by which our judgmentalism is egotistically elaborated and extrapolated. Instead of a single act in which our "head" would need to become estranged from our erotic potential, our socialization and acculturation causes us to internalize all these rules and regulations that tragically alienate us from the enjoyment of our erotic embodiment.

These developments
—from the necessary judgment of incest taboo
to the cult of anti-sexual judgmentalism,
from living in our heart to living "in our head"—
are malicious.
They are the root cause of all human malice—
of our capacity for hostility, aggression, violence and hatred,
as well as our propensity for prejudice, abuse and exploitation.

The confrontation with incest is terrifying. It brings us face-to-face with psychological annihilation. That is, it evokes from within us our deepest fears of, and longing for, "madness."

In philosophical and psychoanalytic terms, it confronts us with the inherent "castratedness" and the "deathfulness" of our subjectivity. (Parenthetically, we may note that this is why we cannot achieve a thoroughly joyful erotic life unless we have fully come to terms with the inevitable "castratedness" and "deathfulness" of our being-in-the-world. It is also why ecstatic orgasming is an emotional and spiritual experience of our deathfulness. However, these are matters that we will leave for the final chapters of this book.)

It is well known that we typically react to traumas, and attempt to alleviate our fears, with an accumulation of aggressive feelings and intentions, along with an acceleration of our egotism's judgmental activities. There are three reasons why this is so:

➢ Judgmentalism takes the erotic energies of the body and, for its own purposes, transmutes them, "aggressivizing" them in the establishment of the representational system in which we live—the representational reality of "good versus bad," or "me versus not-me," of "right versus wrong," and so forth.

➢ Judgmentalism also transforms representations that are about sensual and sexual expression into those that are not. In so doing, judgmentalism advances the aggressive functioning of our egotism in the name of protecting us from the dangers of erotic freedom.

➢ Judgmentalism renders us sensually deprived and sexually conflicted, and then offers us aggressive outlets for this frustration.

The first reason is the most fundamental, but it is perhaps rather abstract since it is opaque to our awareness, involving the origins of judgment that are antecedent to our capacity for reflection. Judgment is always aggressive in as much as the operation of judgmentalism is established by the depletion of erotic energies.

The judgmental mind is alienated from the source of its own "fuel"—it steals its force from the energies of our sensual and sexual body, which it then attacks and repudiates. In an important, even if rather metaphysical sense, the founding of our egotism—the establishment of our judgmentalism—is the primordial act of rape. So the exercise of our judgmental mind is inherently an anti-sexual activity.

Even if the content of the judgment appears to have little or nothing to do with our erotic pleasures, the energy for the act of judgment is "scored" from the erotic potential of the body. Our judgmental mind founds itself by the transmutation of erotic energy, using it to make decisions that separate and subjugate—the one is discriminated from the other, the one is upheld and the other is condemned.

In the act of judgment, erotic energy is transmuted into an aggressive force—something is always condemned. This "aggressivization" of energy occurs even when the decision made appears to be pro-sexual. For example, even when we decide to have sex with this partner, rather than another partner, or rather than no sex, a certain amount of erotic energy has been transmuted into an aggressive force.

If this first point is abstractly metaphysical, this is because it does not concern the content of our representations of our selves and the world, so much as the formation of our representational system in and of itself. However, the content of our judgmentalism always does have to do with some aspect of our erotic potential, even when the apparent connection seems very remote.

All judgments sooner or later involve the disposition of our senses and therefore have repercussions for the possibilities of our erotic enjoyment. It could be pointed out that, by progressively reducing our repertoire of sensual and sexual desires, our judgmental mind buffers us from even getting close to the commitment of an incestuous act. However, the effect of this "buffering" is—as I have emphasized—that all manner of erotic interests come to be suppressed and repressed from our repertoire. Aggression always represents alienation from our erotic sourcing.

The mandate of our judgmental mind is to transform representations that might involve our freedom of erotic expression into those that constrain or constrict our bodily pleasures. Our reactions to traumatization—to the reductive shaping of our erotic potential—always diminish our sensual and sexual freedom. If we examine the five strategies of our egotism's "defenses" against erotic impulses, we can see how each of them has aggressive consequences.

➢ The repression and inhibition of erotic energy causes individuals to accumulate anger that is held both in the representations of unconscious fantasy and in somatic blockages. This anger demands expression and release.

➢ The channelization and segregation of erotic interests—such that "sex" is acceptable here but not there, or this way but not that—causes individuals to become increasingly hostile and angry about the erotic interests that they themselves have condemned within themselves.

➢ The manipulation of the "other"—such that desires are condemned within the self are externalized or projected onto others—causes individuals to participate in the sexual oppression of those who are unlike themselves. Such oppression involves the hostile exploitation or persecution of those who represent erotic interests that these individuals have condemned within themselves.

➤ Turning sexuality into something else typically means that erotic energies are poured into "non-sexual" enterprises such as when individuals become devoted to the acquisition of material advantages, to the synthetic pleasures of titillating media, to religious preoccupations, and to ambitions for familial or political power. All of these pursuits involve, at the very least, the ambition to gain advantage over others, and more often than not they involve the outright intent to exploit and dominate others.

➤ Compulsivities always involve hostile feelings and actions that are directed either toward the self or toward others. When individuals exhibit compulsive tendencies—whether these are phobic or obsessive in their preoccupation with erotic interests—harm is invariably done toward the self or the other.

Finally, let us return to the topic of shame and guilt, which was discussed in Chapter Five. These dynamics involve all of these "defensive" maneuvers on the part of our judgmental mind, and we can see again the extent to which aggression—often directed against the self—is integral to these pervasive and pernicious phenomena.

The defensive representation of shame and guilt can also result in the expression of their apparent opposite. For example, shame and guilt are operative in hostile exhibitions of shamelessness, or hostile exhibitions of a self-righteousness that accuses others of being guilty. This again is evidence of the pervasive and pernicious aggression inherent in judgmentalism.

As we examine all these "defensive" maneuvers that preoccupy our judgmental mind, it might also be argued that each of them may also have a doubly "adaptive" aspect, psychological and sociological:

• Each of them purports to defend us in some way against further traumatization, even if what it defends us against is—typically—only the memory of a traumatization, for our judgmental mind operates solely by representing our past and thus determining our future. This is the psychological aspect.

- Each of these anti-sexual strategies renders us better adjusted to the oppressiveness of the society and culture we inhabit. Becoming increasingly alienated from the open, spontaneous, and free-flowing expression of our erotic nature renders us better citizens. This is the sociological aspect.

However, whichever way we investigate these "defensive" maneuverings of the judgmental mind, it is clear that judgmentalism perpetuates our sexual fear and frustration. Judgmentalism ensures that we are sensually deprived and sexually conflicted. Moreover—and this is a vitally important conclusion—it is clear that erotic fear and frustration are the root cause of all human malice.

The essence of sensual and sexual pleasuring
is a spontaneous, open and free-flowing movement of erotic energies.
If an activity is not safe, sane and consensual,
if it is not freely mutual, it is neither sexual nor genuinely sexy;
rather, it is founded in the aggressivity of our egotism.
All human malice results, directly or indirectly,
from our egotism's fear of our erotic potential
and from the frustration of our erotic desires.

The men and women who instigate incest and other abuses, who instigate traumatizations in others, as well as those engaged in prejudice and persecution of whoever is unlike themselves, may be engaging in an unconscious effort at self-healing, but they are never genuinely "in touch" with their own erotic nature. They never reunite with their own sexual-spiritual source by means of their compulsive activities. In this sense, they are caught in their own repetition compulsions, and can only be healed if their genuine erotic freedom is facilitated. Perhaps, as has been said "everything is either love, or the cry for love."

Rape and other exploitations epitomize acts that are anti-sexual. For sensuality and sexuality is the open, spontaneous and free-flowing energy of our embodiment.

> *All behaviors that assert dominance,*
> *that are in any way coercive or nonconsensual,*
> *that manipulate power relations,*
> *and that exploit or control an "other,"*
> *are inherently anti-sexual,*
> *for they are derived from our egotism's*
> *fearfulness and frustrations.*

As a clinician, the men I have known who have raped women, children, or other men—as well as the women I have known who have committed similar abuses—may have seemed frightening, but they are also, tellingly, some of the most deeply frightened humans that anyone could ever encounter.

In our culture, rape is epidemic—for example, we know that at least one in every four women and female children can expect to be assaulted one or more times in the course of their lifetime. We also know that incest, abuse, and trauma are rampant, and that our children attain adulthood only by means of their multiple traumatizations.

In this sense, what we commonly call rape is only the visible tip of the wider and deeper social phenomenon of traumatization—violence, abuse, exploitation, coercion, and incest. Rape is the horrendous symptom of our ubiquitously compulsive strategy of performing something "sexual" in order to avoid the essence of our erotic energies.

In a disturbing but radically important sense, our society is deeply committed to the ideological motif of domination, exploitation, conquest and control; and, in such a culture, rape is the normative condition of relations between people.

I am not minimizing the seriousness of these matters by indicating their prevalence. Nor am I doing so by suggesting that violent rape is actually the symptom of a society that is deeply committed to the paradigm of rape as a fundamental form of relationship between one person and another, between one group and another, between one country and another. And I am not implying that all abuses are somehow equivalent in their seriousness or malignancy.

However, abuse occurs not only in explicit situations of coercion and violence, but also in the implicit messages all around us, which depict or enact "sex" in an anti-sexual manner, or which imply that power, wealth and domination are somehow inherently "sexy."

A simple example can be seen in the abuse our commercialized and commodified culture commits against us when—through advertising, "artistic" production, misguided medical pronouncements, religious doctrine, or the blathering of "experts"—it proclaims or insists that sexuality is

> ... only for the beautifully-bodied ... only for specified parts of the body ... or only for the legally married ... that sexual beauty is the exclusive prerogative of youth ... or could be enhanced through plastic augmentation ... that erotic pleasures should be forbidden for some ... or forbidden for all unless undertaken in prescribed positions ... or forbidden except on special occasions in which they may be indulged as "smutty" or disreputable pleasures; and so forth.

The list of these abuses seems almost endless, and is indicative of how alienated from our erotic body we have become in this "sexified" society.

Most of us have experienced "sex" that is not erotic, and indeed that is inherently anti-sexual, incestuous or abusive. Sadly, for some of us this is all the "sex" we will ever know.

For example, the majority of us have had intercourse motivated not by the sharing of erotic energy but instead motivated by our egotism's need

> ... to prove that it has overcome its own fears of sensual or sexual activity ... to reassure ourselves in relation to some other insecurity about our self ... to achieve a conquest and prove our powerfulness ... to get our partner to admire us, adore us, and make us feel "loveable" ... or to get our partner to be indebted to us, or intimidated by us.

Most of us have experienced what purports to be "lovemaking" but is actually one of these versions of a basically hostile "fuck." Again, for many of us this is all we will ever know.

Surely we know that when words like "penetration" are applicable—when one partner is "passive" and the other "active"—we are no longer speaking of the mutuality of a sacred sharing of erotic energies. Rather, we are speaking of an anxiety-driven and basically hostile act—an exploitive co-optation of energies, which our chattering judgmental mind passes off as "love." In short, if it feels like one person is "penetrating" another, then we can be sure that something anti-sexual is occurring.

Doing "sex" out of our anxiety over sexuality, performing acts that are orchestrated by our egotism's fear of the free-flow of sexual energies, is fundamentally hostile, and tragically commonplace.

Need it be belabored that all these phenomena are instances of our aggression? Need it be further argued that if we were sensually and sexually happy, we would not be motivated to abuse, to exploit, and to commit acts of physical and emotional violence against our selves and others? Need it be belabored further that the forces of anti-sexuality are the root of all human malice?

SECTION THREE

Choreographies of pleasure

9

Our Sensual Bodies: Becoming Naked

There is something miraculous about the exuberant multiplicity of our naturally sexual responsiveness. The human body is an awesomely sensitive and sensual organism. We are blessed with the ability to find many pleasures through our bodies, and we are blessed with bodies that spontaneously offer us these gifts. Let us now uncover some of these gifts. Let us start by becoming natural.

On the beach at Cap d'Agde, one can appreciate fully the sheer beauty of human bodies moving naturally in the Mediterranean sunlight. As the sea sparkles and bare feet scrunch into the sand, a baby nestles into her mother's breast, suckling, softly sleeping—their nude configuration melting into a unity of bliss, as white clouds go scudding lightly across the azure sky. On this beach, a boy lies nude on his father's naked back, lying on sun-bleached crystals, siesta time—the boy squirms gently, eyes closed, softly smiling, presumably as the friction of his tiny penis feels pleasurable against the firmness of paternal musculature.

The French expression *au naturel* means with naturalness, simplicity, and grace. Here, on the shoreline between land and sea, is the naturalness of prepubescent girls, their cleft modestly hinting at an inner recess of beauty yet to blossom into its fullness—the naturalness of prepubescent boys, their little penises of boyhood projecting, their balls tucked tightly into the scrotal promise of manhood yet to flourish. Here is the naturalness of exposed vulval folds configured between sun-drenched thighs, accentuated by trimmed public hair or a full bush of mature women offering themselves to the gods of light and warmth. Here one can rejoice in the magnificence of breasts, from their small firmness, piquant, to their bell-shaped fullness and fecundity. And here one can revel in the scape and dangle of each penis, nestled in its bush of hair or exhibited projecting from a shaven pubis. Here one can delight in the variations of buttocks, from the lavish to the compact—and yes, here one can feel the sensual pleasure of the sun's rays caressing the anal orifice, blessing it with a healing touch.

Contrary to what is often anticipated by those who have never enjoyed the convivial community of nakedness, there is no need to compare or contrast the "quality" of the bodies presented fully in their naturalness. Rather, there is an invitation to let-go any attitudinal commitment to evaluation, any attachment to some ideal of "perfection" or "what should be"—to set-aside goal-oriented lust, as well as the stickiness of our shame and guilt. There is an invitation to free our selves into the experience of pure enjoyment.

At Cap d'Agde, all sorts of bodies take pleasure in the sensuality of fresh air, whatever their age, race, class, occupation, body-type or muscular-skeletal condition. Many bodies are scarred, exhibiting the ravages of time, unhealthy habits, accident, illness, emotional pain, or stressed-out lifestyle. Yet, all are "skyclad" as some pagans phrase it, naked in the outdoors, and in this, there is a profound beauty.

I am reminded of a nude photograph of the feminist writer, Deena Metzger, taken after the surgical removal of her right breast—her body has been wracked by a terminal disease, her arms are outstretched as she bares herself toward the camera, her face blissful, exultant, life-affirming. She is supremely beautiful, and I wish to thank her for sharing that image with all of us.

I am in gratitude for the sanity of the nude beach, for skipping naked in the sunlight, for dancing unencumbered on the sand—for this sensuality of movement in the moment, and for the opportunity for letting-go some of the obstructions to sensual pleasure with which we are all burdened. Whether one believes in any version of "God" or subscribes to the values of secular humanism, it is surely always true that

> *Our spiritual growth cannot begin*
> *if we do not accept and enjoy the embodiment of our spirit;*
> *becoming naked initiates this acceptance and enjoyment.*

As at least one wise person has said, "if body acceptance is our intention, nude recreation is the way." At Cap d'Agde and at the hundreds of places where I have enjoyed being naked in the open air, the enjoyment of the body in its natural state may readily take us to play along the spiritual "edge" between effort and ease. The nude beach places no premium on compulsive exertion, on activities that take the body "too far" for its own wellbeing. Nor is there any press toward productivity. Indeed, at Cap d'Agde, the only "labor" would seem to be the propulsion of frisbees or the production of sandcastles—their fortress-like character an ironical inscription against the implacable and unstoppable flooding of the tide.

But the ease of the nude beach offers something different from its apparent torpidity. It is a pleasure of sensual enjoyment that may take us to a spiritual "edge." Whether swimming, sweating, or languorously soaking, the leisure of the nude beach—or of any opportunity to be naked in nature, communally or individually—expresses the vibrancy of sensual pleasure, and offers us a unique opportunity for the letting-go of bodily shame and guilt, and for an enjoyment that sets aside judgmentalism.

I know that to be fully present and naked under the open sky, in solitude or with the conviviality of the nude community, is to be skyclad in a process of prayer. It is to be simultaneously in touch with our profoundest divinity and our most natural humanity. It is to commit ourselves to return to innocence.

10

Our Sensual Bodies: Touching Tenderly

Touch is the most basic expression of our human capacity to love, and it is vital to our survival. As someone once wrote, "without touch, a baby dies, the human heart aches, and the soul withers." Science and commonsense both teach us what we know inherently, which is that

We all need touch for our physical welfare and for our emotional vitality, touching tenderly is also necessary for our spiritual growth.

Research has shown how babies fail to thrive if they are not nurtured with touch. And there are scientifically documented reasons—coming from the disciplines of developmental neurology and psychology—that tell us why this is so. However, clinical experience also suggests that adults, from teenagers to the elderly, suffer greatly if they are touch-deprived. In this culture, so many of us are.

Physical illnesses of all sorts, mental disturbances (especially difficulties with hostility and rage), and emotional constrictions (which seem to close down the heart and rigidify the body) are all caused or catalyzed by touch-deprivation. In so many instances that I have seen in my work as a clinician and educator, this deprivation could easily be alleviated if the deprived person could let go of fear and ignorance just enough to take the initiative in joining or convening an intentional community of touch.

We live in a culture that is touch-phobic, and it becomes a serious challenge—especially for those without regular partners—to touch and be touched, to have what we need and want.

About once a week, a small circle of friends was accustomed to meet in my home to perform the rituals of our "consensual touch group." In such groups, there are usually between three and seven men and women aging from their twenties to their seventies. We begin seated around a candle with each person speaking into the candlelight to share from the heart whatever is happening in our lives.

This "heart-sharing" is not a recounting of stories, and avoids factual details, judgments, or "figuring things out." Rather, it is a speaking "from the heart," and in the "here-and-now," about whatever is occurring in the person's life. One person may speak briefly of feeling the challenges of letting-go addictive behaviors and deepening into self-love; another may speak of sadness because a partnership is in difficulties; yet another may speak of the anxieties of facing stress caused by practical and material difficulties. Rarely does an individual's sharing last more than a few minutes, and no one responds verbally to what is shared.

This part of the ritual reconnects us within our transient circle of love. It serves not merely to inform us about what is occurring in each other's lives. It also serves to release feelings by speaking them into the circle and thereby helps, at least to some degree, to set aside the preoccupations of the chattering mind during the sharing that is to follow.

Then we all undress completely and move into a sacred space that has been prepared in advance—a warm, softly lit room, with gentle music, and a double futon that functions as a "massage table." Each person has ten to twenty minutes receiving the group's touch in any way that she or he requests. Some ask for a deeper massaging of tired muscles; some for light stroking all over the body's surface. Genitals may be brushed inclusively, but genital stimulation is not the focus of this particular practice. My friend, Bill, a beautiful man in his mid-seventies, used to say

> With our touch group, I love the opportunity to be giving, as much as I love receiving the soothing caress of as many as a half-dozen pairs of hands gently stroking my body—the whole experience is sensual and spiritual, and addresses my needs for nurturing touch in a way that my current dating life does not—I feel that this sort of ritual of shared touching gives me an experience that is profoundly Holy—I always leave our group feeling more loving and loved, more centered within myself, and more ready to face the challenges of my life with joy in my heart.

So this is, in the most profound sense, an act of worship. And we might recall here that it is a method of worship that many wonderful spiritual teachers, including Jesus of Nazareth, are known to have enjoyed—from the touching associated with the "laying on of hands" to the washing of feet.

Sadly, many of us have suffered abuse and trauma in such a way that our enjoyment of being touched has closed down. Perhaps, to some degree, this happens to us all.

For example, many of us—especially in adolescence and young adulthood—will "fuck" hard and fast without being aware that we are doing so in order to avoid the intensification of being touched. Others of us may regrettably avoid sexual contact altogether for fear—so to speak—of what will be touched off when we are tenderly touched.

Clinical experience shows that for those of us suffering any of these syndromes, what is feared may also be what is curative and restorative. Here we can consider the "skin-brushing" methods that nurses or other therapeutic practitioners sometimes use to elicit the responsiveness of autistic and other emotionally closed-down individuals—often with wonderful results.

But we can also consider how often the provision of healing touch is a major aspect of the sacred work of "sensual-relational educators"—temple prostitutes, sacred whores, sexual surrogates, and so forth. It is also the reason many of us receive massage—sometimes including genital massage—with heartfelt gratitude for the services we receive. We will discuss these matters later.

Whatever our background, whatever our personal reasons, the impulse to return to touching and being touched is a cry for love—and, whatever else it may also be, it expresses the wish to reground ourselves in our capacity for love, to *return to Love through the basic capacities of our embodiment.*

At the end of their busy professional weeks, my friends, Pamela and Steve, reconnect through the process of a Friday evening ritual—they wash and massage each other's feet. Jennifer visits her demented grandmother each week just to massage the elderly woman's hands and stroke her hair. Joe and Michael exchange back-rubs regularly—"just to keep each other sane!"

In these encounters, we see healing and worship in action. We see a reverence for both the humanity and the divinity of the bodies that touch. In this, we may be reminded of the example of Mary Magdalene washing and massaging Jesus' feet. It seems very unlikely that Magdalene limited herself to Jesus' feet—and indeed, *for heaven's sake,* why would she?

In this context, we honor those who dedicate their lives as massage therapists, psychosomatic healers, and bodywork practitioners. We may also honor the example of Magdalene whose dedication was perhaps not so much therapeutic, as it was a simple act of connection and erotic worship with which to offer both pleasure and relief. All these services remind us how the blessings of touching and being touched flow not only to the one who receives, but also to the one who gives.

Let us consider further the healing and worshipful dimension of bodily touching. Our spirituality—and the most precious aspects of our humanity—involves compassion, appreciation, and grace. There is an obvious compassion involved in relieving weary limbs with the tenderness of touch. Appreciation is evident when we revere the holiness of the other's embodiment.

Touching bodies may evoke the same reverence, only in a more intensely connecting modality, as when we greet someone by gently placing our palms together over our hearts and murmuring *"Namasté"*—which means "the light within me honors the light within you."

And in touching bodies there is grace—the grace to which Bill testifies when he says that his group experience enables him to feel more loving and loved, more centered within himself, and more ready to face the challenges of his life with joy in his heart.

However, there can be yet more to the spiritual practice of touching and being touched. There is a dancing of energies, a sharing of the flow of our spirits and, with the cultivation of touching, there is a stirring and a deepening of sexual-spiritual momentum. For example, ancient mystics have taught the practice of *nyasa*—a ritual in which all parts of the body are touched methodically, usually accompanied by the chanting of mantras or prayers, in order to heal and protect the person's sexual-spiritual energies. The same ancient mystics, as well as many contemporary sexual-spiritual practitioners, know methods of touching that can elicit the most powerful movements of our erotic energies.

For example, my friend, Juliet, is famous for her acting in erotic movies, and is also a longtime practitioner of *vipassanā* meditation. She had been very ill most of her childhood and, to relieve her severe chronic pain, she intentionally cultivated her full-bodied orgasmic capabilities, which she self-administered. From these experiences in childhood and adulthood, she developed a type of bodywork she called "tender loving touch." Although she has a beautiful body with intact and sensate genitals, Juliet is now a vibrant older woman who has chosen to diversify her orgasmic capacities, beyond the genitals, in several ways.

For example, I have been privileged, as her friend, to facilitate her enjoyment of full-bodied orgasming by lightly stroking under her armpits (we will again mention some of the ways in which delicious experiences of orgasming may be invited to occur without genital stimulation, in Chapter Twenty).

It is from these kinds of experiences—from her compassion and appreciation for her own body tormented with childhood illnesses that have followed her throughout adulthood, as well as from her extensive career as a "porn star"—that Juliet has developed an exceptional wisdom about the sensuality of touching and being touched.

The basic principle of practicing Juliet's method of "tender loving touch" is a gentle, sometimes almost imperceptible, and always varied stroking of what some psychoanalysts have called the "skin envelope."

Our bodies are blessed with the most sensual surface, our skin. This sensuality is available all over the body and not just in the special areas of sensitivity that we typically know such as nipples, anuses, genitals, fingers, palms, armpits, and soles of feet.

Juliet teaches a method of touching that not only connects our sensitivities with the lightest stroking, but does so in a seemingly erratic manner. There are, so to speak, "deliberate vagaries" in her touching, and a delightful whimsicality to any encounter with her. The variability she advocates both in the direction of light rhythmic touching, and in the manner of its delivery (by fingernails, wrists, surface of the whole lower arm, hair, nipples, tongue), elicits a distinctive experience.

This variability makes it virtually impossible for the person being touched to anticipate the sequencing of sensations. As the mind can no longer control or attempt to "master" the experiences by anticipating or "making sense" of them, the person is taken "out of mind." As in any meditation, what is thereby invited is a letting-go of the hold of the chattering mind and—when such touching is administered proficiently—a deep and delicious orgasming of the entire body usually comes into play. Whenever I have benefited from Juliet's offering me a session of her touch, I have always left her presence feeling lighter in my heart, more centered in the love that flows within as well as without, and blissful throughout my body.

Later we will further discuss some aspects of orgasmic experience. So here we will simply note how orgasming may be initiated or facilitated by the lightest touching of our bodily surface. The skin envelope, which is the marginal surface where our bodies seem to end and the rest of the world seems to begin, is a miraculous conduit for spiritual experiencing. Whether one touches oneself or a partner, it is by reverence for this conduit that the deepest and highest sexual-spiritual energies may be remobilized, and this brings us into alignment with compassion, appreciation and grace.

11

Our Sensual Bodies: The Glories of our Genitals

As we proceed through childhood and adolescence and become adapted to this culture and to our social circumstances, there are many ways in which we tend to become less wise rather than more so.

This is because the procedures of acculturation and socialization effectively coerce the pleasures of children into the darkness of secrecy—where shame, guilt, anxiety, and conflict perennially fester. This occurs not only through mechanisms of oppression, in which certain erotic behaviors are externally subjected to prohibition and persecution. It also involves a range of subtle psychological processes in which we suppress and repress our own sexual desires, and thus internalize social codes by inscribing them within us— cognitively, emotionally, and somatically.

Our desires become the cause of a deep sense of shame and guilt about our selves, as our erotic potential becomes subject to our own processes of suppression and repression. We become psychologically conflicted, intrinsically anxiety-ridden, and somatically blocked.

If we become successful products of our socialization,
we become profoundly alienated from ourselves;
nowhere is this more evident than in our erotic lives,
and especially in our relation to our own genitals.

Typically, as we develop, the natural sensuality of our genitals—as well as the excretory structures associated with urination and defecation—becomes the focus of our sexual shame and guilt. The glories of our genitals become the major arena of our sexual secrets. This is central to our acculturation. All cultures seem to recognize that there is something "special" about the genitals. Most cultures subject the genitals to some special modes of inhibition and prohibition, although in some cultures, this recognition inspires reverence rather than contempt.

The tradition from which our contemporary society has developed is one in which the procedures of oppression, suppression and repression alienate us from the glories of our genitals. Our socialization forcefully induces a sense of conflict about *"going down there"*—as one eminent sexologist humorously phrases it. In brief, we continue to be raised to experience our own genitals as if they were foreign, and "other" than the wellspring of our spiritual energies.

This cultural induction of bodily self-alienation occurs on many levels of daily life and is communicatively transmitted in ways both blatant and subtle. It is powerfully supported both by "experts," including an educational system that refuses to teach children, in elaborate and celebratory detail, about their "nether regions" or their sexual life, and by "folklore," including the moralizing strictures of caretakers who prevent or punish children for their solo self-explorations and for their mutual genital examinations.

It is a grievous crime against our humanity—and against our spirituality—when we are discouraged from the benefits of self-pleasuring, and when our children are prevented from the benign and joyful wisdom of playing "show-me" with peers.

As a consequence of these specific spiritual-educational failures and the cultural triumph of anti-sexual ideologies, most of us proceed into and through adulthood understanding rather little about our sexuality in general and our genitals in particular.

Our tradition of self-alienation is tragic to the point of absurdity. In America today, most men are less well informed about the functioning of their penis and testicles, than they are about the operation of their automobile or the state of their bank accounts. Most women experience their vulva-vagina as if it were a tenuously occupied foreign territory, and are often better informed about matters of international politics—let alone about matters of sartorial elegance—than they are about "what goes on down there."

Although slang terms, and sometimes personal pet names, pertaining to the genitals are common—ambivalently indicating their importance to us—neither gender receives more than an uncongenial smattering of information about their own genitals or the genitals of "the other gender." And this smattering is usually communicated in a manner that is more deterrent than invitational. Almost none of us are aware of the variations of genitals—let alone about the fact that there are more than two genders of human being, including some delightful intersex configurations that nature contrives (and that frequently evoke a lifetime of viciously prejudicial treatment).

Walt Whitman once wrote, "If anything is sacred, the human body is sacred." Yet American culture has never recognized this wisdom, especially when it comes to our genitals and their functioning.

As I well know from my own experience, sexuality educators, who offer educational seminars and workshops for adults, often find that their students are remarkably ignorant, and are fearful of talk about the genitals. The vast majority of adult Americans cannot give coherent and correct answers to very basic questions such as

> ... How does a penis become erect?

> ... How does a vagina become lubricated?

> ... What causes sexual desire?

I have asked these three questions to many thousands of adults—not only to nonprofessional members of the public, but also to physicians and university faculty. Only a fraction of a percentage of this population—including those who are healthcare professionals—can provide even the semblance of an adequate answer to these questions.

Interestingly, the question about penile erection sometimes receives no better than a fumbling response, even from specialists in urology. The question about vaginal lubrication is almost always answered incorrectly, even by 90% of specialists in gynecology.

The question about desire is, of course, more complex, since desire depends on so many factors and yet is still, in so many ways, awesomely mysterious. However, since every human being experiences desire—and indeed since desire is the source and origin of our existence as humans, as well as the wellspring of our daily lives—one might have hoped that the average individual would be able to offer some sort of an educated account of its nature. Yet this is far from the case.

In a sexually healthy society, surely every high-school student would be able to give coherent and more or less correct answers to such questions? The issues are, after all, so central to our lives as human beings.

And surely, in a sexually healthy society, the work of teaching basic facts like these would be the responsibility of the mainstream—of families, schools, nurseries, playgrounds, colleges, or professional training programs—and not left to a small and courageous group of specialist educators in sexuality? However, although there are occasionally some small signs of social progress, those who actually do this sacred work of remedial teaching continue, in large measure, to swim against the cultural mainstream.

In America today, there is considerable evidence that we are becoming more ignorant, and more fearful, of our sexuality, rather than less—and this is despite all the "sexified" hubbub of the media that surrounds us.

In this chapter, we are concerned with the celebration of our sensual potentialities. I will later discuss why this celebration is so sacred for, as I have written elsewhere, it is a matter of profound importance for our spiritual lives that we maintain a reverent and even worshipful connection to our genitals. This spiritual connection is quite contrary to the secrecy, shame and guilt, with which these precious body-parts are customarily surrounded.

At this juncture, let us briefly portray some of the joys of genitals, and thus point to the spiritual, emotional, and educational value of "going down there"—of going beyond our most elementary sexual secrets, and beginning to transgress or transcend our acculturation into shame and guilt.

There is an amazing variability in the look and feel of the vulval and vaginal structures—but, when we approach with appreciation and reverence, there is invariably an incredible breathtaking beauty. It is so perfectly understandable that artists and poets of all persuasions, and through all the ages, would wish to lyricize the wonders that are offered from between a woman's thighs. The vulva-vagina, or *"yoni"* as it is called in my spiritual practice, is meant to be worshipped, and is given to us to bring pleasure to ourselves and to our partners.

It is such a pleasurable privilege to gently run a tongue or moistened finger up from the sensitive area of a woman's perineum, along the labial folds, and so to softly encircle her clitoral glans . . . or to hold this tiny nub glistening with its thousands of nerve-endings gently between the lips and caress it with a lateral sweeping movement of the tongue that excites the especially sensitive points that are usually to be found on this tiny glans. The clitoral glans is so impressively sensitive for some women that it is only pleasurable if stroked by circumvention. As excitement increases, special areas of the pelvis may become delightfully sensitized—the inner thighs, the labial folds, the anal aperture, and the vaginal entrance. And as arousal intensifies, the labia moisten and enlarge, sometimes pouting open playfully and provocatively to reveal the entrance to the vaginal canal.

This glans is only the tip of the clitoral structure, which actually extends deep into the woman's body, and especially around the urethra and back towards the anterior wall of the vaginal canal. Vulva and vagina are thus functionally and anatomically united. Engorgement of this long clitoral tube is usually accompanied by a lubricating of the vaginal surface as every cell seeps with a plasma-like fluid. This fluid is, in conditions of health, usually delicious to taste. The clitoris is a sensitive tube of blood-filled spongy tissue that is richly endowed with nerve-endings. Connected with the clitoris, the labia are also highly sensitive.

Most women find that their clitoral structure has two especially sensitive areas. These are the nub of the external glans, and a dense internal area between the anterior wall of the vaginal canal and the urethra. The latter is called the "G-spot" (or Gräfenberg-spot), although in some women it feels like an area rather than a localized "spot."

It is especially pleasing to caress this spot rhythmically with a moistened finger, penis, or toy. Women who maintain healthy pelvic muscles, or who deliberately tone the walls of their vaginal canal, are able to invite the finger, penis, or toy, into its embrace, actively pulling it into their body, and then caressing or massaging the vaginal envelope around the solidity of the invited guest . . . just as the stroking and pulsating movements of this guest—back and forth, in and out, or gently from side to side—may create a mutually pleasurable rhythm of stimulation and escalating excitement.

When orgasming occurs throughout the vulval and vaginal structures, there is often a delightful rippling movement of energy and muscular spasms. When orgasming occurs in this manner, some women spurt a clear fluid from their urethral opening just below the clitoral glans; while, for others, this expulsion is not detectable because it is spurted backwards into the bladder.

The female orgasm always involves much more than the pleasuring of the genitals—their clitoral and labial suffusion as well as their vaginal rippling. It always implies the blissful release of chemicals in the cortex and the release of neuromuscular structures throughout the body—it involves multiple creative openings for intense, full-bodied, and ecstatic movements of energy. The potential joy of this, its healing nature and its unique access to our divinity, cannot be estimated, let alone adequately described in words.

Like the female genitals, penises and testicles come in an impressive array of shapes and sizes. When we approach these genitals with appreciation and reverence—setting aside our fantasies that penises are aligned in some sort of hierarchy of worth—we find here a miraculous beauty and a whimsically playful aspect of ourselves. There is an amazing variability in the look and feel of the *"vajra,"* as it is called in my spiritual practice. Like the female genitals, the penis and testicles are to be admired and adored, with an attitude of careful attention to the profound truth that, as men, our penis and testicles are, above all, given to us that they might worship the universe by bringing joy to our selves and to our partners.

It is such a pleasurable privilege to softly run a tongue or moistened finger up from a man's sensitive perineal area between the anus and testicles, to caress the balls as their scrotal sac tightens with excitement, and to proceed along the underside of the penile shaft to lightly strafe the frenulum at its head. It is a pleasure to hold a flaccid penis, circumcised or uncircumcised, gently between the fingers, or take it fully into the mouth and then, as stroking it in a swirling motion, to feel its surge of engorgement and the enjoyment this brings.

The entire penis does not, of course, have the same density of nerve-endings that are gathered in the clitoral glans. But even so, having one's penis stroked and caressed, whether in a lighter or heavier massaging, creates an impressive crescendo of pleasure. As excitement intensifies, the foreskin of an uncircumcised penis may retract playfully, provocatively exposing the sensitized head. Special areas of the genitals may become increasingly delicious to touch and have touched—the tightened sac of the testicles, the anal aperture, the inner thighs, and the underside of the penile shaft. As an erection fills and then intensifies with pleasure, men expel a clear "pre-ejaculate" fluid from the urethral opening. This is usually tasteless but may contribute to the slipperiness of the excited organ.

Engorgement usually flexes the penis up and away from the torso. Men who keep their pelvic musculature healthy are able to wiggle or flex their organ up and down or from side to side, and this increases the versatility with which the penis may give, as well as receive, pleasurable stimulation. As the pleasures of genital stroking increase, most men are familiar with the experiences of their ejaculatory climax. Sadly, far fewer men know the pleasures of multiple full-bodied orgasming.

Ejaculation involves several rhythmic contractions of several internal muscles, usually resulting in the expulsion of seminal fluid. Depending on individual variation as well as the man's health and several other factors, this expulsion may ooze or spurt, weakly or strongly, in small or large amounts, and the fluid itself may be thick and creamy, or watery and whiter, sweet or salty.

However, male orgasming involves much more than ejaculatory responses, and may even be intensified or ecstatically prolonged if ejaculation is averted. Indeed, male orgasming is actually attainable without any penile erection at all. Men who cherish their capacity to receive and to give sexual happiness, and who have maintained their sexual health well, can delay, retain or bypass their ejaculatory responses so as to orgasm more extensively and intensively.

This orgasming involves muscular spasms through all the limbs and torso, with the blissful release of chemicals in the cortex and throughout the neuromuscular structures of the entire body, creating the possibilities of dramatic, full-bodied, and ecstatic movements of energy. As with female sexuality, the potential joy of these multiple creative openings of men's orgasming cannot be estimated, let alone adequately described in words, for its healing nature and for its unique access to our divinity.

Ancient texts of spiritual wisdom have occasionally offered classifications as ways to consider the wonderful variability of human genitals. For example, the well known *Karma Sutra* and the less known *Ananga Ranga* suggest that there are several types of male and female sexual organs, distinguished mostly by their dimensions, the changes they undergo when aroused, and their taste or smell.

The American Native teachings of Quodoushka offer a more complex system. Male genitals are differentiated by several characteristics such as the length and thickness of the penis on erection, the frequency of spurting contractions on ejaculation, the consistency and taste of the ejaculate, as well as the activity of the scrotum and testicles during arousal. Female genitals are differentiated by several characteristics such as the anatomical configuration of the labia and clitoral hood, the distance of the glans from the vaginal entrance, the nature of the vaginal canal including how far up the G-spot is located, as well as the consistency or taste of vaginal secretions.

Other spiritual traditions—Sufi, African, Kabbalistic, and many indigenous doctrines—suggest similar considerations and classifications.

The spiritual-erotic intent of these considerations is to celebrate the miracles of human diversity. The intent is not to construct typologies in order to discriminate genitals that are "better" or "worse"—nor is the intent to demote homosexualities by speaking here of the ways in which male and female genitals may belong together.

Rather, it is to be noted how the traditions of genital classification, far from establishing a pernicious hierarchy of "better" and "worse," may actually serve to help us honor our genitals with greater appreciation. No one type of penis is best for the pleasuring of all types of female genital—for example, "bigger" is definitely not always "better," although it may be "better" for certain types of vulva-vagina. And likewise, one type of vulva-vagina is not best for the pleasuring of all types of male genital.

Ancient teachings make clear that certain specific types of male genital tend to be best suited for the pleasuring of certain specific types of female genital, and vice versa. That is, for every type of male or female genital, there are perfect erotic partners. For every type of male or female genital, there are perfect ways to achieve erotic ecstasy.

Every human being has the potential for a joyous sexual life. But the fear and ignorance with which we are accustomed to experience our genitals aborts this potential. Only by moving against our socialization, by overcoming our fear and ignorance—for example, with the commitment to learn and to teach what have been sexual secrets—can we facilitate an appreciative admiration of all our genital arrangements, can we promote their worship, and thus support our sensual enjoyment in a way that moves us toward spiritual bliss. As tantric spirituality teaches us—and as we will later discuss—the glories of our genitals are the altar for spiritual practice.

12

Playing with Power and Pain

Chapter Ten described touching encounters that are characterized not only by consensuality but also mostly by "mutuality" or by reciprocity between participants. However, we know that, when two or more people are in relation, it is rarely under conditions of mutuality, and often consensuality is also in question.

Very often, there is a significant disparity in the power relation pertaining between those participating in any relationship. Indeed, "mutuality," as I use the term here, is a challenge that is only achieved by diligent spiritual practice—by working and playing through the power differentials that operate between us in order to transcend them.

Moreover, in the previous chapters, we emphasized touching that is "pleasurable" in the ordinary sense of this word. But we know that our bodies offer many modalities of sensation including those to which the ordinary notion of "pleasure" might initially seem unsuitable. So we now need to investigate further the conditions of human "pleasure" which are, we will find, notably complex.

The topics power and pain are intrinsically connected on several levels. To discuss them, we turn to a diverse range of common and uncommon sexual practices that, at the source of their imagination, express the intention to work and play through the identities, positions, stories and roles that imprison us within fixated patterns of power, pleasure and pain.

> *Since issues of power and pain*
> *are so often aspects of our sexual traumatization,*
> *practices that play with power differentials and pain thresholds*
> *in ways that are safe, sane and consensual*
> *may be profoundly healing.*

"BDSM"—"bondage-and-discipline" or "dominance-and-submission" or "sadism-and-masochism"—are perhaps popular but rather misleading labels covering a broad range of many different sorts of sexual practice and ritual. The prospect of exploring and experimenting in these areas often seems forbidding to those who have never entered the communities associated with them.

When I initially researched these practices and rituals, some years ago, I was mostly aware of my feelings of aversion. These were evident in my wish to distance myself "scientifically" from the phenomena I observed, and by my—private but still entirely unethical—tendency to concoct presumptive "diagnoses" or "psychodynamic formulations" of those individuals I was observing. As I became more familiar with these activities, moving tentatively from observer to participant, I was granted the awareness that there may often be spiritual value to these activities—a spiritual value that is unlikely to be perceived by anyone who has never entered this experiential domain.

Research sexologists have found that many of us with sexual partners—probably as many as 20%—have, at some time or another, enacted fantasies of bondage or restraint. For example, one of the partners is tied up, sometimes blindfolded, while being stimulated in some way by the other.

When our playing such a "scene" of a master/slave dialectic is consensual, respectful, and procedurally safe, it may be mutually freeing. Whether we are in the passive or the active role—receiving restraint or giving stimulation—such play may evoke a thrill and precipitate personal growth in a way that is perhaps unparalleled by activities that appear more interactively balanced.

For the psychology of the person who appears to be in the "passive" role, at least one central reason for this is obvious. If my capacities for pleasure are inhibited by unconscious shame and guilt, then it is as if, while being tied up, I tell myself that I have "no choice" but to accept the stimulation I am receiving (even when I may appear to be physically struggling against such acceptance). It is as if, since my body appears to be under someone else's control, my mind lets go the controls that my unconscious shame and guilt routinely wield over its functioning.

Here we may note in passing a remarkable feature of how our procedures of imagination and belief operate. For these effects usually occur even if I "know" that I am physically strong enough to break the tethers on my wrists and ankles, or even when I "know" that there is a pre-arranged "safety word" (as indeed there always is, if the play is to be undertaken safely and sanely) which, if uttered aloud, will immediately cue my partner to interrupt the scene and promptly release me.

Thus the effects of being blindfolded and bound during sexual activity have to do with the importance of letting-go the mind's persistent but futile tendency to try to "master" the sensuality of erotic experiences. My own experiences corroborate this. Earlier in my adulthood, I found that being blindfolded could significantly intensify pleasurable excitement precisely because my mind would be less able to anticipate the next sensation to be experienced. Being tied to a bed or similar structure for a "session" in which my partner offered to play with my body without my reciprocation would help both to release me from my mind's customary worries whether I was doing enough for my partner, and to allow me an increased acceptance of receiving and enjoying pleasure.

For the psychology of the person who appears to be in the "passive" role, another attraction of such activities is evident. For those of us who have been wounded by experiences of terrifying helplessness or traumatized by mistrust—which is to say, almost all of us—scenes of this character offer us a safe, and even whimsical, way to explore and experiment with deeply conflicted feelings.

Fantasies are not only expressions of our emotional wounds, they are also curative or restorative endeavors. So, when conducted with care and communicative deliberation, the playful and safe enactment of our fantasies of being coercively "made to do" a sexual act can have a profoundly growthful impact, and afford us an opportunity for insight into our conflicted impulses. This intentional enactment of scenes that bring us to our "edge" around issues of trust and mistrust, as well as powerfulness and powerlessness, is thus potentially an adventure in healing as well as in enjoyment.

This applies also to the psychology of the other person, the "master," who appears to be in the "active" role but who is, if such a scene is well conducted, both "in power" and yet "at service" to the "slave," the partner who is restrained.

Experiences in which our partner asks to be tied up and "ravished"—that is, for us to enjoy a "session" in which we would agree to act as if one of us were solely in control of the experience—provided an exaggerative performance that helps in providing an opportunity to gain insight into exactly how controlling we are during our more typical, interactive lovemaking. This spurs our personal growth and the realization that having a controlling attitude, trying to be mentally "in charge" of erotic experience, is perhaps the most deceptive and pernicious way in which our minds inhibit the fullness of our sexual pleasures.

We know that, in this culture, the craving for power—the entire motif of domination and subordination—is etched dramatically in the operations of our egotism. We know that this craving is founded on our fearfulness, and that its indulgence leads to much of the world's suffering—violence, exploitation and oppression of an "other" or "outgroup" by an "ingroup," irreversible desecration and destruction of the planet, and so forth. As has been said, "the greater the power, the more dangerous the abuse." And we know that much of our lust for power, and our terror of powerlessness, originates in the abuse and traumatization of our childhoods—as Erich Fromm wrote, "the lust for power is not rooted in strength, but in weakness."

Given that the craving for power and the fear of powerlessness is etched in our chattering mind, what better can we do with this dangerous preoccupation than to transform it alchemically into the protocols of whimsical playfulness—to experiment with these feelings in a manner that is safe, and that places them within the context of love? This then seems to be a major dimension of our interest in the mode of sexuality that is colloquially labeled "BDSM."

When I first visited Mistress K, a vivacious woman who lives fulltime in her "alternative" lifestyle as a highly successful professional dominatrix, I was ushered into the austere elegance of a downtown loft, and "commanded" by her assistant to remove all my clothing and to kneel—which I did. What occurred in our hour-long session may be unremarkable for those who live in this alternative community. Yet for those who live, as most of us do, in a lifestyle that is unfamiliar with this sort of playfulness and is unfamiliar with its range of sexual practices and rituals, what I experienced seems noteworthy. So I will describe just two aspects of this—submissiveness and sensation.

When Mistress K appeared before me, dressed in the exotic regalia of her profession, her eyes were playfully alive, her smile sweetly embracing, and her breasts—scarcely concealed beneath her red bodice—luscious. There was something so exciting about the anticipation of the scene that I was erect even before her black high-heeled leather boot gently stroked my penis. She caressed me with apparent affection, asking me if I was a "dirty little boy" even as she stroked my penis with her delicate fingers.

In may be noted, in passing, that Mistress K is petite in comparison with my broad 74" frame, and that she is exactly half my age—she appeared, however, completely "in charge" of this scene and, at least in my participatory imagination, I felt entirely "at her mercy."

Even the effect of her, so to speak, "warmly chastising" me for being a "dirty little boy" (and subsequently leading me around the room by a leash fastened to my genitals) was quite remarkable. It was as if her words, and this emblematic enactment of my "enslavement" to her, conjured up from not-so-distant memory the frequent occurrence of genital humiliation, the derisive treatment of my boyhood sexuality, and other emotional abuses of my childhood. Yet, simultaneously, the manner of her delivery enabled me to feel exquisitely rehabilitated, as if my sexuality was for her an essence of me that she admired and adored.

Later, having been "commanded" to maintain eye contact with her, my eyes drifted downward to the attraction of her breasts. She caught this "infraction" immediately and again succeeded in making me feel that she liked me for it—even while she "punished" me.

This playful enactment of fantasy—being placed in a situation of submissive sexual humiliation and then treated as if loved for my sexuality rather than despite of it—had a marked impact on me. This surprised me.

I had benefited personally from well over a decade of psychoanalytic therapy, and had been inclined to believe that I had extensive insight into the neurotic and psychotic aspects of my personality. In two full psychoanalyses, I had explored and re-experienced much of the pain of the sexual humiliations and other abusive experiences that I had endured as a child. I had intensively "worked-through" the emotional conflicts derived from these and other childhood experiences.

Yet, for all that, the dramatization of sexual humiliation and redemption, played out as I submitted to the commands of this dominatrix, had a pronounced impact on me, and this impact was, in the most important sense of the term, healing. I believe this suggests something about the motive that impels many of us toward such experiences.

Mistress K cuffed my wrists, my ankles, and my genitals, and proceeded to fasten me spread-eagled to a rack. She then proved herself extraordinarily talented at playing with my "skin envelope" by administering many and varied types of tactile sensation and thus by modifying my thresholds of pain and pleasure. At different times, she would utilize her teeth (sometimes teasing my nipples softly, at other times biting me aggressively and unexpectedly), her palms (smacking me frequently with gentleness, occasionally with unanticipated ferocity), ice cubes alternating with moderately hot wax, and an impressive variety of scourges, whips, ticklers, and paddles.

What I believe is noteworthy is that, under this regimen, my mind quickly lost its reflective ability to discriminate pain from pleasure. What might be delightful in one moment might feel aggravating the next, and even seriously unpleasant a second or two later. What might commence as an unpleasant sensation could readily shift into something that felt quite delicious. Moreover, when she "threatened" me with a particular sensation, I frequently could not tell whether my pain or pleasure was to the anticipation of the stimulation or to the stimulation itself. By the end of our session, as I was cuddled in her arms, my hair stroked, and soothing compliments whispered in my ear, my mind felt very still and my entire body felt—as the phrase goes—"blissed out."

As an Arabic saying goes, "there is no gathering the rose without being pricked by the thorns." Many of us have grown out of childhood either having experienced significant physical pain or having had experiences that lead us to fear physical pain. Yet the experience of pain is far from simple, for in ways that are complex, we now understand that pain is neither merely the absence of pleasure, nor merely its antithesis. Rather, human sensuality offers us profound experiences in which the thresholds of pain and pleasure are mutable and continually in flux.

I believe that some of the appeal of these "BDSM" experiences has to do with our compulsion to repeat our traumatizations, and with the way in which freeing our selves from these compulsions is the source of our capacity for bliss. Some of the appeal of these phenomena has to do with the fearfulness of our chattering mind—our egotism's vain belief that an analgesic attitude toward life will succeed in the avoidance of pain and loss, and might even achieve our escape from the inevitability of what psychoanalysts call our "castratedness" and our death. Our egotism is interested in conquering—or, more precisely, believing it can conquer—any experience that threatens it.

My brief enslavement to Mistress K exemplifies a mild exploration and experimentation with sensory thresholds. I believe such a session would be sufficient to convince almost any skeptic that the sensations of pain and pleasure are not fixed, nor are they either/or experiences—and indeed, that there is profound spiritual healing involved in these experiences by which we gain insight into the influence of power relations in our lives, and into our capacity for pain and pleasure.

I have witnessed heavier "scenes" at clubs in Detroit, New York, Chicago, San Francisco, Los Angeles, and Amsterdam.

In such scenes, men and women plead to be flogged until their skin is red and raw, as they cry in an ecstasy of what is ordinarily called "pain." There are individuals who choose to have their bodies cupped, hooked with needles, laced and suspended by wires. There are lovers who slit open their skin, drawing blood in syringes, and squirting it over each other's faces as they seemingly move into their state of bliss. Some of these scenes are performed in the elegant surroundings of affluence; some in grungy cellars with bodily excretions spattered on the floor. In most cases—with men or women, young or old—there is often an extraordinary sense of delight and devotion to their chosen performances.

I remember, for example, one man's arrangements for his 40th birthday celebration at a famous "S and M" club. In a performance that lasted well over an hour, bare breasted women beat drums in an increasingly pulsating crescendo, while he was stripped naked, his arms bound behind him, anchoring him to an upright pillar. As the drums gained rhythmic speed and volume, his female partner slowly inserted forty hypodermic needles under the skin of his upper arms, his shoulders, and his chest. Initially, he appeared in agony at each insertion—but gradually an amazing peacefulness and light suffused his face. This performance continued with forty candles being attached to the end of each needle, set alight with wax dripping liberally onto his skin, and then the attending community sang a poignant rendition of "Happy Birthday."

With the processes of play, pain converts to pleasure, or at least to something that is "beyond" the usual thresholds of pain/pleasure experience. Adrenaline "highs" and endorphin rushes, as well as mediating fantasies, are the concomitants of these remarkable phenomena. While some of these rituals are exceptional, the same processes enter, to some degree, into the sensual pleasures, and the shifting experiential thresholds, that characterize our everyday sexual practices.

Whatever we conclude here about the vicissitudes of pain and pleasure, it would be a mistake to suggest that the devotees of "S and M" experiences are not finding their particular bliss, their enjoyment in bodily experiences, and their pathway towards a transcendence that may well have an inherently spiritual momentum.

13

The Economics of Sexual Service

At this point in our deliberations, an objection probably arises for many readers, and it is one that we must address forthrightly. It concerns the highly charged issue of "sex for money."

At Cap d'Agde, one pays admission for the privilege of nudity on the beach and, although the provision of fully "free beaches" would be preferable, the fees paid do not detract from the spiritual veracity of enjoying this opportunity for nakedness, the opportunity to be in skyclad celebration. For Juliet and for Mistress K, the services they offer are not only their spiritual calling, but must also provide their livelihood. Even if genital intercourse is never an aspect of their professional repertoire, they are, in a certain sense, "sex workers"—constituents of a longstanding community that offers some of the most honorable and ancient modes of human service.

There are many who moralistically condemn this calling. These individuals usually claim that they would "never perform sex for money," that this is somehow an absolute immorality. I believe this boast is not only viciously arrogant, it is also self-deceptively hypocritical, because in our society and our culture, any and all sexual activity *always* occurs within the nexus of power and economy. There is no escaping this fact, even though there are ways in which moralizers contrive to deceive themselves about it.

Those who condemn "sex work" usually idealize marriage as the singular context in which sexual sharing should take place. Marriage is, after all, an economic and sociopolitical arrangement that legitimates our sexual partnering, especially in relation to the use of sex for reproduction. Although ideologically rationalized as "the best possible" or "the one right" context for sexual expression—and as the only means by which to prevent the citizenry from falling into moral turpitude—the basic function of marriage is the regulation of social reproduction. That is, one arrangement of sexual partnering is endorsed—and all others, to greater or lesser degree, condemned—so that the structure of the social order may be stabilized and perpetuated.

In our culture, both traditionally and contemporarily, the legitimated "ideal" for sexual partnering is a legally constituted, religiously ordained, dyadic heterosexual unit, which is sexually exclusive (at least for women, men are traditionally allowed more latitude), and which is then treated as the basis for all social functioning as well as for the construction of "family life."

If all sexual activity occurs within the context of a political economy,
to propose an 'absolute moral distinction'
between 'sex work' and 'conventional marriage'
is mostly delusional and seriously hypocritical.

In relation to the traditional framework of marriage, we owe to Karl Marx and Friedrich Engels a brilliant critique of the ideological precepts and standards of "bourgeois marriage." Specifically, this critique shows it to be a myth that, in such legalized partnering arrangements, sex is ever freely given.

Although marriage has changed a smidgeon since Marx and Engels' writing—particularly with some advances in the status of women—more recent scholars have provided similar *exposés*.

Marital legitimacy does not provide a context in which sexuality may be freely shared, even when it has the underlying purpose of creating a "family unit." On the contrary, since marriage is a context in which partners become economically and sociopolitically dependent, sexual sharing can never be free in this context. That is, even today—when some women have a slightly greater social status than would have been possible in the nineteenth century—it would be erroneous to imagine that sexual activity can ever take place without money being directly or indirectly involved.

In clinics and counseling centers across the country, we very frequently learn of situations in which the wife cannot be fully "at choice" whether to accede to her husband's demands for intercourse—simply because she, and any children she has or may wish to have, are at least to some degree dependent for their welfare on his material provisions and his legal protection. Although the circumstances are rarely "equal and opposite," the husband is also not fully free to decide whether to accede to his wife's demands.

Not only are wives and husbands coerced or compelled to negotiate sex in a context in which there are all sorts of serious consequences to the failure of this negotiation, there are also various prohibitions—and economic or sociopolitical consequences—to any wish they may have for sexual expression with partners other than their legally endorsed spouse.

In short, marriage forces a couple to "make a go" of sex together—and the solution at which many married couples arrive is that they will embark on relatively sexless lives.

Of course, I am not simplistically assuming that at this historical juncture all women are financially dependent and men independent, although this is still often the case. But I am asserting that—as Simone de Beauvoir wrote over fifty years ago—"the curse which lies upon marriage is that too often the individuals are joined in their weakness rather than in their strength . . . each asking from the other instead of finding pleasure in giving."

Marriage is a legitimated arrangement for sexual partnering that subordinates sexuality to the coercion of anti-sexual forces. Although feminist dissent, and the voice of sexual minorities, has—thankfully—instigated significant social reforms, and the tone of some contemporary marriages may have been modified, sexual relationships today are no less influenced by the context of their political economy. Indeed, all human connectedness and all social phenomena are steeped in their political economy.

In capitalist social formations, money readily becomes, as Marx observed, the "alienated essence" of our existence—despite the fact that it is mostly transitive and evanescent, or merely, in Jean Paul Sartre's phrasing, "made to unveil the object, the concrete thing." In this context of a society that continues to uphold the bourgeois ideal of marriage, and that continues to reify, commercialize and commodify, all human relationships, there is still validity in Marx and Engels' insight that "*all* sexuality *is* prostitution." In this respect, matrimonial as well as quasi-matrimonial moralities or ideologies merely serve to inscribe and institutionalize the economic and erotic exploitation of all of us who must accede to them.

Within our extant cultural codes, our bodies are property—bound by relationships and rules of transaction always involving power and money—and indeed, as we have discussed previously, state regulations as well as ideological forces determine the options for the disposition of this property. In our world today, sexual pleasure can never be totally free because of the sociopolitical context in which money is always in some way involved.

It may well be that, if I visit a massage parlor for the comfort of human connection and for the experience of genital caress, money directly changes hands; whereas, if I visit my lover or have sex within a marriage, this does not appear to be the case—at least, not directly. However, we are seriously mistaken if we imagine that this distinction is fundamentally significant or that it carries some sort of moralizing validity.

Throughout the planet, *every* human behavior has a financial dimension, an economic context. And in many respects—unlike the socially ordained arrangements of marriage, or the conventionality of "love affairs"—there is a degree of honesty and integrity in the explicitness with which "sex workers" request their fees and are paid willingly for their sensual services. This is an honesty and integrity that is egregiously lacking with all other interactions in which the economic aspect of the relationship is disguised or deliberately obscured.

Moreover, in addition to the honesty and integrity of such professions, we must recognize that *service* is indeed what sex workers perform for their remuneration—that, very often, they are the ones who caress our bodily humanity and who rekindle its divinity, when our energies have been insufficiently touched.

> *In the practices of 'sex work,'*
> *there is an honesty and integrity*
> *to the recognition that every human behavior*
> *occurs within the context of a political economy.*
> *Such honesty and integrity is lacking*
> *in the moralizing ideologies that attack this sacred profession.*

Not only do I recognize that all my relationships are permeated by the political economy of my culture, but, like the majority of the citizenry, I have paid for sex activity and I have been paid for it.

In addition to this direct exchange of money for explicitly sexual services, I am untroubled by the frequent criticism that, as a psychotherapist, I work as some sort of "paid friend." Indeed, not only am I unfazed by this criticism, I feel honored by it—especially since it implies that my patients experience me as their friend, even if they have to accept some degree of obligation to contribute to my livelihood. Moreover, especially as a professional sexuality educator, sex therapist and psychoanalyst, I feel frankly privileged to see myself as a sort of "prostitute" and to acknowledge my anomalous place in the community of sex workers.

Perhaps even more saliently, it must be recognized how many "prostitutes" are actually healers, including those who hold a place in the precious tradition of "sacred prostitutes," temple dancers, surrogates, and erotic priests or priestesses.

As I see it, my livelihood, as a healer and a teacher, involves sincerely offering my emotional engagement and cognitive reasoning in the service of the personal growth of my patients and students; whereas the livelihood of other sex workers involves sincerely offering their caresses.

This distinction seems irrelevant in relation to the common spiritual intention of being "at service." And I believe those who make so much of the distinction—between selling one's capacity for emotional and cognitive engagement with another human being, and selling one's physical ability to offer pleasure to another human being—are merely giving voice to a prevalent and perniciously anti-sexual ideology.

In many people's minds, it is somehow acceptable to offer the services of one's head, or even one's heart, and to ask to be remunerated for what is given—but it is unacceptable to offer the services of one's body, especially if any pleasurable genital contact in involved. Psychotherapists may touch a person's feelings or fantasies very deeply. Massage therapists may touch a person's skin—anywhere but the genitals. Physicians, if they are trained and licensed, may touch a person inside the genital, oral or anal orifices. And all these practitioners receive money for services rendered. But a professional who touches a person's genitals in ways that give pleasure, or who offers his or her genitals, mouth, or anus in the service of the other's enjoyment, and who receives fees for these practices, is viewed by many as "morally contemptible."

This is the epitome of moralizing judgmentalism as the expression of what I call sex fascism. It is a vicious expression of our sexual shame and guilt that becomes evident in the form of judgments that make the genitals, mouth, and anus, the locus of an "absolute moral distinction."

The moralizing condemnation of "sex work" is thus an expression not only of the generality of anti-sexual attitudes, but also, specifically, an expression of our genital self-hatred. If we were to allow ourselves to fall into love with our genitals, then these specious discriminations—that would single out certain parts of our erotic body and make them the locus of an "absolute moral distinction"—would evaporate. Rehabilitating our genitals, indeed falling in love with our genitals, is an essential aspect of humanity's spiritual path.

SECTION FOUR

The freedom to be healthy—

Visions of erotic liberation

14

Visioning our Birthright

In the first section of this book, we discussed the definition of sexual health and arrived at a useful, but minimalist, definition: Sexual health is any erotic activity that is safe, sane, and consensual. We briefly examined the implications of each of these, especially the third criterion which raises important questions about the importance of observing the incest taboo, particularly in relationships that are, by extension, incestuous in their conscious, as well as unconscious, connotations and ramifications.

Then in the second section, we examined in somewhat more detail why we lose the full experience of our erotic potential in the course of our "maturation"—our socialization and acculturation. We also began to delineate some of the practices of sexual healing and its spiritual implications—a discussion to which we will return in this book's final section.

In our third section, I introduced—perhaps more by anecdote than by argument—various experiences of healthy sexuality as spontaneous, open, and adventurous. That is, healthy sexuality as a free-flowing movement of erotic energies, within our own sensual body, and between our self and our partners, our self and nature, our self and the universe! Essentially, the idea of sexuality as a sacred energy movement that embraces all manner of sensual activities—and that includes, but also goes beyond, genital intercourse—was elaborated. That is, the discovery that sexuality is not only the vehicle to emotional wellbeing, passion, and joy, but that it is also inherently a spiritual-existential experience.

In this section, we will return to the issues of sexual health and its inherent connection with erotic freedom. We will engage whatever vision we might have of living in a world that supports our being sexually healthy and erotically free—instead of a world that imprisons us within the forces of anti-sexuality.

In Chapter Four, our definitions of sexual health were still somewhat hemmed by our knowledge of what is sexually unhealthy. In this chapter, and in this section, we will attempt to go further with this inquiry, by trying to specify what a sexually healthy and erotically free world might look like.

Almost no country in today's world can claim cultural practices and social policies that come up to the standards of sexual health stipulated by the World Health Organization. Let us start by honoring two definitions that were endorsed by this multinational establishment. In 1975, the following definition was published:

> "Sexual health is the experience of the ongoing process of physical, psychological, and socio-cultural wellbeing related to sexuality. Sexual health is evidenced in the free and responsible expressions of sexual capabilities that foster harmonious personal and social wellness, enriching individual and social life. It is not merely the absence of dysfunction, disease and/or infirmity. For

sexual health to be attained and maintained, it is necessary that the sexual rights of all people be recognized and upheld."

In 2002, the World Health Organization expanded its pertinent definitions as follows:

> "Sexuality is a central aspect of being human throughout life and encompasses sex, gender identities and roles, sexual orientation, eroticism, pleasure, intimacy and reproduction. Sexuality is experienced and expressed in thoughts, fantasies, desires, beliefs, attitudes, values, behaviors, practices, roles and relationships. While sexuality can include all of these dimensions, not all of them are always experienced or expressed. Sexuality is influenced by the interaction of biological, psychological, social, economic, political, cultural, ethical, legal, historical and religious and spiritual factors."

> "Sexual health is a state of physical, emotional, mental and social well-being related to sexuality; it is not merely the absence of disease, dysfunction or infirmity. Sexual health requires a positive and respectful approach to sexuality and sexual relationships, as well as the possibility of having pleasurable and safe sexual experiences, free of coercion, discrimination and violence. For sexual health to be attained and maintained, the sexual rights of all persons must be respected, protected and fulfilled."

> "Sexual rights embrace human rights that are already recognized in national laws, international human rights documents and other consensus documents. These include the right of all persons, free of coercion, discrimination and violence, to: the highest attainable standard of health in relation to sexuality, including access to sexual and reproductive health care services; seek, receive and impart information in relation to sexuality; sexuality education; respect for bodily integrity; choice of partner; decide to be sexually active or not; consensual sexual relations; consensual marriage; decide whether or not, and when to have children; and pursue a satisfying, safe and pleasurable sexual life. The responsible exercise of human rights requires that all persons respect the rights of others."

In many ways, these definitions are excellent, and we could only wish that the world paid more attention to their precepts.

What a world would be created if it were recognized that "sexuality is a central aspect of being human throughout life" —let alone the central spiritual source of our being human?

Perhaps this is a utopian exercise, but I believe it would be helpful if we all set ourselves the task of imagining what a world devoted to play and pleasure would be like. It would certainly be a world less preoccupied—or not preoccupied at all—with ambitions and interests in domination, in exploitation and gaining advantage over others, in prejudice and persecution, or in abuse, violence, warfare, and planetary destruction. And why cannot a world devoted to—

or at the least more devoted to—play and pleasure, to sexual health and erotic freedom, be achieved?

The *Midwest Institute of Sexology* was founded in 1996—between the publication dates of the two World Health Organization documents just quoted. The Midwest Institute was an effort to offer clinical and educational services that were not being otherwise provided in the Great Lakes Region. It operated for a few exciting years, offering lectures, workshops and seminars to diverse communities, including

> ... teaching sexual medicine in the primary care setting to medical students and residents,

> ... facilitating workshops on tantric sexual and spiritual practices, as well as offering methods of working and playing with the bodymind's subtle energies,

> ... giving demonstrations on condom usage and other risk-reductive methods at parties for swingers and at gatherings of others involved in multiple partnering,

> ... offering seminars on sexual enrichment and wellbeing, as well as orgasmic enhancement, for men, for women, and for couples,

> ... lecturing to professional conferences on a multitude of sexual topics, including presenting research on diverse topics such as: the psychodynamic significance of body piercing and mutilation practices; the practice of sexual medicine in the primary care setting; clinical methods in sexuality counseling; the psychological significance of boundaries in

relation to the incest taboo; and the genesis of men's anxieties as illustrated by the legends of Isaac, Ganesh, and Oedipus.

Lacking any sort of building of its own, the Institute also operated as a referral network, helping thousands of individuals and couples by connecting them with suitable professional resources to find the assistance they needed (using the pool of clinicians and educators certified by the *American Association of Sex Educators, Counselors, and Therapists*, as well as calling on the help of other qualified psychoanalysts and bodyworkers). In certain limited circumstances, the Institute was also able to offer educational consultations by email and telephone.

Through the website, over a thousand email questions and requests were received each year from all over the world. These were sent by men and women, including adolescents, crying out for help—unable to communicate with their partners, suffering sexual difficulties and disorders, anxious and ignorant about their own erotic functioning. All were heartbreaking—especially since the recommendations that can be offered by email are extremely limited in their usefulness, and most of these requests were from people who did not, and likely would never have, the resources available for an in-person consultation and therapeutic assistance. Some were extremely heartbreaking. For example,

> . . . the woman from a third-world country whose genitals had been ritually mutilated, and who wanted to know what chances she had of every achieving orgasmic pleasure;

> . . . the man in charge of an agency that sheltered over three thousand orphaned adolescents, who wanted to know what he

could do, without adequate funding or personnel, to help these young people enter their sexual lives free of diseases and unwanted pregnancies;

... the adolescent girl raised in a Midwestern community, valedictorian of her high-school class and a very successful student at a major university, who believed that she urinated from her vagina, and who wanted to know how she could overcome her fears of intercourse;

... men and women, from every corner of the country, wanting to know how better to communicate with their partners about their sexual longings, or concerned because their local physician had been at a loss to help them with a specific sexual problem or dysfunction;

... individuals, from every part of the United States, worried about how to handle their "peculiar" sexual fantasies, or about their "obsession" with particular forms of sexual activity.

I continue to provide all these clinical and educational services. But the Institute successfully provided them for a only few years before it floundered, mostly because of a serious lack of funding. Eventually it had to close down.

However, during its brief heyday, the Midwest Institute of Sexology functioned under a "Vision and Mission Statement," the intent of which was to articulate a manifesto for sexual health and erotic freedom that would go beyond the World Health Organization's 1975 proclamation and that would be more sex-positive in its pronouncements. I will reproduce this "Vision and Mission" here, without further commentary, because I continue to believe that every precept in it is still worthy of serious consideration, and because my hope is that it will inspire others to reflect on their own vision of sexual health and erotic freedom.

The vision and mission of the Midwest Institute of Sexology (legally registered as the "Michigan Sexological Center") is to promote sexual health, healing and happiness, by offering clinical, educational and research services that affirm the following five human rights:

- *The right to enjoy complete freedom of sexual thought, feeling or fantasy, and to pursue actively the erotic pleasures of our sensual bodies in any way that is ethical, safe and self-determined.*

- *The right to engage, or to refrain from engaging, in all sexual activities, free from any coercion, nonconsensuality, hypocrisy or deceit, and to seek socially and psychologically a gratifying sexual lifestyle without fear of punishment, condemnation, intimidation or harassment.*

- *The right of every individual to regulate his or her bodily functioning and livelihood, as well as the right of peoples of all ages, backgrounds and circumstances, including all those who are disadvantaged, disabled, ill, impoverished or impaired, to be appropriately encouraged and supported in the development of their sensual and erotic potentialities.*

- *The right of all those suffering any form of sexual distress, disorder or dysfunction to biopsychosocial care and personal growth opportunities that are competent, compassionate and accessible.*

- *The right of every individual to develop his or her potential for playfulness as an intrinsic function of the human spirit like the capacities to love and to work.*

The intent of the Midwest Institute of Sexology is to pursue this vision and mission by creating and implementing programs that are ethical, humanitarian, and spiritually grounded, and that meet the highest standards of personal and professional conduct.

The exercise of creating one's own vision of sexual health and erotic freedom is helpful. It supports our personal examination of the extent to which we suppress and repress our own erotic potential. It also enables us to confront more clear-sightedly all the sexual oppression that occurs in the society around us.

Sexual liberation on the social and cultural level will not happen without our working and playing individually to release our selves from the psychological devices by which we imprison our own erotic potential. In the quest for erotic and spiritual emancipation, personal transformation must precede, or be concurrent with, our efforts to confront anti-sexual forces in the social and cultural arena. At both the personal and the political levels, visioning our sexual liberation is an essential step toward its achievement.

15

Five Styles of Sexual Partnering

At the end of Chapter Fourteen, I suggested that, in the pursuit of sexual health and erotic freedom, personal liberation has to precede, or to proceed concurrently with, our emancipation from the oppressive forces that confront us in the social and cultural arena. In my journey toward sexual health and erotic freedom—a journey which, as I have already indicated, I view as an essentially spiritual path—I find it useful to review all the varieties of being human.

Everything that has ever manifested in a human being is an aspect of who we each are as individuals. So to consider all the many and various styles of sensual and sexual activities engaged by other human beings actually helps me to understand what I am suppressing or repressing within myself. Reviewing the panorama of human sexual expression helps me to recognize how I am blocking, diminishing, and dishonoring my erotic potential.

Although, by and large, our society holds up a single style of erotic partnering as the exclusively acceptable model—the paradigm of the sexually exclusive and sensually constrictive heterosexual marriage—there are actually very many varieties of partnering. If we drop our anti-sexual ideologies and all the moralizing judgmentalism by which we uphold some sexual arrangements and condemn others, we can learn more about what it means to be human.

In this chapter, I will review and describe some of my learning experiences with five styles of sexual partnering: solo sexuality, cruising, partnering intensively, sharing extensively, and tantric partnering. These "styles" apply to both homosexual or same-gender, and heterosexual or other-gender erotic connections.

> *Solo Sexuality:*

Pernicious religious doctrines, political legislation, social convention, cultural mores and folkloric dogma all focus on our genitals in an adverse manner. "Masturbation" and "fornication," both heterosexual and homosexual, are usually designated the paramount "sins" against which all sorts of moralizing ideologies are promulgated.

The most prominent religions typically propound that the "sins" of sexuality are even more serious, and more severely punishable, than actions involving violence against life. Consider here the teachings of fundamentalist Christianity and Islam, as well as certain aspects of orthodox Judaism, and also many of the Hindu, Confucian, and Shinto traditions. Strident warnings against the perils of self-pleasuring and the dangers of illicit sexual liaison are also issued by prevalent folklore in traditional as well as contemporary cultures.

My personal journey with self-pleasuring is commonplace. Although I can only recall genital self-stimulation from the age of about six years, I assume that I had tried to touch my genitals for pleasure ever since my infantile hands were sufficiently coordinated to grasp my penis, or my body sufficiently coordinated to press, rock and rub my pelvis against a suitable object. Unless actively prevented from doing so, children naturally engage in these delightful pursuits, from infancy or early childhood onwards—although memory of these pleasures, like almost all memories before the age of about five years, tends to disappear.

In my case—as is often the case, even today—I was discouraged, punished, and shamed for this practice, even as a very young child. Thankfully, I experienced nothing like being beaten, having my hand chopped off, or being publicly flogged. Also thankfully, the prohibitions and restrictions to which I was subjected never seemed to stop my pleasure in the practice.

However, I also know that, while still young, I became psychologically conflicted about self-pleasuring. And I have invested a significant portion of my adolescent and adult journey of personal growth struggling to overcome this conflict. I have succeeded in this to the point where I am now able to express openly my gratitude for the great blessing of being able to honor myself through self-stimulation. An honoring of the self is indeed what it is.

Despite my early history of personal conflict, I know that the activities of self-pleasuring have been a "saving grace" in my life. Since the age of about six years, I know that I have stimulated myself genitally at least once a day, and often several times daily. This has continued throughout my adulthood—alongside the privilege of enjoying partnered sexual activities of all sorts.

Solo sexuality actually has many psychological benefits. I know, very surely, that I might be a rather vile and violent man today if it were not for this persistent practice—which is, of course, not to suggest that my personal growth has been facilitated by this practice alone. However, the healthful and healing power of self-pleasuring has yet to be sufficiently acknowledged by our society or any other.

If you doubt the pervasiveness of the anti-sexual messages and mystifications in our contemporary world, consider the fact that almost everyone can identify at least half-a-dozen beliefs about the dangerous consequences of "masturbation"—even if they claim that they are not themselves believers in these myths. For example, it deforms one's genitals, it deranges one's mental capacities, it detracts from one's ability to work and to love, and so forth.

Also, almost everyone within range of a television satellite can name at least a half-dozen movies, worldwide box-office successes produced within the past decade, that take as their motif the dire consequences of extramarital dalliance or sexual "excess." For example, there are stories of workplace sexual encounters that destroy a family life that otherwise appears perfectly ordered. Other stories describe irresistible erotic passions that wreck careers that are, in all other respects, rocketing to exemplary success, and still others depict pleasures relentlessly pursued to their "inevitable" denouement in madness or mayhem, and so forth.

Against these prevalent cultural messages, let us now embrace these "sins" for what they indeed may be—an emotional healing and a spiritual practice *par excellence*. Let us begin by appreciating the physical, emotional, and spiritual benefits of "masturbation."

In Chapter Ten, we already emphasized how much children—and anyone who has ever been a child—need to be touched. We mentioned how being touched is essential to our physical welfare, our emotional vitality, and our spiritual growth. However, none of us would thrive if our being touched remained dependent on the love of others—the love of our self is prerequisite.

It is an important line of childhood development that, as we grow from babies into toddlers, we are able to assume some responsibility for our need to be touched, as we become sufficiently coordinated to be able to touch ourselves intentionally. This does not mean that the need to be touched by others disappears. Quite the contrary, it remains strongly important to continue to be touched by others, especially since we know that being touched by another human being has pronouncedly different energy dynamics than touching ourselves—an issue we will mention again. But it does mean that, as our child develops, touching can become reciprocal and then, if these developments proceed well, touching can become energetically mutual or "synergistic."

Very importantly, it means that our child becomes able to administer the gift of touch to ourselves—moving from being simply a recipient, to the possibilities of being interactively or transactionally tactile, and to the possibilities of being actively self-giving. This is an enormously important shift for physical and emotional development as has been demonstrated in many ways that are documented in the literatures of developmental psychology and psychoanalysis. It is also the foundation of our human capacities to receive love, and therefore to be able to give love.

Self-pleasuring is the foundation of our potential to love and be loved.

Self-administered touch integrates, soothes or comforts, and gives us a psychologically fundamental sense of worthiness and competence—which is commonly called "self-esteem." It is the antidote to shame. The "skin envelope" defines where, and how, we are in our sensual and existential foundation—the capacity to engage in active self-stimulation of our own skin envelope is thus essential to the formation of a healthy and happy sense of "self" in at least five ways.

First, self-stimulation "in-forms" or integrates our child. It informs us where the sensual space of our "self" has its margins, that sensual boundary where—so to speak—"self" appears to end and the rest of the "world" appears to begin. Thus, returning to the processes of self-stimulation, and knowing one has the intentional ability to choose such a return, centers our "self" in a profoundly healthy sense.

Second, pleasurable self-touching soothes or comforts us when we are distraught, by alleviating our fearful anxieties, and indeed by helping us—at least to some degree—to achieve a letting-go of our judgmental mind, our fear-based patterns of thinking. The gentle enjoyment of touching grounds experience in the present moment, and quietens the chattering mind.

Third, these abilities, which serve reliably to ground ourselves in our bodies and to center ourselves in pleasure, are the wellspring of our sense of being loveable. By this, I mean that we come to feel basically worthy and competent in our sense of being-in-the-world. As this occurs, we become able to experience more clearly the extent to which our world is trustworthy.

When these three contributions of self-touching are facilitated, self-pleasuring constitutes and catalyzes our most basic human capacities of feeling loveable, of being able to love and of finding sexual-spiritual bliss. However, when these three contributions of self-touching to physical and emotional development are interrupted, egotism substitutes for what I am here calling a "healthy sense of self."

Disturbances in these developments of self-touching, the progression from being touched to touching ourselves, lead to profound unhappiness throughout our lives—by which I refer to the extent that we all wrestle with psychotic, neurotic, and addictive processes. Psychoanalysis shows us how everyone suffers, to some degree, from these constituents to our personality. We also know that the psychotic, neurotic, and addictive components of our mental functioning are indicative of the operation of our egotistic, judgmental mind.

Psychoanalysts, as much as other scientists and spiritual practitioners, know that, against the development of a "healthy sense of self," egotism is precisely what is exacerbated when our natural tendencies to self-pleasuring are thwarted by suppression and repression, and thence by compulsivity. It is as if, when self-pleasuring is prevented from blossoming as the fount of our emotional and spiritual growth, the chattering mind repetitiously substitutes incessant narratives about how immortal this "me" is (or how terrified I am of my mortality), how "reasonable" this "me" is (or how terrified I am of my madness), and how "superior" this "me" is compared with others (or how terrified I am of knowing the emptiness of my being). The chattering mind spreads like the virulent disease that it is—whenever our natural sensuality is obstructed.

Fourth, when self-touching blossoms into genital self-pleasuring, we are at the source of our capacity for happiness, our capacity to love others as well as ourselves. Without self-love, we cannot truly love another person—if our capacity for self-love is restricted, so too will be our authentic ability to love anyone else. Without self-pleasuring, we cannot truly learn how to facilitate the sensual and sexual pleasures of another person—if our capacity to stimulate our selves into orgasmic bliss is restricted, so too will be our authentic ability to facilitate the orgasming of anyone else, or to receive the gift of another person's facilitation of our orgasming.

Fifth, it is always through genital self-pleasuring that we become able to access the divine gifts of our erotic joy, bliss and ecstasy. This is because, in terms of the subtle energies for which our embodiment is a conduit, the genitals are at our "root chakra." This "chakra" is a powerful vortex of energy, and hence the emotional and spiritual source of our being-in-the-world.

We have now indicated how self-touching grounds, or centers, our "self" in a fundamental way, fostering our ability to look outwards with compassion and appreciation. Simply expressed,

If we cannot enjoy the naturalness of pleasuring our own bodies,
how then can we ever develop a happy sense
of the sensual and experiential space
that we occupy within the world,
and how can we love the world and love others in the world
—love them, that is,

as embodied, sensual and emotional, human beings and not merely as abstract propositions?

Self-love is the prerequisite of our capacity to love others. There is no loving without this grounding in loving the self, and self-love must include—indeed start with—the love of our own genital pleasuring.

Foremost, love is not discriminatory—Love does not divide, separate, and exclude. We cannot become able to love if we love our own bodies *except* for our genitals. Love does not blossom under such a condition of alienation from the central source of our capacity to receive and to give pleasure.

The capacity to love others, and to accept love, does not develop out of hateful self-experiencing. The prototypical act of self-hatred, the origination of shame and guilt about our sensual self—by treating the genital source of our joy under the aegis of a moralizing ideology of exclusion—is the perpetuation of this alienation within our selves. To manipulate ourselves into any attempt at "loving" others, without first accepting, finding our enjoyment in, and fully loving all aspects of our self, is foredoomed to a hollow outcome.

Moreover, as we described in Chapter Eleven, the genitals are, for most of us, the most touchable area of our bodies, the most intensely pleasurable of all the many gifts our bodies provide. They are where self-love takes root. Self-pleasuring is the basis for our bodily potential to blossom into our bliss.

In passing we may note that this is why when patients, who have orgasmic difficulties, solicit my services as clinical sexologist, therapy begins with working and playing to access more deeply the joys of self-pleasuring. This healing process continues intensively and extensively before partnered sexual activity ever becomes the therapeutic focus.

We may also note that "marathon" sessions of self-pleasuring have been advocated—even if only in the secret teachings of ancient and contemporary spiritual leaders—as a premium route to the transcendent experiences of bliss and ecstasy.

Self-pleasuring invites our erotic energies into their dancing. Genital touching stirs the *"kundalini"*—libidality, *"prāna"* or sexual lifeforce—that has its roots from the soles of our feet, through the rectum, perineum, and genitals. Here is our sexual-spiritual sourcing, the vibrationality that can sweep through our bodies, in a way that warms our hearts and uplifts ecstatically the crown of our heads. Here is our sensual source that enables us to set-aside the tyrannical governance of our judgmental minds, and moves us toward divine bliss.

Self-pleasuring is meditation—"masturbation" is the epitome of prayer. It is not merely that "masturbation" is *not* sin—whatever "sin" may be—it is that this joy of sensuality is essential to all spiritual practice.

Genital self-pleasuring is
the most fundamentally human expression of love
and the most fundamental manner in which we learn to love.

Whether we are aware of it or not, awakened to it or not, whenever we stroke or caress our bodies, whenever we play with ourselves genitally, we are worshipping the divine. With his characteristic bluntness, the Reverend Laird Sutton, an eminent director and producer of erotic videos, once stated this poignant truth: "The kid in the bathroom, jacking himself or jilling herself off, while reading a two-bit erotic novel or holding up a sexy magazine, is in the process of approaching God."

As I stated in Chapter Eleven, "the glories of our genitals are the altar for spiritual practice"—we will elaborate this spiritual dimension in the final section of this book.

➢ *Cruising:*

"Cruising" is a way of seeking sensual and sexual contact with another human being. It is an adventuresome way of reaching out for interpersonal connection, often culminating in brief sexual encounters with strangers.

Although often condemned by prevalent moralizing ideologies, the phenomenon of cruising merits serious discussion. For it is the most profound spiritual privilege to experience erotic pleasure in the presence of another person—and it is a profound emotional and spiritual privilege to have the honor of facilitating another person in their pleasuring.

Sensual and sexual arousal, and its orgasmic climax, involves a mysterious movement of spiritual energies, and we know this truth from deep within ourselves. Sharing these mysteries creates emotionally and spiritually profound connections—including when these mysteries are shared with strangers. So let us now discuss some of the pleasures of genital sharing.

We know that the mysteries of climactic sexual sharing have prompted men and women through the ages to copulate in the fields as a prayer to make the crops grow and the cattle prosper. These mysteries have prompted men and women to attend to the stewardship of their sexual energies as the essential way to facilitate gratitude throughout the ventures of hunting, fishing, and gathering. And these mysteries of climactic genital connection are why the rituals of May Day, and similar festivities all over the globe, involve orgiastic sexual couplings that set aside the social prerogatives and cultural mores of stable partnership—liaisons that may occur with someone else's designated partner or with a stranger. These mysteries are also why men and women orgasm in front of images of the Goddess, the men spilling their ejaculate, in an offering of propitiation and gratitude.

Sexual pleasuring celebrates the interconnectedness of the universe—and the mysteries of its climax mark the spirituality of this interconnectedness.

Sexual connections are always prayerful. From the pleasuring of our own bodies, we are able to turn outwards with compassion and appreciation. Sexuality not only reconnects us within ourselves, it reconnects us with others, and it conjoins earth and heaven. From the base of self-pleasure, we reach out to others and to the universe—we take the emotional and spiritual energies that arise within us and return them to the universe, in acts that connect our selves with others around us, both intimates and strangers.

Cruising is a reaching out to others. It is an adventure in sensual and sexual connection. Cruising begins in the sandbox and the playground of our childhood. As we enter adulthood, it diversifies the arenas of its operations. Cruising moves the adventurer out of the solitude of his or her home, and into the public arena. In every region across the globe, there are locations where we may go as individuals to seek encounters with other individuals—woods, beaches, parks, bars, clubs, churches, military installations, or street corners.

The encounters that we seek may be of many kinds. But, in a certain sense, cruising is essentially sexual, even when it appears to take a non-sexual form. Almost by definition, and even when they involve full genital sharing and climactic experience, the connections we make in cruising are usually transient—although durable partnerships do occasionally result. So, now let us briefly consider the emotional and spiritual meaningfulness of sex with strangers.

Many of us have had sex with strangers. All of us have fantasized about the thrill of such transient anonymous pleasures. And most of us have had the experience of sexual sharing in relationships that we imagined were characterized by intimacy and integrity, only to be later disillusioned.

In this society, there is an enormous cultural pressure to restrict our sexual life to partners with whom we are—supposedly—emotionally intimate. Or at least to restrict ourselves to partners with whom there is an illusion or delusion—or at least the public presentation—of emotional intimacy. Here again, we find the hypocrisy of our culture's anti-sexual ideologies. The notion of sex with strangers elicits—or is supposed to elicit—the full force of our shame and guilt about being sexual.

*The benefits of cruising consist
not only of reaching out for connection,
and for the pleasures that may be shared within this connection;
cruising is also an expression of integrity.
It involves taking responsibility for our sexual desires,
and is thus an expression of our intention
to free ourselves from sexual shame and guilt.*

Yet cruising is challenging. For heterosexual connections, cruising locations are everywhere available, but the social disapproval is also everywhere present. In most areas, cruising locations for finding homosexual connections are physically dangerous, and making them dangerous is one of the main ways in which society manifests the viciousness of its homophobia. For lesbian connections, cruising is even more complex. For those who are transgendered, or those interested in connections associated with the many varieties of alternative lifestyle ("s and m" devotees, swingers, aficionados of paraphilias or fetishes, and so forth), cruising is, sad to say, an especially high-risk endeavor.

From my personal experience with cruising—as well as from my professional experience listening to many accounts of cruising told to me by patients, clients, and students—I learn much about human nature. For example, I know the assumption that brief sexual encounters with strangers are necessarily "meaningless" is presumptuously dismissive. It dismisses the potential emotional and spiritual impact of such liaisons. Encounters with strangers, enacted under conditions of safety and respect, may offer a wonderful reconnection with the divine energies that flow within, between and around us. Perhaps this is even *especially* the case with strangers—because, if we cannot find the divine in every stranger, how can we imagine that we are truly finding the divine in those whom we profess to "love"?

Not only is bodily pleasuring the most basic way to reach out lovingly, but the anonymity or unfamiliarity of not being acquainted with our transient sexual partner may facilitate a momentum that is relatively uncluttered by the repetitive mechanics of our judgmental mind. This is essential to the emotional and spiritual impact of cruising experiences.

Cruising, as the practice of brief sexual encounters with strangers, potentially offers a pleasurable experience "out of ordinary time." That is, it is unfettered by the accumulation of previous interpersonal transactions, by the delusions of "intimacy," or by the expectation of future affairs. It is thus spontaneously disinhibiting in its celebratory abandon. Of course, the importance of honoring such moments by ensuring that they are entirely consensual or mutual, and by the practice of risk-reductive modes of sexual contact, cannot be overemphasized.

In this context, cruising for sex with strangers may evoke the same reverential grace as any mutual touching of bodies— the reverence with which we greet a stranger by gently placing our palms together over our hearts and murmuring *"Namasté,"* meaning "the light within me honors the light within you."

As a practice that brings us genital to genital with strangers, cruising is, in what is perhaps a more intensive modality, an instance of meeting the "other" face-to-face.

In this respect, as the philosopher Emmanuel Levinas has discussed, we express a fundamental dimension of the humanity of our being-in-the-world, and perhaps also we express the fundamental dimension of our connectedness with the divine.

Cruising seeks the divine within our selves
as we connect our selves erotically
with the divinity of the human stranger in front of us.

There is a prevalent—moralizing—attitude, which requires that we should only have sexual contact with those whom we "know" and for whom we have allegedly cultivated a history of affectionate feelings. As I have already indicated, there is an obvious anti-sexual implication to this precept. It implies that sexual connection is not, in and of itself, emotionally and spiritually enhancing, or that it is only acceptable if subordinated to the prerequisites of some sort of cognitive-affective bonding. The assumption is that sexual contact is somehow "dirty" or "morally contemptible" unless the protracted rituals of an intimate or pseudo-intimate relationship have somehow sanitized it.

The notion that sexual contact should be limited to those with whom we are allegedly "intimate" is flawed, especially when we consider how our abilities to "know" our selves cognitively and emotionally, let alone to "know" anyone else, are *always* both severely limited and seriously distorted. This is a sad truth contributed by many psychological researches, including the insights of psychoanalysis. So, if we wait to "know" another person before we love them—if we delude ourselves into imagining that "love" is a consequence of judgmental evaluation—then we will never truly fall into Love.

Although to some this may seem a pessimistic outlook, there is something profoundly important here. To value, compassionately and appreciatively, the experience of cruising for sexual connection is to open ourselves to the emotional and spiritual practice of refusing to "wait" for the "right" person in order to express our capacity for love. Far from pessimism, cruising is the quintessential act of spreading the vibration of love to those with whom we most urgently need to share love—those who are strangers to us.

When we cruise for sex with strangers, we are reaching to connect our self-pleasuring with that of the divine "other"—"God" is in every man and woman.

> *Partnering Intensively:*

Please do not misunderstand me: Durable partnerships that permit a deepening cognitive and emotional intimacy, within the integrity of the truthfulness of love, are both a blessing and a miracle in which to rejoice. Such "bonds of love" take many forms, such as lasting friendships, durable "affairs," or longterm relationships such as marriage.

Contrary to popular myth, when these intensive partnerships are happy arrangements, this does not "just happen" alchemically. Rather, happy human relationships, including durable sexual partnerships, require diligent nurturance, attentive work and play, especially in their sensual and sexual dimension, if they are to remain alive. We indeed honor our selves whenever we choose to work and play in such relationships, and we need to honor whatever degree of success any of us achieves in this venture.

Here I will use the term "marriage" as a general label for all such "durable partnerships"—which is not to imply anything about their legal status, and definitely not to imply that such relationships only pertain heterosexually. In our culture, "marriages" are embedded in a series of beliefs and values about the "commitment" of each partner to the procedure and progression of the relationship.

In passing we may note that rarely are such "commitments" well explicated, even though sometimes a couple will embark on a "commitment" that is utterly inhumane, and still left implicit. For example, couples will commit to continue their relationship even if it is the cause and catalyst of suffering and unhappiness. This is often implied by marital declarations, even if such an implication seems absurd when scrutinized. And rarely is it well considered or discussed whether declarations of commitment could ever be realistic or are merely delusional.

For instance, "I will ensure that you are clothed and fed for as long as it is feasible for me to do so" seems like a plausible commitment, but rarely are "marriage vows" so honest in their limitations and their specificity. Declarations such as "I will be in love with you forever" or "I will always feel sexually passionate toward you" are unquestionably delusional. As appealing as such declarations may be in their expression of an ardent wish for permanency, it remains profoundly true that "love" and "passion" cannot be legislated, and can never grow out of our resolve, however well intended this resolve may be.

Love cannot be "made to happen" by human egotism, just as sexual passion cannot be manufactured. Rather, *Love is a vibration into which we may surrender*, at the price of our egotistic grandeur and with the sacrifice of our longings for attachment as well as our craving for permanency.

So often the commitment to a marriage actually carries an emotionally-defensive and fear-based, spiritually-unacceptable and anti-sexual implication. In actuality, the "vow" means something like "I will continue this liaison even if its passion evaporates, its sexual energies dry up, and the vibration of our connectedness is no longer that of love."

In a profound sense, the only "commitment" that our judgmental and chattering mind knows that it can keep with any consistency is its commitment to keep on chattering with judgments. Since our judgmentalism is promulgated on the basis of past-pain and future-fear, we are indeed able to make an authentic declaration of our commitment to keep on acting judgmentally. However, all other declarations made by our chattering mind are more illusory and delusional.

Letting-go the tyranny of our chattering mind, living in the present, implies an acceptance of the spontaneity of our spirit. It implies that we accept that we cannot control the future. Although we can commit ourselves to the endeavor of living life in Love, and we can commit ourselves to the spiritual path in which our egotism is sacrificed, we cannot realistically anticipate our future feelings any more than we can eradicate our past thoughts. So we cannot control the outcome of our relationships, unless we intend to fall out of living in the present and stay together with our partners on the basis of fear rather than Love.

In this context, two rather unpalatable facts about marriages, both traditional and contemporary, need to be briefly confronted. These facts are witnessed, again and again, by those of us who offer clinical services to couples, and by those of us who conduct sexological research. Whenever we avoid addressing these facts, preferring instead to cling to the falsehoods of popular myth, we merely undercut our own potential for the personal growth of developing our capacity to live life in Love.

The first fact is that, because our judgmental mind lives so insistently on the basis of past-pain and future-fear, we tend to make commitments that we are incapable of fulfilling. That is, we attach ourselves to the illusion or delusion that our persistent mental efforts will be able to stipulate and regiment our feelings and energies at some later point in time. This is the illusion or delusion that our chattering mind will take charge of the outcome of our lives and be able to determine the "end of our story." In this respect, most of us actually deceive ourselves most of the time into imagining that our readiness for cognitive and emotional intimacy with another human being is far greater than it actually is.

In one strategy, we dupe ourselves into believing that we are far happier in our marriages than we actually are. In another strategy, when relationships go awry, we believe that the only reason we have not achieved a "perfect partnership" is because our partner has let us down, or because the "true love of our life" has somehow not yet arrived on the scene.

Thus, it is sad but true that, even when they endure, most of our marriages are far less intimate, far more lacking in personal integrity, and far more sensually and sexually depriving, than we, as participants, wish to believe or proclaim.

Perhaps we enter marriages because we are steeped in shame and guilt over our wish to cruise for sex with strangers. Because the second fact is that—contrary to the popular myth that marriages enable both partners to develop and deepen their experiences of sexual sharing—the commitment of most marriages is actually fear-based, even when it has the glossy appearance of being founded on love. Ultimately, marriage rarely supports an exuberant and spontaneous sexual-spiritual life—even when it may appear to do so initially.

> *More often than not, we embark on marriages*
> *with collusively unconscious intentions*
> *of containing and curtailing the resourcefulness*
> *of our sexual-spiritual exuberances.*

More often than not, we enter marriages not to grow spiritually and sexually, but to alleviate the painful challenges of profound growth and personal adventure.

Note that this collusion to contain, curb or curtail personal growth is unconscious. Rarely do we marry someone with the conscious intention of diminishing our partnered sexual lives. Rather, we delude ourselves thoroughly. We begin a "honeymoon" in which we believe that the liaison is going to enable us to overcome our shame and guilt. But as time passes, our shame and guilt "get the better of us." Thus begins the downward spiral of the relationship into sensual and sexual frustration, conflict and deprivation.

Obviously, entering a regular partnership may indeed sometimes increase the "frequency of coitus," as researchers would call it, or of "sexual intimacy" as others would have it. But this is, so to speak, precisely beside the point. What typically occurs is more along the following lines.

With the development of cognitive and emotional "intimacy" in a relationship, with the advancing belief that we "know" our partner, the judgmental egotistic mind attempts to take charge of sexual interactions. Then sexual sharing becomes routinized, as mental maneuvering takes priority over the spontaneity of erotic synergies. Routinization of sex is adverse to the essential sensuality of erotic or spiritual sharing. That is, commonly in marriages, when "sex acts" occur they do so in a deceptive manner that is fundamentally anti-sexual. Sadly, there is extensive clinical evidence how frequently this is the case.

Our mistake derives from our belief in commitment. To what are we actually committed? Consciously, the "purpose" of partnership may be the deepening of love, as well as enjoyment of the opportunities that a regular relationship provides for the intensification of sexual ecstasies. But, unconsciously, the "purpose" is usually a retreat from the challenges of spiritual-sexual growth. It is a decision to live in the consistency of fear-based thinking and feeling, rather than to accept the uncertainties of living in the present, living life in Love.

The mistake here is also the hegemonic presumption, peddled on multiple levels in our social and cultural belief systems and ideologies, that sexual passion follows from interpersonal "commitment." In actuality, the passion of sharing sensual energies is prerequisite to any genuine intimacy.

As has been well said, "Love is not an idea, rather it is a vibration to which we may be attuned." It needs to be added that "love" is not a decision or commitment that can be made by our judgmental egotistic mind. Here is the profound truthfulness of Love.

To enter a marital commitment is therefore, in actuality, to undertake the perilous risk of falling out of love, and out of sensual bliss. Despite the truthfulness of this, couples ignore it. I have been, personally, an example of this ignorance, as someone who has "failed marriages" in my personal history. Although these relationships brought me many wonderful blessings, the idea that one can realistically make a commitment to maintaining the permanence of passion, in the sharing of sensual and sexual energies, proved fallacious.

As a sexuality educator and sex therapist, I have been consulted by and counseled a very considerable number of couples of all varieties. It is exceedingly rare to find a marriage that honors the sexual-spiritual energies of its participants. The very aspect of marriage that one might imagine to be its sexual promise—the ritualized time and space to explore and experiment exquisitely with the passion of sexual desires, to deepen and intensify the sharing of an erotic-energetic momentum, to facilitate each other's movement toward bliss—proves to be quite the reverse. Instead, the opportunity is either increasingly ignored altogether, or the sexual sharing becomes increasingly routinized and anti-sexual.

Instead of attending to the cultivation of their capacities for ecstasy, marriage partners typically act as if their partnership should operate like a prolonged episode of cruising. They act as if, once married, their chattering minds would politely step aside to allow the spontaneity, the mystery, and the ecstasy of erotic bliss. They do not attend to the evolution of their sexual partnership. Rather, out of their unconscious shame and guilt, they act as if the sexual component of their relationship should just keeping running satisfactorily without attention. This does not happen.

Our egotism never aborts itself, and our shame and guilt never evaporate, just because we have deluded ourselves into believing that we have found a partner who will liberate us from their clutches. The chattering anti-sexual mind never steps aside to allow our sexual energies to flow freely, openly and spontaneously. On the contrary, only by freeing the intensity of our sensual resources can we access the power to dissolve the spiritual obstructions concocted by the shame and guilt of our chattering mind.

In sum, our anti-sexual minds compulsively use the repetitiousness of durable partnerships and "commitments" as if they were an opportunity to seize complete control. As a consequence, "love" is gradually immobilized within this interpersonal routinization or stagnation. The very aspects of marriage that we believe to be a blessing—the opportunity to spend time with a regular partner, to augment sexual sharing with a deepening cognitive and emotional intimacy within the truthfulness of a relationship that has extensive integrity, and the opportunity to intensify erotic connectedness—often prove to be its greatest liability. Knowing the other, or believing we "know" the other, readily comes to obstruct the flow of sexual energies rather than to enhance it as the deepening of love.

> *Sharing Extensively:*

Unlike the socially idealized arrangements of marriage, as our culture supposes it should be, there are dyadic partnerships that retain elements of cruising, precisely by not committing themselves to the agreements of sexual exclusivity.

From the "circle jerks" and "slumber parties" of our childhood and adolescence, to the adult activities of polyamory, "swinging," and orgiastic celebrations, it is often found that sharing sexual secrets, and sharing sexual energies, in a community may be emotionally and spiritually beneficial for all participants. My personal and professional experience suggests how often this is the case.

Not only can our erotic energies be mobilized magnificently in a circle or community of sensual sharing and multiple partnering, but such sexual practices often serve profoundly in the healing of the suffering caused by our shame and guilt.

Lifestyles involving multiple partnerships are not to be condemned automatically, as if they are invariably motivated flights away from the challenges of intimacy and integrity. Rather, they often may be understood as ways of honoring the spirituality of sensual sharing, ways of celebrating the flow of erotic energies, and thus deepening the challenges of falling into the vibrationality of Love.

I recall a joyous evening when my lover, Puja, and I shared our sexual energies with Zoë and Gavin. As our verbal "heart-sharing" drew to a moment of closure, Zoë, giggling deliciously, announced that she was going to take off all her clothes and get into our bed. All of us had been naked together many times at various gatherings—and, at a previous date, our conversation had turned to the pleasures of sexual sharing. We had discussed the limits within which we would all feel comfortable should such sharing spontaneously arise within our foursome. Now was clearly the right moment for this to occur. Enjoying the warm fragrant breeze that wafted through our windows in the summer's night, Puja, Gavin, and I quickly shed our clothing. We lit candles around the spaciousness of our bed, and we put on some gentle music.

I always loved looking at this lover's body. Puja was lithe, with strong legs and long elegant arms. Her long dark hair would cascade over the sweet firmness of her breasts, and her eyes were soulful even when they shifted with apprehension. Now I enjoyed looking at Gavin, a slim, handsome man, with a beautiful penis that harmonized his torso. His face always seemed fresh and open, inviting, and his luminous hazel eyes would often swim with tears when the soft depths of his tender heart were touched. Zoë had a vivacious demeanor that had often appeared in my fantasies of lovemaking with her. Now she was naked before me, I reveled in the delicacy of her smile as much as I delighted in looking at the delicacies of her rounded buttocks and breasts offsetting the trimness of her hourglass waist.

Seated next to each other, Gavin and I side-by-side, facing Zoë and Puja, we each began to massage our partner's feet, murmuring phrases of gratitude for our time together—Puja and I expressing our appreciation at the sight of Zoë and Gavin's bodies, and they each expressing their enjoyment of ours.

It may be noted that, in the anticipation of this scene, my mind had been somewhat focused on the fact that Puja and Gavin had been partners some years previously. My mind had also been preoccupied with my frequent fantasies of making genital love with Zoë, with a slightly obsessive preoccupation as to whether such an event would ever occur, and with my knowledge that she had never seemed to be interested in genital intercourse with me—a "limit" that she had stated with exemplary kindness and clarity. But now, almost to my surprise—as our stroking and caressing of each other's bodies progressed ever more affectionately—my mental focus and my chattering preoccupations evaporated. Any jealous defensiveness that I had harbored about Puja and Gavin's history together, and the goal-oriented lusting for Zoë that I had held onto, simply dissolved in the precious pleasures of the moment.

Now lying side-by-side, Zoë and Gavin licked and kissed each other's bodies, as Puja and I played lightly with our tongues. Gradually, as our arousal increased, genitals erect and moistened, we were fully lovemaking, together, apart, side-by-side. Puja and I contributed to Zoë and Gavin's pleasures as they pleasured each other—we stroked Zoë's hair and shoulders as she and Gavin genitally embraced. We lightly scratched Gavin's testicles, as we enjoyed the sight of his penis and moving inside Zoë as her vulva and vagina enveloped his organ. It was a thrill to be watched admiringly as Puja and I engaged each other in coital union, and it was a special pleasure to feel Zoë and Gavin caress me as Puja and I felt our climaxes oncoming.

It felt as if the entire bed vibrated, and the room was suffused with warmth and light, as we finally all cascaded into our various orgasms. It felt as if the love within our circle was inscribed in the stars as all four of us snuggled in post-orgasmic embrace. We felt wondrously, cosmically united, our chattering minds stilled, and the darkness of our sexual shame and guilt banished from the celestial moment.

I have deliberately described this scene in somewhat graphic detail because I know that it is easy for those who have not enjoyed such situations to assume that expansive sexual sharing only occurs in dangerous or distasteful circumstances.

What this foursome achieved could be called the delights of "soft swinging"—meaning an open sharing of sexual pleasures with genital intercourse only occurring between primary partners.

Soft swinging occurs in various ways all over the world—with "straight" or gay participants—and sometimes in groups much larger than four. There are also "heavier" swinging scenes—orgies at which genital intercourse outside of primary partnerships is a frequent occurrence.

Tuesday evenings at Dan's place are usually a glorious celebration of male energies, reminiscent of the traditional theater of "sex-night" at the bathhouses. Men of all shapes and sizes, freshly showered and wrapped only in towels, bask in the warmth of his living-room. As the superficialities of chitchat become exhausted, oils are provided and the tender firmness of massage ignites the erotic energy in the atmosphere. Penises become exuberant. Men smile with enigmatic beauty. Genitals are caressed and kissed. There are no rules here, except those of gentleness or decency, of respecting those who request limits, and of diligence in risk-reductive sexual practices.

As the scene becomes yet hotter, orgasming is fierce and loud, ejaculate flows, and men who had looked tight and tired, soften into a centered, peaceful demeanor that is extraordinary. As the evening draws to a close, the joy that has been created is palpable.

At swinging clubs, there is occasionally a rather frantic, goal-oriented attitude of "let's get laid as much as we can." This sometimes contributes to a "meat market" atmosphere in which, for example, men treat women as if they were property to be bartered and swapped. The slogan of one organization I used to visit occasionally was "Use it or lose it!"—a sentiment that expresses some of the sexual anxiety and obsessive compulsivity that underlies much of a predominantly male attitude, which subordinates sexual pleasure to the competitiveness of racking up conquests.

But not all swinging is like this. Rather, my experiences suggest that this is merely the grungy side of the community. This side promotes itself more assertively and has received more media attention. Against this, swinging groups are often relaxed, contagiously friendly, frequently celebratory and adventuresome in their sexual attitudes, and scarcely dominated by male conquistadors.

Rather, the heterosexual swinging community provides an invaluable haven for bisexual women. Often, swinging preserves marriages by acknowledging openly the non-exclusivity of our sexual desires.

We know that bisexual men in heterosexual marriages tend to conduct their same-gender affairs surreptitiously, often with dangerous physical and emotional consequences for themselves and for their female partners. Outside the gay swinging scene, direct sexual contact between men in the swinging community tends to be ambivalently regarded—although clearly there are enormous homosexual gratifications for men in heterosexual swinging, even if they occur mostly on voyeuristic and exhibitionistic levels.

However, much swinging activity is led by women in order to enjoy having sexual contact with other women, while retaining the enjoyment of male partners, and without involving direct sexual contact between men. In this respect, for bisexual women in heterosexual marriages, the swinging community offers opportunities to be open with, and applauded for, their sexual interests.

In orgiastic revelry, the extensive sharing of sexual interaction illuminates both the abundance and the "transpersonal" nature of our erotic energies. As has been discussed in many anthropological writings, almost every culture is known to have—ritualized or spontaneous—episodes of collective release from the constraints against sexual expression that are imposed by all social organizations. Such episodes are transgressive, breaking the "normal" regulations by which culture constrains, curbs or curtails the expression of our erotic desires.

In providing this occasion for impulsive release, these episodes also serve to revitalize the community. Thus, from the viewpoint of anthropological or sociological research, it becomes evident that orgies serve seemingly paradoxical functions. These transgressive occasions are both ways in which the human spirit bursts the bounds of social organization, and ways in which cultures or communities rejuvenate themselves and their membership.

These sociological or anthropological aspects are interesting. However, what is also noteworthy is the emotional and spiritual dimension of orgiastic revelry. For such revelries are a celebration of the abundance and the transpersonality of our sexual-spiritual energies—those very energies that flow through human communities as much as they flow through each human individual.

I remember—a recollection that is both deliciously hazy and dramatically vivid—a gathering honoring the occasion of my birthday at which I was the "object" of the most wonderful surfeit of sensual attention. As the culmination of the evening's ceremonies, I was tenderly undressed and laid out on the soft expanse of an enormous cushion in a warm candlelit room suffused with the pulsating rhythm of some of my favorite music. Naked, laughing, dancing, the celebrants—about twenty of my dearest friends and lovers—gathered around me, clearly delighted with the gift they were about to deliver.

Joining in, one at a time, they "addressed" my body in an accumulation of sweet sensations. Initially, only my limbs were stroked. Then, added to this pleasure, the souls of my feet were massaged, my toes tickled and sucked. A little later, several celebrants began gently to scratch the palms of my hands, to play sensually with my wrists, and to caress each of my fingers.

Sensations piled onto sensations as, one by one, each celebrant took up a "station." Two women preoccupied themselves with each of my nipples. Another attended to my scalp, my hair, my ears. A small group of women and men attended to my genital pleasuring—licking, fondling, sucking, and vaginally embracing my erect penis, sequentially and together. Two celebrants played with my anus, teasing around the sphincter and perineum, tickling the tightness of my scrotum, softly entering my rectum and gently rubbing my prostate. Finally, my lover kissed my lips, and our tongues played in a tantalizing dance. As they achieved their cumulative crescendo, these sweet ministrations delivered me into a delirious melting stream of sensations.

Let us pause for a moment to consider the benefits of this experience, and to question whether it has any deleterious effects when considered from a scientific point of view. Let us note here how the gift I experienced both was, and was not, what clinicians sometimes call "overstimulation." The latter, as every clinician knows, typically has detrimental or traumatic consequences for both children and adults. For example, this is one of the many reasons why we insist that children should not be exposed to adult sexuality for, whatever its other consequences, such an exposure is almost invariably overstimulating and traumatizing for them. They cannot "handle it." A flooding of sensations ruptures, or at least temporarily overwhelms, our capacity to organize the excess it is receiving, and on whatever scale this occurs, it can be traumatic.

However, overstimulation is a condition that depends on its context, and is relative to the organization that is being challenged. What is detrimental in other circumstances may be a blessing—at least under certain special conditions. For example, with an emotionally prepared adult, who fully trusts the circumstances of its delivery, a flooding of sensations can offer an experience that is transcendent. This paradox is similar to that of the dangers, and the potential blessings, of experimenting with hallucinogens.

Sensual excess may offer a profoundly spiritual momentum, silencing the chattering mind, dissolving the bounded structure of our egotism, and delivering us into bliss. In this way, it may be *ecstatic*—taking us out of the stasis of our mental imprisonment. Excess may deliver us to ecstasy—at least if we are emotionally ready for it to do so. When my celebrants gifted me with all their sweet attentions, I ascended. As my pleasuring melted into its cumulative crescendo, I dissolved into the blissful flow of a delirious timespace that is extraordinary and ecstatic. Herein lies, I believe, the enigmatic spirituality of my celebrants' sensually excessive gift.

More often, orgiastic revelries are for the benefit of all participants, rather than being so focused on a particular celebrant. On other occasions, I have seen mattresses replete with an extravagance of writhing naked bodies—orgies in which the libidinal dynamics of collective passion sweep away the distinctiveness of each individual, and where the gyrations of entwined limbs and the undulations of swaying torsos make the pile on the mattress appear as if it were a single gigantic organism that unifies the collective in its rapturous eroticism.

At their best, the exuberance of such occasions highlights several features of the energies of our erotic repertoire. Orgies comprise a breaking of taboos. They break the propriety of social conventions and cultural mores that, under "normal circumstances," bind the community by constraining the possibilities for erotic expression. Orgies are also transgressive in another sense that is sacred. They offer each participant the opportunity for an erotic experience that dramatically deconstructs the enclosure of individual identity—although, again, it must be emphasized that the realization of this potential depends very much on the emotional preparation and readiness of each particular individual.

The communal sharing of carnal desires invites the experience of "ecstatic loss." Erotic excess facilitates a process in which egotism dissolves into delirious bliss as each celebrant is swept into the flow of energies that are—as we will discuss further in the final section of this book—far greater than the bounded construction of the individual bodymind, and indeed far greater than life itself.

Here we glimpse yet again the emotionally passionate and spiritual abundance of sensual energies, how sexuality is always surfeit, overflowing and overwhelming our egotism. We glimpse that it is an energy flowing within, through, and beyond our individual bodymind. This sexual-spirituality of our erotic potential is thus always an abundant and transpersonal momentum.

> *Tantric Partnering:*

The four styles of sexual partnering that we have described above—partnering with oneself, the casual or transient liaisons involved in cruising, partnering in the context of an intensive or committed relationship, and multiple-partnering—are not exclusive of each other. For example, solo sexuality occurs throughout our lives, regardless whether we are partnered with another person or not; cruising often occurs alongside other sorts of sexual arrangement; and, as will be mentioned in Chapter Sixteen, committed relationships are actually never sexually exclusive.

However, each of these four styles holds something in common—namely that the sensual and sexual activity is understood to be personal or interpersonal. That is, in each of these styles of erotic partnering, the experience is framed as interactive or transactional. However, as indicated in my descriptions, each of these styles is not only an expression of our erotic potential, it also manifests a spiritual momentum. This suggests the following conclusion.

Erotic partnering of every lifestyle, orientation and preference, whether alone, in a twosome, in a threesome or more, always has the power to be an expression of our spiritual potential. When our bodymind's energies are not recruited by our egotism such that "sexual" activity is aggressivized and rendered non-sexual, the expression of our erotic potential is always a spiritual momentum.

This is an important conclusion, to which we will devote the final section of this book. Here we will merely mention the fifth style of partnering in which sensual and sexual sharing is consciously engaged as a spiritual experience.

Although there is some risk of my being misunderstood—because the term "tantra" has become frequently misused, partly as it has been westernized—I call the fifth style of erotic sharing *"tantric partnering."* Whether practiced solo, with a single partner, or in groups, tantric partnering is distinctive in that it embraces the mobilization of our erotic energies consciously as a spiritual experience.

In tantric partnering, sensual and sexual sharing is performed with an awareness of its spiritual potential to release our being-in-the-world into joy, bliss and ecstasy. Sexuality is appreciated as a way of living in meditation, freeing ourselves from the imprisonment of our egotism and mobilizing us in the naturalness of an ethical existence. Tantric partnering begins with the awareness that the energies of our erotic freeing provide the momentum of our spiritual enlightening.

With tantric practice, erotic activity is engaged not so much as a personal or interpersonal experience, but almost as if an "impersonal" one. That is, it is embraced as an experience that can free us from our egotistic attachment to our personhood, our equation of our self with all the identities, positions, and stories established by our judgmental or chattering mind.

More precisely, in this awareness, generated by tantric sensuality and sexuality, is an appreciation of erotic activity as a transpersonal experience. Erotic activity may be cultivated precisely as a freeing, accessing and cultivating, of the subtle energies that flow within, through and around our bodymind. And our awareness of this flowing dissolves not only our egotism but also the boundaries between us.

*Tantric practice involves the conscious discovery,
cultivated experiencing,
and spiritual awareness,
that the human bodymind's subtle erotic energy is Holy Spirit.*

Tantric partnering must be discussed as distinctive from other styles of partnering because, unlike mundane erotic activity, it intentionally and consciously focuses on the fact that sexual and spiritual energy are one-and-the-same. We will postpone further discussion of this until the final section of this book—because, at this juncture, more needs to be said about the parameters of the mundane.

16

The Ten Keys to Successful Sexual Partnering

Sexual partnering—whether with oneself, in the casual or transient liaisons that are found by cruising, in the context of an intensive relationship, or in the context of multiple relationships—is inherently healthy, even though any of these arrangements can, of course, be conducted in an unhealthy manner.

For example, risk-reductive practices may be abandoned, physical and emotional interaction may become nonconsensual, sensual and sexual activity may become compulsive, and "sex" may be aggressivized and recruited by our egotism to non-sexual ends. By these means, the emotional, existential and spiritual momentum of our erotic potential may not be honored.

Our socialization and acculturation does not support our learning to engage in sexual partnerships in ways that ensure their health—in ways that ensure that they are healing experiences, promoting our happiness. On the contrary, we are raised fearful and anxious, wracked with shame and guilt about our erotic desires, and we are not helped to learn how to make our sexual partnering healthy.

So in this chapter, I offer, for your consideration, ten "keys" to successful—that is, healthy, healing, and happy—sexual partnering. These are actually very simple suggestions, but for most of us, our upbringing makes them quite challenging to implement. Although some of these ten keys address certain styles of partnering more than others, most of them apply in some way to all situations, and all of them apply to all manner of sexual activities—to all lifestyles, orientations, and preferences.

Key #1: We commit to explicit verbal communication. One aspect of the "sexification" of our culture is that we are encouraged to snicker about sex, to giggle about sex, to laugh about sex, to be silent and secretive about sex, or to be outraged and indignant about sex. But we are not encouraged to talk freely, clearly and in explicit detail, about sex, and we do not often do so—even with those who are our regular sexual partners. With our partners, we often proceed almost wordlessly.

As an illustration of this, I invite you to consider, for a moment, your first kiss. I will describe this scenario in a heterosexual context, although it applies similarly to most gay and lesbian encounters. If you remember the circumstances of your first kiss, it is more than likely that the event went something like this.

> He (or whoever is the initiator—it is traditionally incumbent on the man to take active responsibility for initiating the event, and it is often the case that women hide their desires behind their "passive" role) is thinking something like: *"I want to kiss her, but how will she respond, should I go for it or should I wait, what if she doesn't want me that way?"*
>
> She is thinking either something like: *"What is with this guy? Why doesn't he get on and kiss me*

already? Perhaps he doesn't like me that way?" Or something like: *"I hope he doesn't try to kiss me! I just don't want that with him. How will I deal with it if he does?"*

A kiss is now completed, perhaps with mutual satisfaction, and the silent interaction continues.

He is thinking either something like: *"I wonder if she'd go for some tongue play. Should I try it, or should I leave it at this for now? What if this is enough for her and she's turned off by my tongue?"* Or something like: *"This is fine by me, but if I stop here, will she think I'm less of a man, or will she think I don't want her?"*

She is thinking either something like: *"This is such a chaste kiss! I wish he'd make it more exciting already."* Or something like: *"This is sort of okay, but I hope he doesn't try anything with his tongue. I don't want that!"*

Tongue play is now undertaken, perhaps with mutual satisfaction, and the silent interaction continues.

He is thinking either something like: *"I wonder how she'd go for it if I tried to touch her breasts outside her clothing?"* Or something like: *"This is fine by me, but if I stop here, will she think I'm less of a man, or will she think I don't want her?"*

She is thinking either something like: *"Oh God, this is good! I wish he'd fondle my breasts already!"* Or something like: *"Oh God, I hope he doesn't go for my breasts next!"*

Breast caressing outside of clothing is now undertaken, perhaps with mutual satisfaction, and the silent interaction continues.

He is thinking either something like: *"I'd really like to feel her breasts under her clothing, would that be going too far for her? Perhaps this would be the point at which she rejects me."* Or something like: *"This is good but I'm so nervous! I really don't want to go further than this, at least for now. But if I stop here, will she think I'm some sort of 'dweeb' or that I don't know what I'm doing?"*

She is thinking either something like: *"Why doesn't he undress me already!"* Or something like: *"That's far enough already! I really hope he doesn't want to go under my clothing next. How am I going to put a stop to this?"*

So perhaps the interaction then proceeds, from breast caressing to the question of genital caressing, and so on and so forth.

Obviously, there are many variations and permutations to this scenario, but its general characteristics have remarkable veracity. One might think from this scenario that human linguistic skills were insufficient for the construction of simple sentences, such as

— "Would you like to kiss?"
— "Can we play with our tongues?"
— "I would like to touch your breasts, would you like that?"
— "Can I caress you under your clothing?"
— "I would really like to be naked with you, how do you feel?"

In the course of my schedule of lectures and workshops, I estimate that I have presented this vignette to over two thousand people. Almost everyone nods and laughs knowingly. One way or another, it resonates with their recollections of their earliest sexual encounters. That is, fraught with anxiety, and conducted with minimal, if any, explicit verbal communication.

I usually perform the vignette somewhat dramatically, and then ask my audience how well this corresponds to their own experiences. Invariably, there is more laughter, even applause. Sometimes I specifically inquire whether *anyone* in the audience had a first experience that diverged significantly from this scenario. In all the years in which I have used this vignette as an illustration, only three individuals have ever come up to me later, and told me that their early experiences were unlike this scenario, that they and their partners did at least talk about what they wanted with each other, before they proceeded to action.

In any context, sexual or otherwise, communication has three ingredients:

➢ *Listening Respectfully.* In general, this is perhaps the most challenging aspect, especially when our emotions and our sexual heat are aroused.
➢ *Expressing Truthfully.* In sexual matters, this is often extremely challenging, since it requires us to overcome our inhibitions about our erotic desires.
➢ *A Dynamic and Evolving Balance between Listening and Expressing.* Specifically in sexual partnering, this is essential for the preservation of full consensuality.

In our society, despite the culture of sexification, people are very inhibited about talking about sex—at least in so far as "talk" involves the explicit verbal communication of their specific desires. Indeed, people mightily resist the fact that

Explicit verbal communication enhances sexual partnering, especially when it is done as frequently and in as much detail as possible. Indeed, explicit verbal communication is essential for sexually healthy interaction.

Few people find it easy to embrace this key to successful sexual partnering. Rather, many people make a mystique out of the—usually entirely mistaken—notion that partners who are really "in sync" can, and should, communicate without words. They often claim that the verbalization of erotic wishes makes an encounter "unromantic."

This is an utterly bogus rationalization for a major piece of resistance. These same people do not claim it is unromantic if someone says to a partner:

— "You are so adorable, I love you!"

So why is it somehow "unromantic" if someone says

— "Would you like me to take your clothes off?"
— "Your vulva is exquisite, can I kiss it?"
— "I like the way your cock quivers, can I take it into my mouth?"

Refusing to commit ourselves to explicit verbal communication with our sexual partners almost always has three anti-sexual consequences.

First, not only is it motivated by our shame and guilt about our erotic desires, but it endorses and reinforces these anti-sexual forces within us.

Second, it ensures that sexual encounters will be anxiety-ridden, particularly in the early experimental phase of a partnership, and it also makes it very likely that interaction will not proceed mutually and fully consensually.

For example, it compels the beginning phase of a relationship to proceed on what I call a "trial-and-error" basis—meaning "you try it until you make an error, then you are told about it, and your feelings get hurt!" More exactly, the active or "agential" partner tries something, and the other partner silently acquiesces, which permits the first partner to continue or to try something else, but sooner or later the receiving or "target" partner dislikes what is happening and criticizes or rejects the move made by the initiating partner.

For agential partners, trial-and-error is a nerve-wracking way to pursue sexual pleasures, because, sooner or later, rejection and criticism of their desires is almost guaranteed—since they never have the opportunity to listen and respond to their partners' desires.

For target partners in such scenarios, trial-and-error indeed relieves them of whatever shame and guilt they would experience if they had taken responsibility for their own desires, but their pleasures are limited to receiving whatever their partners happen to offer, because their opportunity to express their own desires is annulled.

Men in traditional heterosexual relationships, especially if they are sensitive to the feelings of their partner, often feel victimized by this silent trial-and-error protocol. When the man is supposed to be the agential initiator and the woman the target or recipient of the moves he initiates, this amounts to putting the man in a difficult situation. He tries something and, if "successful," he is met with no opposition, so he then tries his next move. In short, he keeps trying until he makes an error, at which point his partner becomes active in criticizing or rejecting him.

For the woman in the passive role, such trial-and-error has, as I stated, the dubious advantage of allowing her not to need the courage to overcome her shame and guilt by expressing her own desires. But this is obviously also profoundly disadvantageous because, if she does actively express her own erotic wishes, she will very likely disrupt the man's routine, and expose herself to the possibility of his criticism or rejection.

Let us note here how *the "trial-and-error" procedure for initiating sexual activity often accounts for the way in which this activity becomes aggressive.* From the standpoint of our egotism, it can appear to the man that his anxieties about rejection in response to his having to be the one to "make the moves" can be alleviated if he adopts a pushy or aggressivized—"Let's just fuck the bitch"—attitude toward the encounter. And from the standpoint of the recipient's egotism, it can appear to the woman that her anxieties either about having her sexual desires made evident, or about having to be the one to reject her partner's advances, can be alleviated if she adopts an acquiescent—"I have no choice"—attitude toward the encounter.

In these interpersonal liaisons, we see how readily our erotic inclinations are turned into something anti-sexual. Additionally, as is well known, many women then like to take revenge for their apparent disempowerment by becoming the seductress who incites men's wishes in order to frustrate them. These interpersonal dynamics illustrate well—in my opinion—the sad consequences of our failure to be open and free with our sexual desires. That is, our failure to be verbally explicit in our communication of these desires.

Third, the avoidance of explicit verbal communication about sexual interaction almost always means that partnerships, if they get beyond the initial anxiety-ridden trial-and-error phase, become routinized. Routinization is—by definition—never spontaneous, open, adventurous or free-flowing. It turns "sex" into something inherently non-sexual. So it invariably makes a sexual relationship spiral downwards. Couples fall into a set pattern of erotic interaction that appears not to be overly riddled with shame and guilt for either of them, but is actually structured by their largely unconscious sense of shame and guilt.

Consequently, the sexual dimension of the relationship descends to what is, in effect, their "lowest common factor," rather than the "highest." By this, I mean that, by arriving at this unconsciously negotiated and routinized pattern of sexual interaction, the couple has certainly not supported each other in realizing their erotic potential. On the contrary, they have effectively reinforced each other's propensity for shame and guilt.

In sex therapy, I have regularly found that couples fall into routine patterns of interaction for entirely anti-sexual reasons. Usually these patterns are sustained by a variety of rationalizations, such as that: these same activities once did bring pleasure into the relationship; they are necessary because daily life is so overcrowded with other matters; they are each sure that this is what the other partner wants, and that he or she would not tolerate anything more intensely erotic.

To give a more specific example, a couple might act as if their particular routinized pattern "simply is the case"—and the pattern that has evolved has never been discussed. For instance, they usually hold hands when on a Sunday afternoon walk. They kiss each other when they leave for work and when they return. They have genital intercourse on Saturday nights. And they hug each other intermittently while cooking or doing the dishes together.

They resist the idea that it would be helpful if they communicated with explicit verbalizations about what they liked and did not like together. Sometimes, even though neither partner is happy, each member of the couple still claims to be sure they know what their contribution to the relationship's unhappiness is or is not, and still claims they are certain they know their partner so well that they are well aware what he or she likes or dislikes, would or would not accept, and so forth.

However, almost invariably with such a couple, if they agree to my proposal that, for a three day experiment, they will have no physical contact unless it is explicitly verbalized, the resultant shift is astounding. Suddenly they find that one of them does not particularly enjoy the hand-holding while walking in the park; that both of them wish the perfunctory kiss "hello" and "goodbye" would either become more meaningfully passionate or be given up altogether; that one of them finds Saturday night intercourse a bore or a chore, and wishes that it could be wilder and more spontaneous, perhaps even being accomplished on the kitchen table or under the moonlight in the backyard; and both of them agree that they treasure the fact that they feel like hugging when doing kitchen tasks together.

With longstanding partnerships, committing ourselves to explicit verbal communication regenerates genuine intimacy and erotic energy. It safeguards the full consensuality, of the shared sexual activity. Perhaps this seems like a paradox, but it also ensures the spontaneity of the experience, because it protects partners from falling into a pattern of routine acquiescence with activities that, in the particular present moment, are not enjoyed.

With new partnerships, committing ourselves to explicit verbal communication advances intimacy and erotic gratification. For example, safety and intimacy are promoted if a person asks his or her partner, as if for the first time, "Can I rub your back?" and waits for explicit permission, rather than merely hoping and groping. Perhaps this also seems paradoxical to some, but explicit verbal communication can be accomplished in such a way that it heats up the sexual encounter, rather than cooling it down.

Because most of us have such resistances to committing ourselves to explicit verbal communication in our sexual interaction, I must be careful not to overstate my case. Obviously, with some partnerships, communication does not always have to be explicit or verbal. Partners who know each other well can use explicit nonverbal cues—a nod, a gesture with one's hands, a squeal of delight, a murmur or satisfied sigh, and so forth—in ways that are adequately communicative. Partners who know each other well can also use inexplicit verbal cues—such as privately shared allusions or codes—in ways that adequately safeguard the health of the encounter.

Moreover, if surprise is an important element in an erotic encounter, it is sometimes possible to undertake explicit verbal communication in advance; for example, "anytime you want to kiss my genitals while I'm asleep, please go ahead, I would love to be roused that way."

However, these practices are very risky for partners who do not know each other well, and even with partners who are very familiar with each other, ongoing communication is always necessary as a sexual encounter proceeds, since one or other partner's desires may always shift in the moment.

In general, committing ourselves to explicit verbal communication always empowers sexual partnering in three very important ways.

First,

> *Talking freely with our partners,*
> *with our friends,*
> *and with complete strangers,*
> *about our sexual life*
> *is a miraculous antidote to the shame and guilt*
> *that encumber our erotic pleasures*

Shame and guilt fester in the secretiveness with which we shroud our sexual lives, as well as with the culture of sexification that permits salacious talk about banal sexual matters (but censors our interest in really sharing what turns us on, and in sharing with each other our plans to overcome our inhibitions about seeking the fulfillment of our erotic desires). In short, enlightened communication dissolves the anxieties about our sensual and sexual nature. In this sense, sexual communication is hot!

Second,

Explicit verbal communication impels us to take responsibility for the fulfillment of our erotic potential. Talking about our sexuality in "I" statements that are explicit and detailed, liberates us from shame about guilt about being ourselves.

Talking about our sexuality also ensures that we can no longer hide behind routines, perhaps blaming our partner for our frustrations and our conflicts. Rather, committing to the verbalization of our feelings honors our erotic potential by having us claim it for ourselves and bear witness that it belongs to us.

Third,

Explicit verbal communication increases the likelihood that an erotic encounter will be spontaneous and more gratifying, individually and mutually.

As an example, consider straightforward, but specific and detailed, sentences like

— "Your kisses on my vulva feel wonderful. Would you please try licking up and down my labia?"
— "My penis feels so good in your mouth. Would you please try swirling your tongue around its head for a while?"

If you can become articulate in this way, you are far more likely to receive the sort of physical sensations that you most desire. And your partner—if he or she really wants to please and pleasure you—will be delighted to receive the directions.

Finally, it must be added emphatically that there is one special circumstance in which, I believe, explicit verbal communication is not only a key to successful partnering, but is absolutely necessary for any successful partnering. Namely,

> *No one should ever enter another person's body*
> *—vaginally, anally, or orally—*
> *without clearly hearing that person's specific and*
> *freely-given invitation.*

To give a paramount heterosexual example, it is utterly unacceptable for a penis to enter a vagina without *both* the man asking something like "Can I enter inside you?" *and* the woman giving her clear consent.

Our body boundaries are a very sacred and precious feature of our most fundamental sense of our self, and the security of our being-in-the-world. It is never acceptable—indeed it is not healthy—not to recognize and honor this foundational feature of our humanity. When one person's body enters another, a sacred act is being committed, and the importance of the act being safe, sane, and consensual cannot be overestimated.

Key #2: We commit to asking for 100% of what we want with our partners. In most instances, the remaining keys to successful sexual partnering are specific principles that follow the general injunction to commit ourselves to explicit verbal communication.

For most of us, this second key is very challenging. Given our inner shame and guilt over acknowledging that our erotic desires fully belong to us, it often requires courage to commit ourselves to asking truthfully, 100% of the time, for 100% of what we desire, and especially to do so in the moment that we desire it. Yet, endeavoring to do this diligently is one of the surest ways to improve and enhance sexual partnering.

> *Successful partnering requires that we be true to our selves,*
> *and that we take responsibility for our sensual and sexual desires,*
> *by asking our partners for what we want.*

For many of us, who are struggling to overcome inhibitions and conflicts, it is helpful to rehearse. I often recommend that individuals, who find it particularly difficult to ask for what they want, try practicing various lines that they might want to use at a later time. Rehearsing alone, and then perhaps with a friend acting as a "stand-in" partner, it is helpful to practice saying various lines aloud, taking care to remain in integrity so that the lines can be genuinely expressed, from the heart, at the suitable moment.

Perhaps one of the most important criteria for this key to sexual partnering is that we should speak in "I" sentences, so that we fully own our desire, even while we invite and listen for our partners response. For example,

— "I would like to play sexually, would you like to join me?"
— "I would like to lovemake with you, would you like that too?"
— "I want to give you a hug, would you like that?"
— "I want to stroke your hair, would that be okay with you?"
— "I am so hot for you, I want to kiss you passionately, how about it?"
— "Your breasts are so beautiful, may I caress them?"
— "You have a great cock, can I play with it?"
— "I love your vulva, can I touch it?"
— "I need for us both to be safe as well as pleasured, so let's find a condom?"
— "Can I come inside you, I want you so much?"

When I suggest to people that these are the sort of sentences that they might usefully practice saying, they often respond that such utterances feel "artificial." Yet we usually have no difficulty saying things like

— "This is a little bland, please pass the salt."
— "I want to drive to the beach, can I borrow your car?"

So the strangeness of making sexual requests is almost entirely a matter of our inner shame and guilt about owning our sensual and sexual desires.

Once these sorts of sentiment can be expressed without undue anxiety, the next challenge is to use them. Some individuals find themselves unsure what they want, in which case a playful and experimental attitude towards the erotic encounter is especially advantageous. The key here is actually to ask for 100% of what we want from our partners in the present moment, and to witness compassionately our reactions when our partners say "Yes" or "No." This latter aspect, the practice of taking note of our reactions to our partners' responses, facilitates the healing of shame and guilt, as well as enabling us to become more courageous in taking responsibility for our erotic desires.

Key #3: We commit to honoring our partner's "No." It is obvious, from all our discussions thus far, that honoring our partner's "No" is one of the most basic acts of sexual health, in that it preserves safety and ensures that sexual interaction is fully consensual. Simply stated, it safeguards against abuse and rape. However, there are some more profound aspects of this key to sexual partnering.

For example, *honoring* a "No" means much more than merely observing it or complying with it. To honor a partner's "No" implies our commitment to try to empathize with this rejection and yet, so to speak, not internalize it or "take it personally." That is, to try not to hold it against our partner— or against our selves—as the relationship proceeds into the future.

Successful partnering requires that we be true to our partners
by honoring their "no" appreciatively.
Otherwise, all erotic connection is lost,
and an aggressivized relationship is constructed.

Empathizing with a "No"—and trying not to allow rejection to sour our feelings for the partner—does not imply that we have to like it! Of course, if we ask for something and are rejected, we are unlikely to feel positive about the experience. But there is a dual aspect to the honoring process.

On the one side, honoring the receipt of a "No" means that we do not allow the "No" to increase our sense of shame and guilt about our selves. For example, if we ask our partner for anal sex, and are told "No," it does *not* mean that we were wrong for asking or that we "should feel bad" about having this desire. In short, we do not have to take rejections personally! There may be one-hundred-and-one reasons our partners decline our requests or invitations, it is advisable to try to understand that his or her rejection is about him or her, and not about us.

On the other side, honoring the receipt of a "No" means that we do not allow the "No" to affect our ongoing feelings toward our partner. Of course, there are limits within which this is, and is not, possible. For example, if we ask our partner for oral sex, and are told "No," it does *not* mean—unless, of course, he or she specifically tells us that this is what it means—that he or she will never agree to oral intercourse with us. It merely means that our partner is declining our request or invitation in the specific moment that we ask for it.

If we do not "take the rejection to heart" and allow it to make us feel that we should not have asked, then we are surely free to issue this request or invitation again at some later time. If rejections are repeated, then a different mode of communication is required. This might be something along the lines of the following.

> "There is something I would like to discuss with you, are you ready to hear it? [And if he or she indicates willingness to listen, we proceed to say . . .] I've noticed that the last several times I've asked you if we might have oral sex,

you have said "No," which is fine. But I wonder whether you are hoping I will stop asking, whether you anticipate that oral pleasures are never going to be something we can share, and whether there are feelings about this that we could usefully share together."

As in all the examples I have given so far, such wording may seem initially strange. And, of course, everyone needs to find their own wording—a style of discussion that feels genuine and specific. However, in general, explicit verbal communication along these lines is a wonderful gift, and it prevents the accumulation of hurt feelings that can so easily occur in any ongoing sexual relationship.

Key #4: We commit to meaning "Yes" when we say "Yes." Sexual communication—and the possibility that sharing can be genuinely sane and consensual—falls apart if there is any kind of hypocrisy or deceit. It is no service to our partners if we consent to a sexual activity, when we really do not desire it. However, when it comes to sensual and sexual interaction, many people are so anxious and conflicted that they violate their own integrity. This occurs most frequently when genuinely consensual partnering is lacking. It occurs especially with a non-dominant partner who fears failing to please the other.

Successful partnering requires that we be true to our selves and our partners by never saying "Yes" when we mean "No."
Otherwise, all erotic connection is lost,
and an aggressivized relationship is constructed.

It might appear—and in fact this is a common delusion—that giving a partner what they want, when it is "at our own expense," is an act of service. Some would even characterize it as an "act of love." However, quite the reverse is true. If we give our partner a "Yes" to something that is invited or requested of us, when we feel "No," we are actually violating our partner's integrity as well as our own.

On the one side, by saying "Yes" when we mean "No"—by acquiescing in some sensual or sexual activity that our partner desires but we do not—we effectively assume a dominant role in the partnership, even if we appear to be the frightened and non-dominant partner. We passively control the nature of the interaction, and we unilaterally decide that the partnering will be intrinsically unhealthy and non-sexual.

The deceit we perform ensures that what transpires will not be truly erotic, because it will not be genuinely mutual and consensual. Nor will it really be sane, because hypocrisy and deceit are always viciously damaging to our foundational sense of who we are and how we belong in the world. This is true, even when we are dramatically effective at acting the role required by our lack of integrity. Sham participation in "sex" is never authentically sexual.

On the other side, if we desire some act of sexual sharing and our partner says "Yes" when he or she means "No," we are not only the victims of a deceit, we are being coerced into an activity that is actually unhealthy. Although a partner who acquiesces to our requests or invitations in this manner does subordinate himself or herself to our physical urges, they do not do us any service by doing so. Their acquiescence is certainly no gift. For if we are committed to healthy sexuality—to erotic sharing that is always sane and mutual or consensual—then we have been tricked out of our commitment. Whatever physical sensations we receive from the subsequent interaction, we will have been duped into believing that this is genuinely erotic sharing, and that it is authentically sensual and sexual, when it is not.

If we really wish that our partners would abnegate their own integrity and violate ours for the sake of our physical sensationalism, then we are really not committed to healthy sexuality at all. Rather, we have been carried away by our egotism's interest in compulsive sexification, and our "sexual" impulses have actually become entirely aggressivized. Indeed, we are manifesting the mentality of an abuser, who pursues an act of rape and foregoes genuine erotic enjoyment.

Finally, however, the commitment to mean "Yes" when we say "Yes" is not just a commitment never to say "Yes" when we mean "No." It is a commitment to an affirmative and positive attitude toward sexual sharing. To achieve healthier and happier sexual partnering, to enjoy a better sex life, we need to commit our selves to being more sexual—to saying "Yes" to our sexuality and sensuality, saying "Yes" to all the joys that life has to offer.

Key #5: We commit to offering our "No" in a sex-positive manner. Given our responsibility to say "No" whenever we feel "No," successful partnering depends on our offering our "No" in a way that honors our selves and our partners, and that also enhances our sexual connection. There are important ways of declining our partner's requests or invitations, without risking the deleterious effects of rejection to the ongoing relationship. There are three important points about learning how to do this.

First, even when we speak our "No" clearly and strongly, we can also express appreciation for our partner's request. Our partners have, after all, honored us by directing their erotic energies toward us. Additionally, the act of asking may have required their courage because, in order to issue their invitation, they may have had to overcome shame and guilt, as well as whatever inhibitions and prohibitions they customarily experience. So we can express appreciation to our partners for having asked us for some sort of sensual and sexual sharing, even if we are quite adamant that we do not want to participate at this time, or maybe anticipate that we never would.

Second, we can not only speak our "No" even while expressing appreciation for having been issued an invitation, we can also speak our "No" without gratuitous judgmentalism. This is so important that it is amplified as "Key #6" to successful sexual partnering.

For now, it can simply be noted that it is sufficient to tell our partner that we do not wish to share this or that activity with him or her, and it is quite unnecessary to add whatever opinions we may have about that activity.

For example, even if we are conflicted and inhibited about anal sex, we do not have to inform our partner that the idea "disgusts us." Even if we are conflicted and inhibited about oral sex, we do not have to tell our partner that we consider it licentious, immoral and "against God's wishes." And even if we are conflicted and inhibited about penile-vaginal sex, we can refrain from adding that we actually find our partner's genitals "funny looking" or ill proportioned.

Third, we say "No" to one activity and, at the same time, *redirect* our partner, requesting or inviting him or her to perform some other activity that we would enjoy.

The principle of redirection is vitally important to the health of any sexual liaison.

This principle is not only essential for any ongoing partnership, it is important for any sexual liaison that lasts more than a couple of minutes! The obvious examples of this can easily be imagined. For instance,

— If we say to our partner "It's sweet of you to ask, but actually I don't feel up to lovemaking tonight," then we can always add "So tomorrow can we set some special time aside just for each other?"
— If we say to our partner "You know I usually adore having long, languorous lovemaking sessions with you, but I have

to get that report written before I go into the office tomorrow," then we can always add "But I do feel like a quick fuck would be fun, how would that be for you?"
— Or if we say to our partner, "I appreciate how much you want me to do this with you, but I am still feeling too nervous to try going to the swingers' club," then we can always add "Although it might be really fabulous for us to have another threesome with Robin, would you like that too?"

However, aside from these rather obvious examples, there are some far more subtle and vitally important aspects to this principle of redirection. For a moment, let us consider the nature of physical sensations. I believe we can note three rather fascinating features.

➢ A sensation that may start out deliciously pleasurable will sooner or later become uncomfortable, or even painful, if it is continued too repetitively. For example, consider someone gently stroking your lower arm. It might begin feeling calming, exciting, or simply pleasant. But if it continues for too long, it will surely become aggravating, dulling, or even unpleasant.

➢ A sensation that may start out slightly painful can sometimes become pleasurable when it is continued, and as our level of arousal increases. For example, consider someone pinching your nipple. It might be that, as it begins, you can scarcely tolerate even a moderately intense stimulation. But if your arousal increases, and the pinching continues, you will crave the pleasure of stronger and stronger pinches.

➢ As the thresholds between pleasure and "unpleasure" shift with varying levels of physiological arousal and emotional intensity, we also notice how whenever one bodily zone receives pleasure, another zone seems to call out to us for sensual attention. In short,

> *Our erotic body is a holistic system*
> *and the erotic attention we receive*
> *eventually ripples throughout our being-the-world.*
> *The sensual and sexual pleasuring of our being*
> *eventually cannot be localized,*
> *just as Love is a vibration that cannot be sequestered*
> *but that eventually must pervade the entire universe of beings.*

Given these three aspects of sensation, the importance of the principle of redirection becomes even more salient.

Consider it like this: if our partner is stroking our thigh with his or her hand in a way that feels delightful, and the delight gradually fades, or another part of our body calls out to be stroked, how are we going to tell him or her "No"? Words have to be found for this, because if we simply take our partner's hand and remove it from our thigh, he or she will almost certainly feel rejected. Even if, for example, we remove the hand from our thigh and place it on our genitals, this wordless mode of redirection will still almost certainly make him or her wonder whether the thigh stroking was not pleasurable, whether he or she should have proceeded to the genital caress earlier, and so on. So,

> *Given the shifting nature of our sensory thresholds*
> *and our emotional enjoyment,*
> *the principle of redirection —*
> *that is, of saying "No" with both appreciation*
> *and with the offer of alternative modes of pleasuring —*
> *is vitally important for successful partnering,*
> *if feelings of rejection, and sensual or emotional disconnection,*
> *are to be avoided.*

Each of us has to find our own words for this, but the principle of explicit verbal redirection must include both appreciation for what we have received and clear redirection as to what we would next like to happen. For example,

— "Your hand on my thigh has been feeling wonderful, but would you please stroke a little lighter now [a little heavier now, with a more scratchy touch now, and so forth] . . . ?"
— "Your hand on my thigh is making me feel all tingly, I would love it if you would take that wonderful stroking motion up to my genitals now . . ."
— "Your stroking is so lovely, can I give you the same pleasure now . . . ?"

The principle of redirection needs to be followed mindfully, for it maintains the sexual and sensual momentum of an encounter, even when a particular aspect turns out to be not entirely to the liking of one or the other partner.

Key #6: We commit to refraining from judging our partner's desires. The judgmentalism of our egotistic mind is the ultimate foe of our sexual and spiritual nature. To express this at a mundane level, criticism and judgment are an erotic "turn-off."

If our intention is enhanced sensual and sexual partnering, the more we are able to quiet our chattering mind, the greater will be our pleasuring! Our sensual and sexual nature is ultimately a matter of our spirituality—and this will be discussed in the final section of this book.

However, this key to successful partnering touches on a core issue, namely that releasing our erotic potential is essentially a meditative act. Our erotic nature is blocked by our judgmental mind that keeps us "in our heads"—that is, keeps us repetitively and compulsively imprisoned in all our identities, positions and stories—and freeing our erotic potential implies that we release our selves from the judgmentalism of our chattering mind.

If we allow our selves to become alienated from the pleasures of our erotic embodiment, we find that criticisms clog our consciousness and readily trip off our tongues. We criticize others, and ourselves, in almost exact proportion to the amount of criticism we feel we have received in the course of our lives (especially in childhood), or in exact proportion to our fear of our own erotic nature. Criticism is basically our egotism's defective method of adaptation—the goal of criticism is to bolster our egotism's sense not only that it really exists, but also that it can be secure in its sense that it is itself "Right, Proper, True and Effective."

> *Successful partnering is always sabotaged,*
> *if we engage in judging and criticizing*
> *our partner's sensual and sexual desires.*

Our critical and judgmental faculty never enhances our own erotic pleasures, and never contributes to the erotic pleasures of our partners.

This "Key #6" does not imply that we refrain from saying "No" to our partners whenever we feel "No," but it does imply that whenever our partners ask for, or do, something that is not to our liking, we will redirect them without judging or criticizing them for their desires. This is vitally important because—simply stated—judgmentalism suffocates sensual and sexual intimacy, and criticism is the prototypical and paradigmatic anti-aphrodisiac!

Refraining from criticizing our own desires is an important step if freeing our selves from the crippling shame and guilt that most of us feel unconsciously about our erotic potential. Refraining from criticizing the desires of our partners is an essential step toward cultivating a sex-positive partnership.

Key #7: We commit to expressing appreciation for our partners. Psychologists have done some remarkable studies in which they recorded all the verbal messages that young children typically receive in the course of their daily lives. The messages are then coded and sorted for their "positive," appreciative content or their "negative," critical, reprimanding, and punitive content. The latter include remarks that are not only prohibitive, but also shaming, humiliating, and degrading.

The results of this research demonstrate very conclusively that, on average, children typically have directed at them in the course of their day well over five times more "negative" than "positive" messages. Obviously, there may be exceptions to this finding—exceptional children, exceptional families, and exceptional subcultures. But the lesson of these studies is still crucially important. By and large, we all grow up in an environment of criticism, an environment that fosters our shame and guilt about being our selves.

As adults, we tend to transfer and replicate this environment in our relationships and, perhaps paradoxically, we do this especially in our closest relationships. We are prone to treat our partners in the following manner. If they do something "right" by us, we do not feel the need to say anything—"after all," we rationalize somewhere in our egotistic mind, "they are our partners, this is what they are supposed to do." However, when they fail to do the "right" thing, or when they do something that is evidently not to our liking, then we speak up, offering them our criticisms and complaints!

> *Our socialization trains us to express critical judgments far more frequently than we live in the spirit of appreciation. For successful partnering, and for the sake of the universe, it is essential that we break this pattern, and that we do so genuinely "from our hearts."*

In general, the critical and complaining mode of addressing our partners is disastrous for every aspect of the unfolding of any and all of our partnerships, but it is especially disastrous for our intimate and erotic connections. The more we can express genuine appreciation for our partners' sensual and sexual selves, the more powerfully erotic our connections will become. This is simply because appreciative messages, if they come "from our heart and our loins" rather than "from our head," are a powerful aphrodisiac—perhaps the most powerful of all!

> *Successful sexual partnering requires*
> *that we express our appreciation for our partners,*
> *in general and specifically sexually,*
> *and that we do so genuinely and fulsomely.*

When individuals and couples come to therapy, I often propose that, for at least a week, each individual make a private note of how often, in the course of a day, he or she expresses appreciation for something about their partner's body, their partner's erotic desires, or their partner's sensual and sexual sharing. I suggest that such "appreciations" must be genuine, and they must come "from the heart and or the genitals," rather than "from the head." But the "appreciations" do not have to be grand, such as "you are such a great lover." Indeed, they may well be less than grand, but they need to be meaningfully expressed from the heart. A "small" appreciation, such as "your smile seems so delightfully relaxed today," is often far more powerful than a grand proclamation. I also suggest that at least five appreciative expressions daily might be a helpful benchmark.

If the individual or couple agrees to this proposal, the results are usually astounding. Each individual typically arrives at a threefold realization.

— How little they typically notice whatever appreciation they may have of their partner, and how much they do or do not actually appreciate their partner.
— How little they express their appreciative feelings even when they are aware of them.
— How great the impact of doing so is on the erotic and intimate dynamic of the partnership.

Often individuals also report their surprise at how challenging they found the process of becoming aware of and expressing their appreciation—even when they generally feel that they are "in love" with their partner.

It is obvious from all our discussions throughout this book why the commitment to become aware in this manner and to express appreciation explicitly and genuinely is so challenging. Indeed, the more our appreciations are directly erotic in content, the more challenging it is likely to be. This is because shame and guilt—even while they are out of our consciousness—impact us by making us reserved and inhibited about taking the risk of expressing our appreciations. Yet, how difficult are sentences like the following?

— "I love the sensitivity of your nipples."
— "Your broad shoulders look great in that jacket, and even better out of it!"
— "I really like the taste of your juices."
— "It's so wonderful the way your cock fits so perfectly in my vagina."
— "Mm, feels so good."
— "Wow, what you're doing now feels just exquisite."
— "Thank you—that was such a delicious hug."
— "Those earrings are the perfect color to go with your gorgeous hair."
— "I love the way you respond when I massage your feet."
— "I really like the way you run your hands over my stomach."

Many of us feel such sentiments; we just "forget" to say them, because basically we are afraid of the vulnerability of our feelings. Yet, such sentiments, when given voice, juice our sexual connections in ways that may be both surprising and delightful.

Key #8: We commit to addressing the issues of differential desire. There is a prevalent myth in our culture. One major version of it is the story of the Prince and the Princess. After the Prince has fought off all sorts of monstrous obstacles such as dragons, and has awakened his partner with a kiss, or after the Princess has been going around desperately kissing frogs for a while, the couple is fortunately united and they proceed *to live happily ever after.* Although our fairytales are not usually explicit about the sexual messages they convey, this story offers us the following message: When you find your "perfect" partner, you will desire sex with him or her, at exactly the same time and in exactly the same way, "forevermore." In actuality, this never happens.

*All partnerships face the challenge of differential desire,
and successful partnering entails an effort
to confront this challenge communicatively,
anticipatorily and pro-actively.*

The myth of the Prince and the Princess does great damage to sexual partnering, because it implies that, if the partnership were "perfect," erotic desires would always be "in sync." Again, this never happens. Indeed, the myth itself usually trips up the real relationship. If a couple ever has the experience of wanting sensual and sexual sharing in exactly the same way and at exactly the same time, it will be a blessing that is short-lived. And, to the extent that it may set them up for expectations that this synchronicity is going to continue "forevermore," or even into the next erotic encounter, the synchronous event may not be a blessing at all.

Successful sexual partnering depends on explicit verbal communication around the challenge of differential desire, because the couple will not want exactly the same type of sharing at exactly the same time.

In many years of offering sex therapy, I have rarely—if ever—found a couple that addressed this issue in an anticipatory and proactive manner. Instead, couples act as if, because the relationship is a "good" one, the sensual and sexual dimension of it should simply run under its own steam.

This never happens because our erotic patterning as humans is so multidimensional and varied that no two patterns can ever be fully congruent at any one time. And even if an approximation of congruence occurs to the immense satisfaction of both partners, the fundamental fact is that erotic desire shifts and evolves in the course of a lifetime, and indeed in the course of a single day. So a great match at one time will not necessarily be so great the next time, or vice versa.

Almost all partnerships experience this as a major challenge. How to make exciting relationships enduring, and enduring relationships exciting? When divergences in erotic desire arise in a partnership—as they surely will—there is a substantial risk that the resultant pattern of relationship will have been tacitly negotiated on an anti-sexual basis. Hurt feelings, as well as shame and guilt for sensual and sexual wishes, readily accumulate, and so—as was mentioned earlier—erotic partnerships often spiral downwards into sensual and sexual frustration, conflict and deprivation.

The challenge of differential desire is best addressed anticipatorily. Although any amount of anticipatory discussion will not entirely avert the necessity of further discussion during and after episodes in which erotic impulses diverge, such discussions are an important preparation for handling the feelings that arise when divergences inevitably occur. In therapy with couples I always recommend having "what if" discussions. This means that the couple will discuss freely and frankly how they want to address the issue when differential desire arises. Such discussions will have to be undertaken throughout the relationship, and they need to be as explicit, detailed, and loving—by which I mean open and nonjudgmental—as possible.

If such discussions are not undertaken, it is almost certain that one or other partner—or both partners—will simply censor some aspects of their erotic repertoire, at least within the context of the partnership. Shame and guilt will accumulate, or the particular aspect of the erotic repertoire will disrupt and break the partnership. This is an anti-sexual outcome. "What if" discussions maximize the possibility of a sex-positive outcome that will keep erotic desire active within the partnership.

As examples of what I mean, imagine discussions beginning from the following types of questions.

- "What if you were to want intercourse and I just wasn't feeling up to it, how would you like us to handle it? Would you like me to pleasure you with my hands, or to hold you in my arms while you pleasure yourself, or perhaps you would prefer just to tell me that you're going off somewhere private to pleasure yourself?"
- "What if you were to want mostly "quickies" and I were to feel like I'm not getting enough of those wonderful languorous evenings when we cuddle a lot and then lovemake really slowly? How would you like us to work it out together?"
- "What if my wishes to play anally were to get really intense, and you continued to feel that it cannot be done hygienically and safely? How could we address the issue?
- "What if I were strongly to like the idea of having sex in front of, or alongside, other couples who are also fucking, and you were to find the idea sort of scary? Could we talk some more about what it might be like for us to do it in a way that would make you comfortable?"
- "What if my medical difficulties were to continue to affect me to the point where I cannot enjoy genital sex anymore, and I wouldn't want you to be deprived of something you enjoyed for the rest of your life, but I also wouldn't want such difficulties to affect how much

we love each other? Would you consider taking another lover just for recreational sex and staying with me as your primary partner?"

Again, if these sorts of explicit verbal exchanges seem strange, we have to consider how much it is our shame and guilt over erotic sharing that causes us to abstain from discussions that might advance and protect a potentially exciting and enduring sensual and sexual partnership.

Key #9: We commit to addressing the issues of non-exclusivity. Our society idealizes the notion of an exclusive partnership, and in doing so it perpetuates a very dangerous myth about erotic relations.

For the truth is that there is no such thing as an erotically exclusive partnership. It is, of course, correct that there can be partnerships in which an agreement is made that genital intercourse will be kept within the bounds of the relationship. But genital intercourse is only one of a wide variety of activities that are part of an individual's erotic repertoire. And the question of erotic exclusivity is, in reality, far more complex than can be encompassed within any simple—and, for many couples, entirely unspoken—agreement to be "faithful."

All partnerships face the challenge of non-exclusivity, and successful partnering entails an effort to confront this challenge openly, anticipatorily and communicatively.

First of all, no partnership is exclusive in terms of erotic fantasies. For everyone has some sort of occasional fantasy about sensual and sexual sharing with someone outside the partnership, and some people have many such fantasies much of the time.

Moreover, as soon as we consider all the many variations in sensual and sexual activities that can occur in our daily lives, we realize that partnerships are always non-exclusive in terms of a host of erotic behaviors. For example, if a couple has an agreement to keep "sex," by which they mean genital intercourse, exclusively within their relationship, does this mean that

— Fantasizing about genital intercourse with another person while enjoying intercourse with one's partner is forbidden?
— Fantasizing about genital intercourse with another person is forbidden even if it occurs when one's partner is not around?
— Kissing and genitally caressing another person is forbidden when one's partner is available?
— Kissing and genitally caressing another person is forbidden even when one's partner is unavailable?
— Enjoying with a recreational friend a sexual activity, such as oral or anal intercourse, which one's partner for whatever reason cannot or will not do, is forbidden?
— Greeting a friend with a handshake, a hug, a kiss on the cheek, a kiss on the lips, a kiss with a playful exchange of tongue caresses, when one's sexual partner is or is not around, is forbidden?
— Gratifying one's bisexual desires by consorting with a person differently gendered from one's partner, if the sex is casually recreational, or if it occurs in the context of an emotional bond, with or without the knowledge or participation of one's primary partner, is forbidden?

The point I am making here is threefold:

➢ There really is no such thing as an erotically exclusive partnership, if we understand that sensual and sexual connectedness means much more than simply having genital intercourse.

➢ Most couples enter into their partnership making assumptions about exclusivity and non-exclusivity that are never verbalized, and hence never consensually articulated. Yet when it is subsequently discovered that the couple have divergent notions about the parameters of their partnership, feelings can be severely hurt. Shame and guilt invariably accumulate. And the primary partnership almost inevitably spirals downwards in an anti-sexual direction or is broken altogether. Envy and jealousy are, after all, almost the most powerful and destructive emotions that human beings can experience.

➢ The only way that a partnership can protect their erotic connection from the damaging effects that can result from the unavoidable fact of non-exclusivity—or indeed even make non-exclusivity enhance their connection—is to engage anticipatorily and proactively in "what if" discussions, and to do so regularly throughout the relationship.

Contrary to all the myths of our socialization and acculturation that somehow struggling to keep our erotic pleasures all in one place is likely to make for a "better" sensual and sexual life, there is no "right" set of conclusions for a partnership to reach through their "what if" discussions. Let me give some examples.

In terms of fantasies, there are successful partnerships in which there is agreement to make a practice of sharing and elaborating erotic fantasies about individuals outside the partnership. I know one couple, for instance, who enjoy sitting together in a Manhattan coffee shop with each other, "people watching," and exchanging fantasies such as "Oh wow, I'd like to fuck him" or "Man, she has incredibly hot legs." This couple understand that fantasies about other potential partners do not translate into having "affairs" with other partners, and they find that sharing fantasies such as these generates passion and sexual heat in their erotic life as a couple.

There are, however, many couples whose envy and jealousy is such that they find that sharing erotic fantasies has a deleterious effect on the passion and sexual heat of their erotic life together. Such couples successfully protect their partnership either by agreeing to share only fantasies that involve each other, or by agreeing to forego sharing fantasies altogether.

Again, the point here is that there is no "right" solution to the challenges of non-exclusivity, only some strong advice that it is preferable to face these challenges in advance, as much as one is able to do so, and to address them with "what if" discussions.

In terms of behaviors, there are successful partnerships in which it is agreed to invite other individuals to participate in certain aspects of the couple's sensual and sexual activities. They may engage in threesomes, or polyamorous lifestyles, or participate in swinging activities and orgies. And many such couples find that such activities augment their erotic partnership, keeping their relationship both exciting and enduring.

For many other couples, expansion of the boundaries of non-exclusivity in this socially controversial manner is too threatening to their partnership. However, even if such couples agree to forego additional partners for intercourse, the challenges of non-exclusivity do not evaporate.

Such couples still have to discuss a wide range of other non-exclusive erotic encounters outside their partnership that cannot be avoided. Whether kissing a coworker at an office party, or swimming in the nude with the neighbors who have a secluded backyard, or watching erotic performances in movies that are rented on the weekend, the challenges of non-exclusivity have to be addressed if excitement is to endure, and the enduring relationship is to be kept exciting.

As examples of what I mean, imagine discussions beginning from the following types of questions.

- "What if you I go on an extended business trip and want some physical touch? How would you feel if I were to get a massage in my hotel room from a professional, and would it matter to you if the massage was given by a man or a woman?"
- "What if I go on an extended business trip and feel really horny? How would you feel if I were to get a massage in my hotel room with a professional who was also willing to massage my genitals until I orgasm?"
- "What if I go on an extended business trip and want to have intercourse, with all proper risk-reductive procedures, with a casual friend of mine? How would you feel about that? Would it make a difference to you if it wasn't with my casual friend but rather with a professional sex worker?"
- "What if our neighbor invites me for a walk while you are away on a business trip, and then wants to hold my hand, or walk arm in arm? How would you feel about that?"
- "What if our neighbor invites me for a swim while you are away on business, and then wants us to swim in the nude? How would you feel about that?"
- "What if my bisexual desires prompt me to seek a sexual encounter with someone else? Would you rather I did it privately, or would you like to join us?"
- "What if you really feel that you want to try swinging in the next few years? Would you need me to join you or, given my fears about it, would you prefer me to let you go alone?"
- "What if medical difficulties were to continue to affect me to the point where we cannot enjoy genital intercourse together anymore? How would you feel if I encouraged you to have another partner just for recreational sex, and asked you to stay with me as your lover?"

— "What if medical difficulties were to continue to affect you to the point where we cannot enjoy genital intercourse together anymore? How would you feel if I took another partner just for recreational sex and, of course, kept you as my primary partner for emotional intimacy and lots of other pleasurable sensual and sexual activities?"
— "What if your friend continues to greet you with such a full kiss on the mouth, and you know I find it difficult to handle my jealousy whenever something seems to be happening behind my back? Would you consider telling me about it whenever it happens?"

Such conversations cannot, of course, cover all contingencies. But they do provide a forum for respectful and caring conversation in which the realities of erotic desire are addressed. If such forums become a regular feature of partnered life, the possibility of sex-positive solutions to the challenges of non-exclusivity is greatly enhanced. If such conversations are avoided, issues of envy and jealousy, alongside the accumulation of shame and guilt over sensual and sexual desires, almost invariable propel the partnership into a downward anti-sexual spiral.

Key #10: We commit to practicing only risk-reductive sex. One might imagine that this key to successful sexual partnering would scarcely need mention. However, this is not the case. For clinical and scientific evidence shows us that far too many partners are lackadaisical about following "risk-reductive" procedures.

*Successful partnerships are diligently aware
of the need only to engage sexually in a risk-reductive manner.*

This means that sexual activity is always safe, sane, and consensual, that unwanted pregnancies are avoided, and that diseases are not transmitted by the body contact that sexuality usually involves.

Sexual activity is not safe if engaged in a manner that is likely to endanger participants physically or emotionally. It is not sane if its consequence is an unwanted child, who is conceived because the provisions of adequate contraception were ignored. It is not sane if undertaken without clear consciousness and a sense of personal responsibility—for example, if performed when intoxicated or otherwise mentally impaired. And it is not consensual unless all participants are equally empowered and mutually capable of giving their willing consent.

As is well known—but too frequently ignored—one of the most common risks of sexual activity concerns the incidence of sexually transmitted infections, that occur when risk-reductive procedures are not followed. Such infections are not only a medical problem in the physical sense. They also do untold harm to each affected individual, causing an intensification of sexual shame and guilt, as well as the disruption of otherwise successful partnerships.

Risk-reductive sex means that erotic activities are performed in manner that deliberately minimizes the chances of a sexually transmitted infection.

The risk-reductive protocols for avoiding the transmission of sexual diseases are relatively simple:
Consistent use of condoms and other barriers,
along with judicious use of "chemoprophylactic" lubricants
(chemicals that exterminate the microbes which
cause sexual diseases).

Although a certain amount of risk cannot be avoided, most but not all risks of transmission become relatively minimal if "barrier protection"—male condoms, female condoms, and dams—is used diligently, so that infected body fluids are not exchanged during sexual activities. The careful use of lubricants that contain chemical disinfectants—"chemoprophylactic" agents—that kill sperm, as well as the bacteria, viruses, and other entities that lead to disease, is also important.

The body fluids that are most often involved in transmitting infections are pre-ejaculate, ejaculate, vaginal secretions, blood and breast milk. The bodily sites that are most often involved in taking in these infected fluids are the wet tissue inside the anus, vagina, urethra, and mouth, as well as lesions to the skin.

If risk-reductive methods—the consistent and careful use of barrier protection, as well as the judicious use of chemoprophylactic lubricants—were practiced diligently, virtually no one would ever suffer from a sexually transmitted infection.

The only partnerships that can forego the use of barrier protection are those that are risk-reductively "fluid-bonded." Being fluid-bonded means: (1) that the couple has diligently assessed the health status of each partner over an extensive period of time; (2) that they have committed not to exchange body fluids with anyone outside the partnership; and (3) that they then feel safe exchanging fluids with each other, and proceed to have sexual relations without barrier protection. For partners to become fluid-bonded in this way requires not only a knowledgeable assessment of each person's sexual health over an extensive period of time, but also a commitment to engage in a sacred act of great trust and love.

We all need to learn how to enjoy our sexuality safely, and we need to practice risk-reductive sex, consistently and diligently.

Risk-taking is not a thrill to be brought into the sanctity of our sexual lives. Given the pain and suffering that can be caused by indulging in risky sex, we all need to learn how to relax into the safety of risk-reductive sexual pleasures.

If the watchwords of our commitment to sexual health are *safe, sane,* and *consensual,* then to know that we can enjoy our erotic pleasures in a way that is ethically conducted, freely chosen, individually governed, and without undue risk of physical or psychological harm, becomes a wonderful aphrodisiac!

Risk-reductive sexual practices permit us to enjoy our sexuality with such a greater sense of relaxation and security. Frequent and careful practice is needed . . . start now!

Relax into the blessing of
sexual pleasure, safely, sanely, and consensually!
This is an act of love for our selves as well as for our partners.
Risk-reductive sex is hotter sex!
Enjoy!

Endnote: An expanded version of this chapter is available as a booklet, titled *Ten Keys to Successful Sexual Partnering,* available from Xlibris (2005). This booklet includes "Notes on Risk-Reductive Sexual Practices," which addresses in more detail the procedures and protocols for risk-reductive enjoyment.

17

Five Ways of Nurturing Sexually Healthy Children

There is an enormously disastrous myth to which many human cultures have subscribed, and especially those in the western tradition. It is the myth that one can "raise" children to be sexually healthy—the authoritarian myth that a family or society can "bring up a child" so that he or she is sure to develop into an adult who can safely, sanely and consensually enjoy and fulfill his or her erotic potential.

This is a major and tragic myth. Children can be raised to be sexually unhealthy, and we witness that everywhere around us. But they cannot be "raised" into sexual health. By this, I mean that children cannot be coerced or compelled into sexual health—anymore than health can ever result from coercion or compulsion, because health and freedom are always complicit.

Rather, children will be more likely to be sexually healthy if the adult world would cease believing that children can or should be "raised," and if adults would desist from these inherently anti-sexual attitudes of "child-rearing." Children are not born to be "reared" like livestock.

The attitude of "raising and rearing" implies that the adult world has to "make something happen" that would not otherwise occur naturally. It is an authoritarian attitude that, when applied to the treatment of childhood sexuality, both expresses the adult world's fear of childlike pleasures and ensures that children will "mature" into the same anti-sexual fearfulness.

Against the myths of "raising and rearing" children to conform to a restrictive and constrictive image of "sexual health," the world will be a far happier place when the following truth is recognized.

Children begin life with a wonderful erotic potential of their own. This erotic potential can be destroyed by the anti-sexual forces of our socialization and acculturation. Or we can create an environment for children that facilitates and nurtures their realization of their own erotic potential. Authoritarian procedures of "raising and rearing" children never cultivate sexual health in adulthood.

It is characteristic of all societies and cultures that their structures are reproduced ideologically—especially by means of the messages promulgated by political and religious institutions. The anti-sexual forces of our socialization and acculturation perpetuate themselves largely because we are raised to have our erotic potential conditioned and constrained, stifled and truncated, and we then raise our children in the same manner.

Much of the tragedy of "child raising and rearing" ideology stems from the fact that we as adults are invariably envious and jealous of the sensual and sexual potential of our children and adolescents. We have lost so much of our own erotic freedom that the abundant erotic potential of children stirs deep longings within us, and the erotic exuberance of adolescents stirs our deepest fears of our own sensual and sexual capacity.

"Child raising and rearing" ideology
—the mistaken notion that we can train
children into sexual health—
is structured and motivated, consciously and unconsciously,
from the sensual frustrations and the sexual conflicts
experienced by adults.

Adults can, of course, be of great service to children and adolescents, but I believe that the way in which this can happen is actually very different from the current protocols of "raising and rearing" them. The core issue is that

Children and adolescents
both have their own modes of sensual and sexual expression,
and can be trusted to realize their erotic potential.

That is, what the adult world can do is to *facilitate* and *nurture* their realization of this erotic potential. The authoritarian attitude of "raising and rearing" needs to be replaced by the honoring attitude of "facilitating and nurturing."

What follows is a brief discussion of five tenets by which the sexual health of children and adolescents might be facilitated.

➢ *Children have their own modes of sensual and sexual pleasure, and they need not to be alienated from their own erotic activities.*

Western cultures have had a strong tendency to deny that children are sensual and sexual creatures, as well as to denounce and punish any expression of their erotic nature. The generally held—but utterly mistaken—viewpoint is that childhood sensuality and sexuality, if it exists at all, must be considered "perverse" and thus it needs to be controlled and shaped behaviorally so that it "matures" into an "appropriate" erotic pattern in adulthood.

However, what actually occurs by means of this controlling and shaping is that children are robbed of their polysexual potential, and their erotic nature is diminished. That is, this oppressive ideology of adults toward children actually alienates them from the erotic nature of their bodymind, and requires the child to suppress and repress his or her sensual and sexual desires. We discussed this briefly in Chapter Three and elaborated it subsequently.

There is, of course, a sense in which western cultures do recognize the erotic nature of children—despite the fact that the manifest attitude is often one of denial and denunciation. The fact that these cultures tend to react oppressively to children's sensual and sexual exuberance suggests that there is at least a tacit understanding that childhood sexuality is the foundation of adult sexuality. To produce adults who are socially adapted to their culture, to produce "good citizens," it is necessary to alienate children from their erotic potential.

The results of this alienation are unmistakably tragic, because children need to be allowed to enjoy the full experience of their erotic bodies. Children's experiences of their body are central to their foundational sense of their place in the world—a sense that is only made insecure by the cultivation of shame and guilt. Childhood bodily experiences are not only a source of pleasure, but also provide a sense of accomplishment or self-mastery, a way to soothe and comfort the self, and a way to give to others and to initiate closeness with others.

Childhood bodily experience can also be a source of discomfort, an arena for unpleasant or frightening overstimulation and traumatization, as well as the context in which the child becomes vulnerable not only to abusive violation, but also to the development of profound shame and guilt.

In general, the child's capacity to experience his or her erotic body is foundationally significant for the development of a sense of competence, self-regulation and autonomy.

The sensuality and sexuality of the child is magnificent. Children readily receive pleasure from the equilibrated stimulation of the entire skin surface, as well as the mouth, the bladder and urethra, the anus and rectum, and the penis or vulva-vagina. Without the interference of adults, children will naturally give themselves pleasure—and receive pleasure from caretakers—by playing with these various bodily zones. Children are genitally responsive from birth, and will—as soon as hand-to-genital coordination develops—naturally stimulate themselves autoerotically, just as they will naturally stimulate themselves orally as soon as hand-to-mouth coordination is possible.

The child's sensuality and sexuality is exuberant, pervading the entire bodymind. And without the interference of adults, what has been called the *jouissance* of a toddler's erotic nature is evident to any observer. This is the sheer pleasure that we naturally find in our embodiment, in our erotic being-in-the-world, and it is orgasmic in nature.

The child's sensual and sexual potential needs to be honored, rather than reacted against with fear and prohibition.

There is no excuse for shaming children, for embarrassing or humiliating them, for making them feel guilty, or for punishing them for their sensual and sexual inclinations.

Although, pragmatically, it may be necessary to help a child with certain matters—for example, not to play with or ingest feces, and not to stimulate the genitals in front of an unfriendly public—any unnecessary interference with the child's sensual and sexual expression has detrimental consequences.

Such unnecessary interference damages children's sense of self and their capacity to feel joyful about their place in the world, and it alienates them from their embodiment by the accretion of shame and guilt. Such unnecessary interference is not in any child's interests—it is always done to alleviate the anxieties and conflicts of adults, to ensure that each child is as tragically damaged as the adult that "raised" him or her, and thus ensures that our sexually unhealthy culture is perpetuated.

> *Children need to be protected from overstimulation as well as from understimulation, and they need to be well protected from the sexual activities and fantasies of adults and adolescents.*

If children's erotic potential is to be honored, children need to be allowed the freedom and privacy to masturbate, the freedom and privacy to enjoy their naked bodies and play with their peers, and the freedom and privacy to be curious and to explore their sensual and sexual selves. The notion of the child's freedom and privacy is important here for three reasons.

First, children have to be protected from understimulation, because sensory and sensual experiences are essential for their physical and emotional growth, and their sexual health. Understimulation occurs when the child lacks adequate interaction with caretakers and peers, or in those extreme circumstances where children are deprived of experiences with their own bodies.

If not prevented from the opportunity to do so, children will naturally seek out the stimulation they need. This is why it is essential that their freedom and privacy—to masturbate, to enjoy their naked bodies, to play with their peers, as well as to be curious and explore their sensual and sexual selves—be honored and protected.

Second, children have to be protected from overstimulation, and to some extent they need to be helped to learn how to negotiate the social world without becoming overstimulated. As was discussed in Chapter Six, overstimulation is the defining feature of traumatic experience.

Children will naturally learn to self-regulate, and thus can be trusted not to experience overstimulation, if left to their own devices. However, they are compelled to participate in the adult world, and in that world they encounter possible experiences of overstimulation from which they need protection. Examples of such experiences include the following.

- Exposure to witnessing violence or being the victim of violence, including spankings, and other forms of physical abuse.
- Exposure to verbal abuse, including shaming, embarrassing or humiliating, guilt inducing or other punitive behaviors.
- Exposure to witnessing many of the adult or adolescent modes of sexual activity, including intercourse, and from any form of inclusion in adult or adolescent erotic activities or fantasies.

Third, this last issue is crucial, for children need to be protected from what is perhaps the most traumatizing of all forms of overstimulation—along with violence—which is their involvement in the sexual activities and fantasies of adults and adolescents. This issue concerns the observance of the incest prohibition, the critical significance of which was discussed in Chapter Six.

This danger of the child's "involvement" in the sexual activities and fantasies of adults and adolescents is complicated and double-edged. It is complicated because—as psychoanalysts know, although they rarely dare to talk about it—children need to feel, in a limited and safe way, that their caretakers are indeed erotically attracted to them. If children do not get a sense that their mothers, fathers, and other caretakers, enjoy their embodiment, then emotional growth and especially the capacity for intimacy is impaired. However, it is entirely the responsibility of the caretaker to articulate and maintain the boundary of taboo, and to do so not only in a gentle, non-judgmental, and yet consistently firm manner, but also in a progressively graduated or calibrated manner. For example, a caretaker will participate in washing the child's genitals at two years of age, but not at five years, and so forth.

So for the emotional and sexual health of the child, a caretaker needs to be warmly loving and erotically attracted to the child, and yet at the same time to perform the boundary of taboo in a progressive yet non-judgmental manner.

For any caretaker this is a delicate yet vitally important issue, concerning not only what the caretaker needs to do with his or her erotic feelings for a beloved child, but also the way in which the caretaker needs to attend to the nuances of his or her behavior with the child.

This is why Freud referred to parenting as one of the "impossible professions." No one can completely succeed at parenting. One can only be diligent in making a consistent effort, and then hope that this effort is "good enough"!

The danger of the child's "involvement" in the sexual activities and fantasies of adults and adolescents is additionally double-edged.

On the one side, an adult's interference with a child's realization of his or her erotic potential actually constitutes a way of involving the child in the adult's erotic fantasies— even if this is not its surface appearance. As we have already mentioned, adults interfere with children's sensual and sexual pleasures not because such interference is in the child's best interests, but because of their own anxieties, conflicts, envy, jealousy, shame and guilt, that are all stirred up by the erotic repertoire of children.

On the other side, adults also directly recruit children into their sexual activities and fantasies, and this violation of the incest prohibition is extraordinarily damaging to the emotional and sexual health of the child. Intergenerational sexual contact is usually coercive, always exploitive and abusive. This is the case even when the child appears to desire such contact.

Indeed, children need to feel erotic desires toward their caretakers, and need to be free to act seductively—even if they do not exactly know what they are doing. The adults in the child's world need to take responsibility for protecting the child from intergenerational enactments. Children need to be free to express their sensual and sexual feelings, and—for their emotional and sexual wellbeing—they need to feel thoroughly safe and protected from any enactment of all the reciprocal feelings that adults may experience.

➤ *Children need to interact with sexually healthy adults and to know that adult and adolescent sexual expression can be safe, sane, and consensual.*

This issue actually segues between the previous one and the next—because, although it is crucial that the child be protected from being in any way recruited into the sexual activities and fantasies of adults and adolescents, it also facilitates their own emotional and sexual growth to be able to know that sensual and sexual interactions between adults can be vibrant, loving, passionate, and life-affirming.

In a certain sense, the most important factor in a child's sexuality education—in addition to being allowed freedom to develop his or her own erotic potential—is the child's knowledge that the sensual and sexual sharing between his or her caretakers can be healthy, healing, and happy.

That is, it facilitates the child's emotional and sexual growth if he or she has what are commonly called "role models" who are sex-positive—but who do not interfere with the child's own sexuality, and who do not impose their values on the child in an authoritarian manner.

Children need these "role models" to be of both genders. When a child's primary parents are a lesbian couple, there still needs to be significant male caretakers in the child's life; when a child's primary parents are a gay couple, there still needs to be significant female caretakers in the child's life. And I also know that, when a child's primary parents are a heterosexual couple, it is very important for the child to know gay and lesbian couples as "role models" and as a significant aspect of the child's emotional life.

> *Children need "Comprehensive Sexuality Education" throughout the entire course of their childhood.*

Thus far, I have emphasized the need for children to experience their erotic freedom, and the advisability of dropping the traditionally authoritarian, oppressive and anti-sexual procedures of "child raising and rearing."

However, this emphasis does not imply that children do not need the help of adults as they develop. Clearly, children need information, and they need it to be what is called "comprehensive sexuality education."

Children are, from a very young age, naturally curious about sexual matters—including sexual phenomena that are not yet within the purview of their own erotic repertoire. We are all aware of standard questions such as the following:

— "Where do babies come from?"
— "Why do some people sleep in the same bed and others do not?"
— "How are boys and girls made differently?

Most conscientious caretakers and teachers prepare themselves for these routine inquiries—even though they are often uncomfortable and inept in providing the requested information. This discomfort is usually sensed by the child, who then "gets the message" that he or she should censor a multitude of other questions that have come to mind. The latter are vitally important questions that, in their censorship, often contribute mightily to the child's shame and guilt. They include items such as the following:

— "What are those noises that woke me up to last night?"
— "How come my penis sometimes feels all warm and sticks out?"
— "How come my vulva feels all tingly sometimes?"
— "Why can I put my finger in my vagina?"
— "Why don't men have breasts?"

— "Why does Jack live with Jill, when Bob lives with Ted, and Carol with Alice?"
— "Why do women get bloody and have periods?"
— "Will I be okay if I have a period?"
— "What is it when different stuff, that isn't pee, starts coming out of a penis?"
— "I've heard that AIDS will kill you if you have sex, is that true?"

There are three ways in which adults routinely squash the asking of these vitally important questions:

— by being anxious when asked the previous question;
— by answering the previous question partially or untruthfully;
— by telling the child that he or she doesn't yet need to know about all this.

Many caretakers are so anxious and conflicted about sexuality, and so greatly in denial about the importance of such questioning, that they delude themselves into believing that if the questioning ceases, the issues are not pertinent.

In short, we tend to treat children as if they were either fools or political prisoners ready to renounce their cause as soon as a brutal interrogation commences.

Yet the questions that are vitally important to children are indeed vitally important, simply because they concern the life of the child, they concern his or her bodily experiences or observations, and they concern matters of great emotional significance.

If questions are not well answered, they do not dissolve into the ether. In this deplorable situation, either children will deny their curiosity and along with this denial will come the suppression and repression of a portion of their erotic desires, or they will find "answers" elsewhere and probably fall victim to whatever sexual mythology is readily available.

To offer children and adolescents anything other than comprehensive sexuality education is actually an act of abusiveness on the part of the adults in their lives. Comprehensive sexuality education for children and for adolescents has the following ten features:

- Questions will be responded to without prejudice or judgments about the nature of the question or the motives of the questioner.
- The informant may well inquire what the questioner already knows about the topic under discussion so that the question itself may be better understood and answers customized to the needs of the questioner.
- The response to all questions will be full and frank, and an increment of information will be added so that the answer always goes one degree beyond the mandate of the immediate question.
- The information will be given freely and without anxiety on the part of the informant.
- All the relevant biological and psychological-relational facts about sexual functioning will sooner or later be delivered.
- All the relevant facts about the diversity of human sensual and sexual expression—including matters of lifestyle, orientation, preference, and gender—will sooner or later be delivered.
- The information will be delivered in an age-appropriate manner—that is, at a level and in a language that the questioner can comprehend.
- The informant's gratuitous opinions will be withheld, but the tone of the information given will be sex-positive, and it will be made clear that what the questioner does with the information is entirely a matter of his or her choice—that is, the child's and the adolescent's right to determine his or her own sensual and sexual life will be explicitly honored.
- The idea that healthy sexuality is safe, sane and consensual will be presented, and periodically each of these

three notions will be discussed in some depth and with some specificity.

- It will be understood that sexuality education is not a one-time event, but an ongoing process. Typically the same topics have to be addressed again and again as the child reaches each new phase of his or her development. Indeed, the adult informant need not be surprised if the information provided, even when given in an age-appropriate fashion, is quickly forgotten or distorted by the child. Children always have anxiety about matters of their sensuality and sexuality so they too, just like adults, are capable of being "defensive." Questions and answers often need review and revision at each new phase of development (and sometimes this is only an interval of a few months).

➤ *Children need careful, respectful and informative preparation for any visit to a healthcare practitioner and especially if any form of medical procedure is to occur.*

This final tenet is perhaps obvious, although having been a Director in several primary care medical clinics, I have often been surprised at how frequently this matter is overlooked by caretakers and healthcare practitioners alike. It seems that most adults would like to deny what a profound impact any medical event is likely to have on the child.

The unavoidable fact is that there are occasions in which adults have to violate the bodily integrity of a child. Children take a vitally important interest in their bodies, quite correctly treating their bodies as belonging to them. This sense of belonging, a "self-proprietary" interest, is natural. Indeed, if it is absent, then there is something amiss. So it is entirely understandable that children are very interested in "doctors," for at least the following three reasons.

First, doctors are the only adults who are allowed to cross the intergenerational boundary of the incest taboo, and are legitimated in so doing. That is, doctors are allowed to look at, and touch, children's bodies in ways that adults are customarily forbidden. Doctors, therefore, are also role models for the child's legitimate explorations with the bodies of peers (which is not to suggest that children would not explore each other if there were no such adult profession).

Second, doctors intrude upon body boundaries that the child needs to believe are under his or her own governance. In a certain sense, doctors and their assistants are violators. They routinely poke in ears, nostrils, and throats, sometimes in the rectum; they give injections, and so forth. They even cut people open when they are very sick.

Third, doctors are somewhat notorious for making people, who have been feeling "bad," start feeling "good." They even save lives. So their profession cannot simply be dismissed as monstrous. To young children, this presents quite a challenge for their comprehension.

The problems that all this evokes in the child cannot be overestimated. So children always need careful preparation for any medical procedure and even for routine medical visits. This preparation needs to follow similar precepts to those of comprehensive sexuality education—anticipatory accounts about what is going to happen, and why it is going to happen, need to be geared to the child's level of comprehension, and so on—but with three important modifications.

First, the adult will have to initiate the conversation—the issue cannot wait until the child inquires why he or she has to participate in the medical event.

Second, while it is obvious that the child cannot be given a choice about whether to participate in the medical event, it is highly desirable that the child be given every opportunity to be as much "in charge" as possible, in order to counteract the traumatic feelings of helplessness that so often occur.

For example, if it is feasible, it is highly advantageous for the child to be able to tell the medical practitioner when he or she is ready for the needle to be injected—and for the medical practitioner to honor these directives. It is also advantageous if it is possible for the child to handle a medical instrument and be shown its operation before it is inserted in the ear, nostril, or elsewhere.

Third, the child needs anticipatory preparation for the feelings evoked by having to undergo a medical procedure, and this is not always an easy matter for a caretaker since, for many children, even talking about doctors is scary.

Family illness, surgeries, deaths, all need to be "worked-through" by children. As with sexual issues, these matters need to be discussed thoroughly and in a respectful manner suitable to the age and individual characteristics of the child.

Finally, it has to be added that these tenets for facilitating or nurturing sexually healthy children and adolescents are really the responsibility of the community. Sadly, comprehensive sexuality education cannot be left for primary caretakers to implement—because we know from experience that primary caretakers tend to repeat and replicate their own anxieties and conflicts in "raising and rearing" their children. Comprehensive sexuality education has to be the responsibility of every adult, and I firmly believe that any adult who withholds this education from any child is actually committing an act of serious child abuse. Foremost, this must always be held in our awareness.

The erotic freedom of children is the foundation for adult sexual health. Erotically free children will become sexually healthy adults; whereas children, whose erotic potential is oppressed, will arrive in adulthood suffering all the socially normative conditions of sensual frustration and sexual conflict.

18

Notes on Surviving America's Sex Wars

The first section of this book included some rather alarming information about the way in which this country is drifting, or even dramatically shifting, into cultural warfare—a war over matters of our erotic embodiment.

It is a war in which the forces of anti-sexuality cannot ultimately prevail.

However, writing these words in the first decade of the millennium, it has to be said that it is a war that the forces of anti-sexuality appear, at least for the moment, to be winning.

America is already a culture in which "normality" is a condition of severe anxiety and conflict over our sensual and sexual nature—a culture in which most of us are deeply wracked by shame and guilt. It is also an intensely paradoxical culture because, as I argued in Chapter Two, the social dynamics of "sexification" make it appear that, compared with sex-phobic compulsivity, sex-obsessive compulsivity might somehow be an act of liberation. However, on both sides, compulsivity is not freedom. Rather it is indicative of our alienation for our erotic embodiment, and is always symptomatic of deeply disturbing conflicts.

It is alarming to think what might happen in this country if the ideology of "abstinence-only" propaganda continues to advance, if gays and lesbians are coerced into mainstreaming themselves or are compelled back into the closet, if women's rights to determine the disposition of their bodies are further compromised, if the producers and purveyors of "adult" entertainment are further pressured and condemned, or if those in alternative lifestyles are further harassed and persecuted.

If we look clear-sightedly at what is happening in this country, what we see is alarming. Although we cannot fully predict the longterm future of American culture, what we can probably anticipate is that, at least for the foreseeable future, the anti-sexual forces of fundamentalism and fascism will continue to gain ground—regardless of the outcome of the next presidential election.

What we also know is that a compulsively sex-obsessive reaction to a compulsively sex-phobic culture may be better than acquiescence, but it is not a longterm, radical solution. Rather,

We need, more vigorously than ever,
to commit our selves not only to being sex-positive,
but also to advancing our understanding
of enlightened sexuality and spirituality.

So in this chapter, I will simply offer some ideas about how those of us concerned with sexual health and erotic freedom can "survive" the contemporary crises. In what is perhaps a rather haphazard fashion, I have ten suggestions.

1) Let us set our intention, not merely to survive, but to thrive! This may seem like a "new age" precept, but its truth is nonetheless essential. If we become defensive, we will already have conceded to the forces of anti-sexuality. The central intent of this book is to help us quit being defensive in the face of all the anti-sexual forces within us and around us.

2) Let us be very clear that personal liberation from the anti-sexual forces of suppression, repression, inhibition and compulsivity within our selves has to precede, or at least run concurrently with, action against the anti-sexual forces of oppression that operate on the social and cultural level. To release our selves from shame and guilt about our sensual and sexual nature is not only personally freeing, it is a contribution to the welfare of all humanity and to the healing of the planet. We need to attend to our own modalities of sensual and sexual conflict—the ways we hold our selves back from joy. At the end of Chapter Seven, I suggested five avenues of self-inquiry by which we might become aware of our own modalities of suppression, repression, inhibition and compulsivity. For emphasis, I will repeat them here:

> — *Where, somatically and emotionally, am I blocked? Where has my passion and my erotic exuberance disappeared to?*
>
> — *If I am allowing myself certain modes of sexual expression, why am I not allowing myself and experimenting with the enjoyment of other modes of sexual expression, activities not previously in my repertoire?*
>
> — *How are my judgments about others really a reflection of my anxiety about aspects of my own self that I am trying to repudiate?*
>
> — *Where are the energies of my life being diverted to, and what are the seemingly "non-erotic" activities that are so preoccupying to me?*
>
> — *How erotically free am I, or how much are my chosen modes of sensual and sexual expression engaged compulsively, whether in a phobic or an*

> *obsessive manner? And is my erotic life truly orgasmic, such that it propels me on a spiritual and emotional journey of joy, bliss and ecstasy?*

Self-inquiry or self-interrogation of this sort, accompanied by careful listening to the call of our bodymind, can bring us into awareness in a way that is profoundly healing.

3) At a time of escalating oppression, it is a powerful sex-positive act to be visionary. In Chapter Fourteen, I suggested that everyone write their own vision of a sexually healed and healthy world. The exercise is valuable. It encourages us to interrogate any doubt we may have about the achievability of such a world. It motivates us to move in the direction of our vision. Moreover, if we do not become visionary about sexual health and erotic freedom, we will always be in a reactive position in relation to the forces of anti-sexuality.

4) It is a radical act—perhaps even a revolutionary act—to be open about our sensual and sexual activities, and to talk openly about our erotic life. We make a profound contribution to sexual health and erotic freedom every time we "out" our selves in relation to our polysexuality. I do not simply mean that for gays, lesbians, bisexuals, transgendered and intersex people to come out of the closet is important, which it is. I also mean that every one of us who has ever participated in an "alternative" lifestyle can contribute to this culture's health and healing. That is, for example, if we have ever done any of the following twenty-one erotic activities, let us commit ourselves to speaking about it openly and publicly.

- Enjoyed being socially nude in a private setting or in a public place,
- Engaged in sensual touching with someone other than a primary partner,

- Played "doctor" with another adult, just for the fun of it,
- Experienced an activity that might be classified as "BDSM,"
- Paid for sexual services,
- Been paid for sexual services,
- Watched a "porn" movie, or visited a sex museum or exhibit of erotic art,
- Attended an erotic performance, such as a striptease or "live sex show,"
- Masturbated alone, even when a partner was available,
- Self-pleasured in a group setting,
- Used a vibrator, dildo, or some other sex toy,
- Indulged a paraphilic impulse (activities that used to be called "perversions"),
- Had a secretive extramarital affair,
- Participated in recreational sex with a casual friend,
- Cruised for a one-time-only sexual connection,
- Engaged in risk-reductive oral sex,
- Engaged in risk-reductive anal sex,
- Participated in an enjoyable threesome, foursome, or "moresome,"
- Divorced someone just because of being sexually unhappy,
- Experienced a sexual dysfunction, disorder or difficulty,
- Had an orgasm that was so magnificent that life never felt better.

Not only is this sort of "bearing witness" an act of healing our selves, by inviting our selves to be relieved of whatever shame and guilt we harbor within us, it is also a gift to humanity.

The forces of anti-sexuality depend on secrecy and hypocrisy, which breed yet more shame and guilt, so in this context the act of taking a stand for our erotic repertoire is both personally and communally healing. Both literally and figuratively, let us be naked, and unashamed, in word and deed.

5) Let us support, as fully as we are able, the national and international organizations that advocate for the values of sexual health, and that set the standards for sexuality teaching and healing. For example, the following are my personal favorites.

— *The American Association of Sex Educators, Counselors, and Therapists* (www.AASECT.org) trains and certifies professionals in the field of sexuality, advances standards in this field, and advocates in the public arena for sexual health values. It actively promotes its own "vision of sexual health," and offers many educational opportunities accordingly. This organization needs the support both of professionals in healthcare, mental health, and education. It also needs the support of non-professionals who are concerned with the values of enlightened sexual health.

— *The Sexuality Information and Education Council of the United States* (www.SIECUS.org) engages vigorously in the political arena to advance policies and practices for sexual health. It too needs support from the general public.

— Many other organizations are also doing important work in these areas. For example, several national organizations are focused on advancing the rights of sexual minorities, such as gay, lesbian, bisexual, transgendered, and intersex peoples. Various organizations have been established to try and protect the rights of peoples in "alternative" lifestyles such as the "BDSM" community, the swinging community and the polyamory community. Other national organizations focus on women's rights to self-determination, as well as the availability at the local level of resources for contraception and risk-reductive sexual expression.

6) Grassroots activity against the forces of anti-sexuality is also essential. Almost every community across the country is currently engaged in some struggle that affects erotic freedom. For example, Parent Teacher Associations need to be vigorous in their opposition to the abuse of our youth in the name of "abstinence-only" propaganda. Other institutes, such as Planned Parenthood Clinics, also need support. Community "GLBTI" organizations—serving the gay, lesbian, bisexual, transgendered, and intersex populations—always need local support. And so, probably, does any store in our neighborhood that sells vibrators or other sexually-oriented products, as does any "adult" entertainment establishment. Currently, all these organizations and institutions are under attack, all across the country.

7) Let us talk with anyone who will listen about what sexual health really is, and what it is not: *Sexual health is the free enjoyment of erotic activity undertaken safely, sanely, and consensually.* It is not the strangulation of our erotic nature by means of one-thousand-and-one constrictive and prohibitively moralizing rules and regulations. Let us ask our local priest and our designated politician to speak explicitly, and in detail, about his or her sexual values and practices.

8) Let us talk with anyone who will listen about what erotic freedom really is, particularly as it pertains to the sensual and sexual rights of children and adolescents: *Erotic freedom is our right to enjoy the pleasures of our embodiment.* Let us

ask our local priest and our designated politician to speak directly, and in detail, about his or her understanding of erotic freedom.

9) Let us investigate and study tantric sexual and spiritual practices. As will be discussed in the next section, these are practices that honor the subtle erotic energies of our embodiment. Unless we are attached to a fundamentalist or fascistic position, these are not practices that will conflict with whatever belief system we hold. There are Jewish, Christian, Muslim, Hindu and Buddhist practitioners. We will find that tantric practices empower us to live more spontaneously and openly, freer with our selves and more alive in the spirit of joy.

10) Let us consider committing our selves to living more spontaneously, more openly, and more freely with our selves—to be more alive in the spirit of our embodied joy. I do not know what this might mean for each of us. But life would surely be enhanced if we allowed our selves to be more naked with our selves and with each other. As long as everything we do is safe, sane, and consensual, it is a contribution to our own happiness as well as to the healing of the human community if we allow our selves to *"go wild!"* Surely all our lives would be enhanced if we allowed ourselves—literally and figuratively—to dance naked in the moonlight, and lovemake under the sun.

SECTION FIVE

Sexuality is a (the) spiritual matter

19

Human Spirit Incarnate

What is the nature of the human spirit? And what exactly is spirituality? If life is not for celebration, then why are we alive and why are we living?

Perhaps if life is not for the celebration of being alive, and for the celebration of life itself, then it is for nothing.

I have already suggested that, *if we decide to live "in our heads," then our own condition of alienation from the aliveness of our bodymind will ensure that we repeatedly and compulsively barter the freely-flowing presence of our erotic experience for frozen representations of past-futures.*

In this final section, I will also suggest that, *if we seek a direct and immediate experience of our spirituality, then we have both to begin from, and return to, not the representations of our belief systems, but rather the dynamic liveliness of our erotic energies— the kinesis of our desire—this liveliness of the lifeforce that flows within and through our hearts, our genitals, and our entire bodymind.*

That is, the human spirit is to be accessed not "out there" in dubious articles of faith, but "in here" as the palpable truthfulness of our bodymind's erotic experience.

BARNABY B. BARRATT

If life is for celebration,
then our spiritual awareness shows us
that our sensual and sexual experiencing
is the pinnacle and the epitome of that celebration.

But what is meant when we refer to "sensual and sexual experiencing"? Thus far in this book, I have sidestepped any explicit definition of "sexuality," but I have implicitly introduced an understanding of human sexuality that is somewhat unconventional and nontraditional. This is because I am convinced that the definition of sexuality urgently needs to be radically reconsidered, and that the major criterion of this reconsideration needs to be the freeing of our human spirit—rather than the maintenance of social proprieties or the advance of medical knowledge. That is,

Our sensuality and sexuality need to be defined
in terms of the subtle energy systems of our bodymind.
This is an esoteric definition,
which acknowledges and appreciates that
our erotic potential as human beings-in-the-world is sacred.

However, before we proceed to discuss this appreciation of humanity's erotic potential—a discussion which will occupy the remainder of this book—let us review how "sex" is normally defined. This will set the backdrop for a different definition—one that is radical, unconventional and nontraditional—which appreciates foremost the essentially spiritual nature of our sensual and sexual energies.

In an odd fashion, our western culture has always viewed "sex" in terms of whatever is taboo. "Sensuality" is defined as anything that can generate experiences of pleasure, unpleasure or pain, and "sexuality" is that subset of experiences that is delineated in terms of whatever is forbidden. Often the connotation of "sensuality" is that it is a pleasurable experience that may well lead to sex. Consider for a moment, how people commonly think about what is "sex" and what is not. For example,

— passionate kissing is "sex," but planting flowers in our garden is not,
— oral-genital caresses are "sex," but massaging our feet is not,
— deliberately pleasuring the genitals is "sex," but eating a delicious dinner is not.

And contrariwise, watching an elegant ballet performance, swimming on a warm moonlit night, wearing the latest fashions, rubbing a friend's weary shoulders, or picking fresh fruit on a summer's day, are not "sex," but they might be considered "sexy" if these activities lead to aroused feelings of wanting "sex."

It is surely evident that the western tradition effectively defines "sex" as *"anything you should not do with your mother"!*

That is, although we often imagine that we know what "sex" is and is not, our delineation of the topic is unconsciously crafted by our sense of what is forbidden. Even the issue of pleasure is subordinated to this criterion. For example, lying in the sun may be thoroughly delicious but is not sex, even if it is highly pleasurable; whereas pushing a penis into a vagina is sex, even if both participants are exhausted, the vagina feels painfully dry, the penis is entirely numb, and no pleasure is generated.

In this respect, our conventional and traditional approach to sensuality and sexuality prioritizes the faculties of judgment over the qualities of experience. Our definition and our understanding of "sex" has actually become a function of, and subordinated to, our mind's judgmentalism—rather than arising from the sensuality of our embodiment, and our experience of our erotic potential.

To articulate this crucial point another way, the presence or "presentness" of our experiencing, and the ever-shifting realities of pleasure and unpleasure, are subordinated to the representations or *re*-presentations of moralizing ideologies that extrapolate the incest prohibition into one-thousand-and-one anti-sexual rules and regulations. That is, the compulsive repetitiveness of all our identities, positions and stories, which are always about past-futures, decisively take precedence over the experiential realities of erotic energies that flow within and through us.

In this manner, the immediacy of the bodymind's experience, and our present awareness of it, are occluded by or subjugated to our chattering mind's "narratological imperative," as I have called it elsewhere. As indicated the discussions that preoccupied the second section of this book, the mandate of this governance by our judgmental mind is precisely the obstruction of our awareness of the subtle energies of the erotic lifeforce that our bodymind has the potential to express.

Of course, this definition of "sex"—as any activity that falls within the purview of the incest prohibition, and all the anti-sexual laws that purport to be its extensions—is not exactly written in our dictionaries in this manner. In our society, definitions more scholarly or scientific than "anything you should not do with your mother" are available, but they are scarcely any less confused or confusing, and they reinforce the domination of judgment over experience.

These ostensible definitions treat "sex" as a circumscribed set of behaviors, often referring directly or indirectly to procreative or reproductive functioning. Such definitions are usually then augmented by considering how our judgmental mind feels about these behaviors—that is the emotional or affective aspect—as well as what physiological patterns our body exhibits in relation to these behaviors. Let us examine this matter in more detail.

As we have said, in western culture, what counts as "sex" or "sexual"—as opposed to all other, allegedly "non-sexual" behaviors—eventually refers to the forbidden possibilities of genital activity. That is, from a different perspective, it refers to the way in which our chattering mind dishonors our genitals by condemning their sensuality more stringently than we condemn the sensuality of other bodily zones.

For example, if an erect penis is involved in an activity, then the behavior almost certainly counts as "sex"—unless, of course, the erect penis was simply a nocturnal "hard-on," or accidentally induced by ingesting a medication with "priapic side-effects." If the penis is flaccid, for instance, during urination, the activity may not be "sex"—unless, of course, the penis has been released from concealment for the purposes of achieving an erection. Deep kissing without an erection is "sex," mostly because of its common association with getting a "hard-on." And even an activity like urination can become "sexualized," but this is only the case with people who are designated as "perverts."

The confusions do not end here because, if a toddler becomes erect while his caretaker is bathing him, we usually decline to think of this as "sex" and we try to discount the erection—even if it is accompanied by visible excitement—as somehow "merely physiological." Indeed, if we have a fantasy that provokes an erection, which is then allowed to subside without further stimulation, we are quite inclined to talk as if the fantasy was "sexual," but "sex" did not occur. The penis is concealed by clothing, as if it were a secret, precisely because of its propensity to be involved in "sex."

If a vulva-vagina is involved in an activity, then the behavior probably counts as "sex"—unless, of course, the activity is a medical examination, the changing of a menstrual pad, or the vaginal delivery of a baby. Thus, if a clothed woman dances, it is not usually considered "sexual," but if she dances naked, exposing her genitals, then the performance somehow becomes a matter of "sex." Again, there are further confusions here because we tend to distinguish certain functional activities of the vulva-vagina (its role in menstruation, childbirth, and so forth) from its pleasurable or recreational potential (self-pleasuring and shared play), and then we only allow the latter to count as "sex."

The application of this distinction is usually quite phallocentric. That is, "functional" implies that the behavior is unlikely to arouse a man to erection, and the behavior becomes "sexual" if it typically does have this effect. The "extension" of these forbidden zones of female anatomy also raises complications. For example, activities involving breasts—such as playing with them, exposing them, caressing them, or doing almost anything with them except suckling a baby—become a matter of "sex" again merely because of their capacity to arouse a heterosexual's penis. (Note also how, typically, the suggestion that breast-feeding might be a sexual relationship for both parties concerned is strenuously resisted.) Both the vulva-vagina and the breasts are concealed, or semi-concealed, by clothing, as if they were secrets, precisely because of their propensity to be involved in "sex."

All these confusions are magnified when the behavioral definition that attempts to draw a line between conduct that is "sex" and conduct that is not, is augmented by considering the emotion or affect, and the intentionality of the participants. The definition of "sex" broadens when it takes into consideration not just the behaviors themselves, but also how the mind categorizes and then *feels* or has *wishes* about these behaviors. Thus, even if no erections occur, dancing naked in the moonlight would be judged "sexual" if the participants feel it to be so, or wish it to lead to "sex," or it might be judged "sexual"—or "lascivious" to use a derogatory legal term—by an observer even if the participants do not feel or intend it to be so and proclaim its "innocence."

The criteria of context or convention and the intentionality of participants (or merely the vicarious judgments of non-participants) are frequently invoked as if they might clarify these definitional problems. What is statistically normative exerts a hegemonical influence on these definitions. For example, urinating on a partner's belly is not generally considered a "sexual" act, but a "paraphilic individual" may well feel that it is the apogee of sexual excitement—this fact, however, does not extend the definition of "sex" so much as it results in that individual receiving the condemnatory designation of being a "pervert."

Another approach to clarification of the distinction, between conduct that is "sexual" and that which is not, is to augment the definition of "sex" by considering the physiological effects a particular behavior has on its participants. This clarification also raises complications and confusions. On the gross level of physiology—which I will shortly distinguish from the level of subtle energy movements—it is well documented that "sexual arousal" has specific effects on the body's functioning, both "centrally" and "peripherally." These include the following:

- Raised blood pressure and increased heart rate,
- Changes in skin temperature, skin color ("flush"), and electrodermal activity,
- Respiratory change,
- Pupil dilation,
- Involuntary muscular contractions,
- Cortical release of various hormones, neurotransmitters and endorphins,
- Vasocongestive responses ("engorgement" of vulva-vaginal structures, penis, nipples, and other areas).

However, there are major problems with using these properties of "arousability" as part of the definition of what is or is not "sexual." These physiological effects are quite variable between individuals. For example, many individuals have reactions that are definitely considered "sexual" without experiencing any involuntary muscular contractions, and so on. Moreover, many of these same physiological markers shift in rather similar patterns with other states of arousal that are not usually considered erotic—such as fear, panic, or the "non-sexual" excitement that is experienced by "pumped up" spectators at a sporting event or other entertainment.

What if we were to reconsider our sensual and sexual experiencing in a different manner? What if we were to understand our erotic potential in terms of our experience of the movement of subtle energies throughout our embodiment?

Such a definition is not cast in terms of what is forbidden (although the incest taboo and its necessary extensions are, of course, to be respected). And it is no longer so much a matter of deciding that "sexual" means *this* category of behaviors, but not *that*; *this* type of fantasies, but not *that*; or a shift in the pattern of *this* group of measurable physiological indicators, but not *that*.

Rather, sensuality and sexuality are now to be understood and appreciated, most significantly, as moving experiences—experiences of the spiritual mobilization of esoteric energies. Such an understanding is not locked into categorizations or conceptualizations that purport to be *about* experience. That is,

Sensuality and sexuality involve the presence
of a movement of subtle energies within us.
They are not products or projects of our representational mind
that is incessantly preoccupied with matters of past and future.

In no way does this understanding discount the emotional or affective dimension of our erotic nature, since this dimension arises precisely from the movement of our subtle energies, and passion is certainly the concomitant of any movement of these esoteric energies. And this understanding certainly does not discount the gross physiological transformations that sensual and sexual activities usually involve. Rather, this "definition" emphasizes that, foremost and most fundamentally, our sexuality is a spiritual matter.

Subtle energy movements are the *sine qua non* of sexuality, and indeed of life itself. So what needs to be appreciated about sexuality is that our bodymind is a perpetual conduit for these subtle energies. We learn this not so much from western mystical traditions, as we do from the esoteric teachings of the east—especially from the mystical teachings of the Hindu-Buddhist and Jain traditions, and from Oriental methods of healing and personal growth. That is, from Tantra and Tao. Some of these occult insights are also common to Sufism, Kabbala, Gnostic Christianity, and various African traditions, as well as many other indigenous teachings, including Native American cosmologies. In very varied languages, all these approaches to the phenomena of being human show how

> *The sensuality and sexuality of our embodiment is a matter of the lifeforce, of subtle energies that flow within us, through us, and all around us.*

These subtle energies—the lifeforce for which our bodymind is a sacred conduit—have been given various names. I will offer just a few examples.

- *Prāna*—a Sanskrit term from tantric yoga, referring to the lifeforce or cosmic energy that permeates all things, and that is most manifest in the "breath" that flows through all life.
- *Kundalini*—a Sanskrit term from tantric yoga, referring to a specific energy movement that occurs with spiritual awakening, and that is generated in our root and flows upward through our crown.
- *Shakti*—as the Sanskrit term for the "feminine" nature of free-flowing, wild erotic energies that create the entire universe, and that are supported and contained by the "masculine" function of *Shiva*, which contributes form and awareness.

- *Chi*—a Chinese term from the Taoist tradition, referring to the vital, primordial energy that pervades and enlivens all things.
- *Libidinality*—a term from psychoanalytic teachings, referring to the "erotic energy" that pervades and enlivens all mental and bodily functions. According to these teachings, although no mental representation could be meaningful unless invested with libidinal energy, libido is itself a liminal notion. That is, it is neither purely mental (adding no content to the structure of the representation), nor purely physical (not being reducible to neurophysiological phenomena).
- *Spirit*—as is variously translated from many indigenous traditions. Many other spiritual traditions—including Vajrayāna Buddhism and, in a certain poetic sense, the new scientific teachings of quantum reality—also refer to this energy simply as *"Light."* In the Hebrew tradition—that has influenced Judaism, Christianity and Islam—the first book of the Torah refers to *neshemet ruach chayim,* which may be translated as "the breath of the spirit of life."

Parenthetically, it may be noted that these notions entered the western scientific tradition perhaps most decisively with the early Twentieth Century discoveries of psychoanalysis, developed by Sigmund Freud and by some of his followers such as Wilhelm Reich.

"Libido" is a liminal notion—referring to erotic energies that are, so to speak, "in" but not "of" the representations of the mind and the various structurings of the body. That is, the operation of libido can be inferred—we can experience it when a mental representation or a bodily zone is infused with more of it or less of it—but this "investment" of energy does not directly alter the content or meaning of the structure in which it is invested. And yet somehow libido is inherently erotic in nature and it eludes our experience in its "pure" or "uninvested" condition.

Libidinal energies pervade everything; they are the lifeforce without which the human organism, or any other entity, could not exist. They are esoteric and enigmatic because, in a profound sense, they both lack representable content—that is, they cannot be pinned down by the categorizations and conceptualizations of our representational system—and yet are passionately erotic in nature.

Like something that is both a wave and a particle (yet neither a wave nor a particle), or like our contemporary understanding of energy and light, some of this "makes no sense" in terms of the conventional and traditional rules and regulations of logic or rhetoric.

Yet, as inconceivable as its nature truly is, libidinality is not only profoundly natural, but it is also precisely what makes life ultimately meaningful.

The libidinality of being human is alive and real, yet, in a certain sense, inconceivable to our judgmental mind, which builds itself precisely as an obstruction to the free-flow of libidinal energies.

Regrettably, almost all contemporary psychoanalysts have retreated from this radical notion, fleeing into theoretical formulations that keep us very much "in our heads" by denying the seminal nature of our polysexuality and the pervasive desire of the erotic energies that animate all human life.

The distinctions between the various cosmologies that we have just listed are perhaps not as important as the fact that all these teachings express their intimations or their experiences of erotic energies, as the lifeforce connecting all that is. To summarize, there are three important points to recognize about these insights.

First, the movement of these energies can be experienced with awareness, but that does not mean that it can be formulated, controlled or manipulated by the representations of our chattering mind. That is, the erotic energy that pervades all that is in the universe is, so to speak, beneath, behind, besides and beyond, anything that we can govern by the maneuverings of our judgmentalism.

We can experience and become aware of the power and the momentum of this lifeforce, but this is profoundly different from imagining that it can be captured or comprehended by our representational mind's conventional logic and rhetoric. This implies that there is a vital difference between what we can believe we "know" by means of the representational discriminations produced by our chattering mind, and the wisdom of knowing through the discernment of our experiential awareness.

Spiritual discernment and awareness are radically different from cognitive discrimination and the chattering mind's judgmentalism.

We can choose to live "in our heads," alienated from our erotic potential, or we can choose to live as intimately as possible with our hearts, our genitals, and our entire bodymind.

Second, this energy is esoteric, enigmatic and extraordinary, and this compels us to reconsider radically our understanding of sexuality. Our "exoteric" definitions—that is, definitions that focus on externals, on behavioral acts, on what can be designated by our representational mind, and on gross physiological events—are all inadequate. Our understanding of the erotic power of the lifeforce concerns the subtle energies that course within, through and around, our bodymind.

This is an esoteric awareness that we cannot comprehend if we remain "in our heads" about it. Rather, we access it through our hearts, our genitals, our entire bodymind, and our spiritual being-in-the-world. We come to appreciate our selves as conduits for this erotic energy to which we may surrender. We no longer hold to the illusion or delusion that our "self" is an effective executive agency, propounding our identities, positions and stories—as if such repetitive and compulsive narratological productivity could reign over the exuberance of our sensual and sexual nature. In sum,

> *Our erotic nature involves the flowing of powerful yet subtle energies throughout our bodymind, and our emotional and physiological shifts follow from this. The judgmentalism of our chattering mind always misleads us and mistakes the nature of our sensuality and sexuality, because its mandate is to block the free-flow of our erotic energies.*

Third, this energy is one, pervading all that is. In this sense, we have intimations that it is a vibrationality that secures and sustains the interconnectedness of all that is (and all that is not). So this is inherently a spiritual matter, for spirituality concerns the interconnectedness of all that is, and is not. All these teachings converge on this intimation that the lifeforce is inextricably both sexual and spiritual.

What is intimated here is that our sexuality and our spirituality are one-and-the-same, and our erotic potential is not just one spiritual issue among many. It is not a matter for our moralizing judgmentalism to decide its disposition. Rather, it is the ethical, existential and experiential flow of the lifeforce itself—a power to which our egotistic judgmentalism must ultimately surrender. Our erotic potential as human beings is *the* spiritual issue of life itself, and its realization is our naturally spiritual path.

> *Human sexuality and spirituality are one-and-the-same for they concern the erotic energy that interconnects all that is and is not. The freeing of our erotic potential is naturally experiential, ethical and existential, and it is the spiritual path of being human.*

The spiritual experience of being human is naturally ours—it is not a matter of acquiring articles of faith, promulgating a moralizing ideology, or formulating a system of belief. Rather, human spiritual experience is palpable, and available to us all.

> *As human beings, we are spirituality incarnate,*
> *and our erotic potential is Holy Spirit,*
> *that flows within, through and around our embodiment.*

Spiritual experience is thus accessible through the sensual and sexual vibrations of our embodiment. Our erotic nature is indeed a matter of the flesh. The emotional and physical dimensions of our bodymind are, of course, important. But our flesh is essentially the conduit for erotic energies, rather than the origination of our sensual and sexual nature. The erotic potential within each of us *is* Holy Spirit—the Sacred Unity of all vibrationality within us, and the supreme flow of the universe, which is that of the truthfulness of Love.

"Tantra," as I am using the term here, is any practice that attends devotedly to our awakening—or becoming enlightened—to the flow of Holy Spirit within, through and around, our embodiment.

That is, tantric practice concerns our awareness of the Sacred Unity of all that is and is not—our awareness of the supreme flow of the universe that vibrates within our bodymind, just as it is the lifeforce that courses through all the entities around us, in this and the eternity of present moments, here-and-now.

> *Tantra is spiritual practice*
> *concerned both with the weaving*
> *and reweaving of life's sacred energies*
> *and with our awareness of these processes.*

Tantra recognizes both that presence is godliness, with all else subsisting as an illusion or delusion concocted by our chattering mind, and that this presence is the divinity of every human being-in-the-world for it is our experiential, ethical and existential essence.

> *Tantra is sexual-spiritual practice*
> *founded in the awareness that*
> *"God" is not "out there" but here-and-now within each of us,*
> *and that this godliness is the presence of the erotic lifeforce,*
> *which flows within us, through us, and all around us.*

So authentic spiritual practice is never about articles of faith, moralizing ideologies, or belief systems, for in no way can it emerge from this repetitive compulsivity of the chattering judgmentalism that is our egotistic mind. This is definitely what tantric practice is not. Indeed, tantra is not concerned with the distinctions between "good" and "bad," or "right" and "wrong," for its concern is to embrace the liveliness of all that *is*, the "suchness" of existence and nonexistence—and to do so in a way that is spiritually aware and profoundly ethical.

Tantric practice is an incessant experiment, a spiritual adventure into the radical nature of our being-in-the-world, and it is the path of enlightening our selves into the joy, bliss and ecstasy of our being here-and-now as the divine emanation that we are.

I am suggesting that we use the term "tantra" inclusively, as a generic for a wide variety of spiritual practices—some of which have been given other labels. For example, it suits the purposes of this essay to consider Taoism, Quodoushka, and many other indigenous practices, to be essentially tantric.

Tantric spiritual practice comes in many varieties. Although tantra celebrates the aloneness of each individual within the interconnectedness of the entire universe, the daily practices of tantric spirituality may be performed solo, or with a partner, or in a community. At the higher levels of practice, tantric methods may involve sacred intercourse, or the visualization of sacred intercourse, or neither. Tantric spirituality is also associated with a range of cosmologies, modes of expression, and styles of celebrating life.

Through my personal experience of tantric spirituality—which I have elsewhere called "the way of the *bodyprayerpath*"—I understand all its practices as having three intricately enmeshed components. These are three "principles of method," which need to be mentioned briefly.

> *Deconditioning our Consciousness—Releasing ourselves from our Egotism.* Tantric methods work and play to release our selves from the chattering judgmentalism of our egotistic mind. Tantric practice means living in meditation. That is, it means that, by a variety of methods, it get us "out of our heads" and into our hearts, our genitals, and our entire bodymind—and it does so by dissolving our egotism, allowing us to let go the blocks we have constructed that obstruct the free-flow of our sexual-spiritual energies and our awareness of this flow.

These blocks or obstructions are both "in the mind" as all the "defenses" by which our judgmental mind has adapted to our social and cultural circumstances, and "in the body" as all the somatic constrictions and contractions by which our judgmental mind has kept us from the spontaneity, openness and expansiveness of our erotic potential. Thus, the processes of tantra are often transgressive and transcendent. As the edifices of our judgmental mind are deconstructed and dissolved, conventions are flouted as the rules and regulations of our socialization and acculturation no longer entrap us.

What I am calling the "deconditioning of our consciousness" is a deconstruction and dissolution. It implies that our shame and guilt are eradicated, and our anxiety or conflict about being our authentic selves (just as the "suchness" of the being-in-the-world that we are) evaporates as the anti-sexual force of our judgmentalism recedes, and we come to live more and more in the awareness of what is often described as our "Compassionate Witness."

The latter is the pure lifeforce within us, an awareness that witnesses all that arises and dissipates within us, and does so compassionately, yet without allowing us to become entangled in all the identities, positions, and stories, in which our judgmental egotism would have us get repetitively and compulsively imprisoned.

In sum, tantra is a meditative clearing-away of all that has held us back from our joy in life, our bliss and our potential to live in ecstasy. Tantric practice invites us to dance freely in the Sacred Unity of Love—naked, empty and alone.

➤ *Accessing, Cultivating and Mobilizing our Sexual-Spiritual Energies.* Obviously, this process goes hand-in-hand with the clearing-away process of our deconditioning. As our egotism dissolves, our aliveness fires up anew.

The mind's thinking—the discriminative judgmentalism of all the identities, positions and stories that we once took to be our "life"—along with all the emotional obstructions and psychosomatic blocks, which our egotism has used to keep us from our erotic potential, recede.

This liberates us to experience the energies of our lifeforce in a way that is powerfully fresh.

Tantric practice works and plays to release us from the numbing of our erotic nature, our alienation from our sensual and sexual sourcing. Often, tantric methods initially address how traumatized we have become, how much we have lost our potential to touch—both literally and figuratively. By this, I mean "touching" in a profoundly spiritual sense—as practiced in the tantric methods of *nyāsa*—that cultivates an intense energetic connection between the "subject" and the "object" of the touch. In this sense, we surely all need:

—To touch our selves more fully, with awareness of the momentum of our erotic energies, and thus to unite spiritually with our inner Beloved, our Compassionate Witness;

—To touch the earth, the water, the air, and so forth, and to be aware of their energies;

—To touch our partners more fully and in the embrace of Love (which is very far from what is conventionally called "love" with all its expectations of reciprocity, its possessiveness, and our clinging or grasping for an outcome that will gratify our egotism's sense of its own stability and security);

—To touch strangers, and those for whom we would once have had judgments of disgust or contempt, and to find our awareness of the divinity within all;

—And thus, to touch all that *is,* with the prayerful touch of our erotic connection.

Tantric practices involve many methods for mobilizing the erotic energies that flow within, through and around us, for intensifying our experience of these energies, and for facilitating our awareness of this sexual-spirituality.

Visualization methods, for example, are often used in practices that involve no gross physical contact. There are so many methods of tantric meditation—including mantra, mudra, and mandala—that we cannot discuss them adequately in these chapters.

However, it must be said that, as a little about tantra comes to be known in the west, people often imagine that tantric practice is only about having a better sexual connection and greater intimacy with their partners. This may certainly be one part of what tantra contributes. Tantra does indeed work and play extensively and intensively with the orgasmic momentum of our erotic energies—and this will be further discussed in Chapter Twenty. However, tantric practice is not so limited.

Tantric practice is an aligning and realigning
of our spiritual energies with those of the entire universe,
and this involves an inherently erotic connectedness.

Sexual partnering with a special other, or spiritual consort, is only one part of what tantric practice concerns. Foremost, this is because tantric practice appreciates the erotic energy of everyone and everything—appreciating that this energy is universal and transpersonal—such that one cannot sequester the exuberance of erotic sharing, and limit it to a single outlet. When effort is invested in this sort of delimitation, the spiritual quality of sexuality is eventually lost, and "sex" has been recruited for our egotism's fear-based agenda of domination, conquest and possession.

On the path of tantra, our partners in erotic sharing—whether they are plants, trees, the sky, or any number of human beings—cannot be selected by our judgmental egotism. Rather, we are found by the connections that come to us. Enhancing the intimacy of sexual partnering is thus only one part of what tantra contributes not only because of the transpersonal character of our erotic potential, but also, more generally, because this potential is polysexual. It touches us in many ways, above and beyond our coital connections or specific bonds of emotional intimacy.

If tantra were merely about making "fucking" a spiritual event, it would still be a magnificent contribution to our lives. However, it concerns much more than this, for tantric practice appreciates the polysexuality of our being-in-the-world, and the transpersonal ubiquity or universality of the erotic energies that pervade all phenomena.

In sum, tantra is a meditative access to our erotic potential that both celebrates our aloneness and celebrates our interconnectedness with all things and all people, facilitating our awareness of the Holy Spirit that is everywhere at all times, and thus enabling our lives to move into joy, bliss and ecstasy—to live our lives in Love.

➤ *Living in Spiritual Awareness—Living in the Naturalness of an Ethical, Experiential and Existential Adventure.* The methods of tantra—both in the aspect of the deconditioning of our consciousness, and in the aspect of the accessing and cultivating of our erotic energies as well as our awareness of them—are "dangerous." By this, I do not mean that tantric practice is not always safe, sane, and consensual. It is. Rather, its "danger" is the risk undertaken on any authentic spiritual path.

Tantra moves against the mainstream, challenging the precepts of our socialization and acculturation. It unsettles all that are egotism would like to treat as stable, certain, and secure. It shakes the establishment of all our identities, positions and stories, at their foundations. It deconstructs the "narratological imperative" by which we have lived our lives. It challenges every article of faith, every moralizing ideology, and every system of belief—it ensures that our "answers" will all be questioned! It disrupts the tyrannical governance of our egotism's repetition compulsion. And it connects us ever more deeply with our selves and with all the interconnections of the universe that are within us. It opens us to spontaneity, expansiveness, joy, bliss and ecstasy. And thus it frees us profoundly, but it also renders us naked, empty and alone.

Given the vulnerability of spiritual seekers, the possibilities of abuses being committed by egotists who pretend, or who believe themselves to be, tantric experts, cannot be ignored. Emotional upheavals and the breakdown of conventional lifestyles are regular dimensions of spiritual seeking. So anyone who purports to help others move into tantric practice needs to be not only relatively free of his or her own egotism, and thoroughly grounded in the ethicality of tantric practice, but also well versed in addressing the risks undertaken by tantric seekers. Anyone who does not meet these criteria is not a genuine tantric practitioner.

Tantra is frightening or "dangerous" to our egotism for several reasons, and in many respects the confrontation with emotional upheavals and sociocultural marginality are the least of them. As will be discussed in the next chapter, tantric practice is a discovery not only of the erotic energies of our incarnation, but also of the way in which "deathfulness" is inscribed within every cell of our being.

Tantra invests in no past, and promises no future; it allows us to dwell only in the eternal here-and-now of divine presence.

Tantric practices deconstruct and dissolve our egotism, so that we live in the exuberance of erotic energies that are freely and joyously mobile, but inherently empty and, in this sense, "deathful." So we fear tantric practice because

Tantric spirituality threatens our egotism's very establishment, its sense of "reality," and its security in believing itself to be something that is not illusory—something other than a snare and delusion!

Instead of relaxing into tantric practice, we are tenaciously attached to whatever suffering our egotism demands that we experience, as it blocks us from the experience of our erotic exuberance. When people articulate their fear of tantra, they usually speak in three ways.

First, there is the political objection: If we go into tantra, we will drop out of conventional society. There is no resolution to this objection that will satisfy anyone who is attached to the politics of domination, the achievement of a sense of superiority, the acquisition of wealth or power over others, and so forth.

Second, there is the religious objection: If we go into tantra, we will drop all the moralizing ideologies that religions have foisted on the public for centuries, all the anti-sexual rules and regulations by which religion harnessed the populace for the gratification of priests and politicians. This objection—if it is not merely a self-serving rationale for keeping people in synagogues, churches, and mosques—is based on the mistaken assumption that if moralizing ideologies are let go, violence and incestuous abuses will ensue. However, violence—as we have discussed—is actually a consequence of sensual frustration and sexual conflict, and it is these that are the consequences of moralizing ideologies. Moreover, incest—as well as the necessary extensions of it—actually stands against the ethical flow of our erotic energies.

Third, there is a more profound objection: "If I go into tantra, I will fall apart." This objection articulates our egotism's intimation of the truth about tantric practice. Tantra is indeed a confrontation with the deathfulness of our being-in-the-world—a confrontation that is ultimately joyous, blissful and ecstatic.

Tantric practice spells disaster for our egotism. The "me" will indeed fall apart.

Facing the dissolution of our egotism, tantric practice ultimately asks for trust in the erotic energies of the universe. And that the flow of these energies can be trusted is perhaps the most profound discovery that tantra makes about our erotic nature. Namely, tantra demonstrates that our sexual-spiritual energies flow—if they are invited to flow freely—according to an ethical rhythm that is entirely natural. This then is an ethicality flowing without the intervention of judgmentalism.

The spirituality of our erotic potential is naturally ethical, and naturally free of moralizing ideologies.

Thousands of years of tantric spirituality have enabled tantric practitioners to summarize this natural ethicality as if there are "Five Beautiful Intentions" by which we can align our selves with the intentionality of the universe:

- Tantric practice celebrates and reveres all life.
- Tantric practice celebrates and respects the belongingness of things.
- Tantric practice celebrates and honors the sanctity of our passions.

- Tantric practice celebrates and promotes the expression of our truthfulness.
- Tantric practice celebrates and is devoted to the temple of our bodymind.

The knowledge of this intentionality of the universe is the secret of the tantric process of enjoying our relatedness, without being attached to the outcome of our relationships. It is the secret of enjoying being our holiness-becoming-manifest, rather than attaching to outcomes in the business and busyness of our doing. And it is the secret of enjoying, and embracing, the erotic deathfulness of life itself. Through living ethically in meditation—through casting ourselves into life as the adventure of an existential experiment—we find our authentic selves on the tantric path.

These five coordinates of ethicality are essential to tantric practice. And it must be emphasized that each of these intentions follows precisely from the discovery that our erotic energies are the spirituality presented by the interconnectedness of all things throughout what we think of as "time." That is, tantric practice discovers in the natural ethicality of our erotic energies that this sacred sexual-spirituality is our unique experience of the supreme flow of the universe, which is truthfulness of the Sacred Unity of Love.

Endnote: For a more detailed discussion of my appreciation of the "philosophy" of tantric practice, I invite you to consult my *The Way of the BodyPrayerPath* (Philadelphia, PA, Xlibris, 2004).

20

Notes on Tantric Orgasming (and Prānayāma)

Human sexuality is the flow of the lifeforce within and through our bodymind.

"Sex" has been admirably defined as "*S*acred *E*nergy e*X*change." But the notion of "exchange" has to be qualified here.

Sexuality is a spontaneous movement of freeing, opening and expanding of our energies to the universe—a way of aligning, or realigning our selves with the Sacred Unity of Love.

Sexuality is thus much more than what is commonly regarded as *inter-course*—just as intercourse is so much more than genital friction—for sexuality does not require the construction of a relationship in the ordinary "inter-active" sense. Moreover, if sex is an energy "exchange," then the term "exchange" is not to be understood as a reciprocal barter between two entities. In a sense, sexuality is not between (that is, "inter-") anything, because it is the flowing movement that spiritually relates or realigns us with the universe.

Sexuality already permeates and pervades this universe, so we do not generate sexual energy, but we give our selves over to it. This is an important point because, especially as we come to discuss the processes of orgasming, we need to appreciate that erotic energies wave through us ever more powerfully, if we invite them to do so.

We do not generate our erotic energies, or cause them to occur, and we ultimately cannot orchestrate them. The only power of the anti-sexual forces, inscribed by our judgmental mind within our emotional and somatic structures, is that of endeavoring to constrict, curb or curtail the flowing of erotic energy that runs within and through us.

In sum, the anti-sexual force of our egotism's judgmental mind is such that it has a limited power to block, obstruct, or channelize our erotic energies, but it cannot ultimately control them, cannot do without them, does not manufacture them, and cannot prevail over them.

As soon as our judgmental egotism steps aside, or is bidden farewell, we find our sexuality to be as natural to us as breathing. Indeed,

> *Our sensuality and sexuality are well appreciated*
> *if we understand them as the sacredness*
> *of our vibrating,*
> *breathing, touching, moving, dancing,*
> *orgasming erotic energies.*

Our sexuality is indeed polysexual, which is why so many mystics have said that we carry the entire universe in our bodymind.

Every thought, every feeling, every sensation, everything that seems to us to be benign, as well as everything that seems to us to be malign, and everything that has ever happened in the universe—past, present, and future—are, in a certain profound sense, inscribed in, or deeply connected with, each moment of our erotic experience. And certainly, in a more mundane sense, our polysexuality means that every sensual and sexual act that has ever afforded pleasure to any human being is potentially within our repertoire of erotic desires.

We are capable of a wide range of pleasures, and our erotic energies are not naturally sequestered into packages—packages that assume that we are this orientation but not that, we like this part of the body pleasured but not that, and so forth. Such packaging is a testimony to the anti-sexual forces of our judgmental mind. It is indicative of suppression and repression. Those pleasures we know have survived our traumatization, and those we do not know have succumbed to these processes of censorship within us. In this sense, our individual sexuality is profusely polysexual, all human sexuality is one, and all the phenomena of the universe are deeply interconnected.

An authentic spiritual practice is one that opens us to the expression of our sensual and sexual desires, as we come to recognize the sacred nature of this erotic potential.

Spiritual work and play requires
that we surrender our egotism to the dancing of the universe.
We celebrate our erotic nature
by inviting the sacred energies of the universe
to dance within us and through us.
Our sexuality is essentially the movement of these energies.

Breathing, touching and dancing all facilitate the mobilization of these energies within us, and orgasming is the paradigm, the epitome and the pinnacle, of this mobilization.

Orgasming is an essentially spiritual process—abolishing all judgmentalism, it is the zenith of what I call both prayerful sex and sexual prayer. Orgasming is the kinesis of erotic energies that opens and expands the resources of our bodymind, aligning or realigning us with the spiritual timespace of the universe. In a sense, although orgasming begins with our self-pleasuring, we never orgasm alone, for orgasming testifies to the interconnectedness of the entire universe. And, of course, sharing these mysteries creates spiritually profound connections. It is the most profound spiritual privilege to experience orgasmic pleasure in the presence of another person—and it is a profound spiritual privilege to have the honor of facilitating another person into their orgasming. Orgasming involves a mysterious movement of sexual-spiritual energies, and we know the truthfulness of this from deep within our selves.

*Our sensuality and our sexuality
are the kinesis of erotic energies within and through our bodymind.
Orgasming is the pinnacle and epitome of this momentum,
and it is the spiritually essential process that
aligns or realigns our erotic energies with the entire universe.
Orgasmic movements are the essence
of prayerful sex and sexual prayer.*

As mentioned earlier, we know that there are special mysteries associated with the pleasures of orgasming. These mysteries have, through the ages, prompted men and women to appreciate copulation as prayer—as a modality of worship by which the divine may be accessed. This is why sacred festivities all over the world have often involved orgiastic sexual couplings, freed from the strictures of sociocultural conventions and expectations. These mysteries are central to the sanctity of worshipping the images of the Goddess, and of understanding orgasmic ecstasy as the pinnacle of such worship. Orgasming is the ultimate human expression of celebration and gratitude for life.

All sensual and sexual pleasuring celebrates the interconnectedness of the universe—and orgasming illuminates the spiritual significance of this interconnectedness in which we each participate. Sexuality not only reconnects us within our selves, it reconnects us with others, and it expresses the integrality of earth and heaven. From our initial experiments with self-pleasuring, we reach out to others and to the universe. We take the spiritual energies that arise within us and return them to the universe, in acts that connect our selves with others around us, both friends and strangers. In this sense, all erotic connections are prayerful.

Orgasming is the supreme gift of our sexual energies, an abundantly overflowing kinesis, an exuberance of ecstatic pleasures, and the vibrational alignment of heaven and earth.

However—in answering the question, *What is an "orgasm"?*—we are often deceived into thinking of orgasming as something other than an essentially spiritual momentum. Indeed, the pivotal illusion or delusion perpetuated by the egotism of our chattering minds is that orgasming is merely a bodily state engineered by our egotism's activities. By "pivotal" I mean that it is crucial or foundational because, without this illusion or delusion, our egotism would shatter into our enlightening. This specific notion is prototypical of the general deludedness by which our egotism operates, namely that the presencing of death-in-life could be averted by the compulsive and repetitive recitation of identities, positions, and stories.

This is the basis of the illusions and delusions in which we ordinarily live. Our egotism likes to think that it is substantial, is king of its domain, and could perhaps live forever. So it gives credence to all the productions of our narratological imperative—the compulsively repetitious production of identities, positions and stories, by which our egotism embellishes itself. This incessant productivity keeps us from realizing that the only reality is Love, and allows our egotism to believe that, by means of its chattering judgmentalism, it could be master of all. This is the core of its illusory and deluded condition.

Contrary to this mandate, orgasming not only presents the deathfulness of life itself, it entails the relinquishing of our egotism's ambition of mastery. This is why, when it comes to orgasming, our chattering mind is most insistent on its efforts to appear able to cause and control the very streaming of sexual-spiritual energies that sweeps away its prerogatives—and this fearfulness of our egotism is why so many of us fail to experience orgasmic pleasures or experience an "orgasm" that is severely diminished.

Let us now elucidate further some of the spiritual significance of these rippling pulsations of energy that can sweep through and throughout the bodymind. Three aspects of orgasming need to be noted, before we can turn to a discussion of orgasming in tantric practice.

1) Orgasming is dependent neither on genital sensation in particular, nor even on gross physical stimulation in general. Rather, an orgasm is simply a pleasurable rippling of subtle energies, somewhat or entirely unimpeded by the blockages and obstructions that our judgmental mind constructs emotionally and psychosomatically.

Orgasming occurs in very diverse ways—perhaps as diverse as our individuality. When we reflect on our experiences of orgasming, we usually arrive at the perception that, most of the time, "having an orgasm" is facilitated or initiated by sensual arousal of specific areas of the body. Typically, most of us consider genital stimulation to be the "royal road" to orgasming. In this, our reflections are partial and misleading. As has already been mentioned, the stimulation of any and every bodily zone may invite orgasmic responsiveness. Orgasming does not have to be genitally instigated, nor genitally localized.

Indeed, although this may be less frequent, orgasming does not have to involve the genitals at all. For example, we know that men and women who are genitally insensate (for instance, due to spinal cord injury), or men and women whose genitals have been accidentally or ritually excised (as, for instance, with the victims of genital mutilation practices), frequently develop exquisite "hypersensitivities" in non-genital zones, and these areas may then be aroused to invite orgasmic responsiveness.

Moreover, we know that those of us with intact, sensate genitals (and thus without these compensatory hypersensitivities) can also develop a similar orgasmic responsiveness through stimulation of other bodily zones such as our necks, feet, hands, breasts, limbs and torso.

Finally, we know that orgasming may occur without any sensual stimulation of our bodies at all. For example, it may sometimes occur in a manner that appears facilitated or initiated solely by our "unconscious minds." Especially during sleep—when our egotism somewhat relinquishes its delusions of mastery—orgasming may happen with only the concurrence of our free-flowing imaginative creativity. Visualizations—as well as sounds and other sensual experiences—can invite the movement of our erotic energies. Thus, if we are open to it, orgasming can occur without even the appearance of intentional or conscious elicitation and, as we will soon see, orgasming is actually a capacity of the "unconscious" bodymind—a capacity to which egotism's only real contribution is to allow itself to cease its obstructionism.

2) The physical characteristics of orgasming usually involve the conjunction and coordination of cardiovascular, neuromuscular, and physiochemical phenomena. Scientifically, we know that the special responsiveness of orgasming requires cortical triggering, and cooperation of both "peripheral" and "central" aspects of our neuronal and hormonal systems. However, let us emphasize again that this involvement of central and cortical functions does *not* imply that orgasming is somehow under our "mind's control," or ever really could be.

Physically, the responsiveness of orgasming usually entails the complex interplay of several bodily systems. For example, cardiovascular changes entail not only the suffusion of vasocongestive tissues, but also alterations in heart activity and respiration. Neuromuscular changes involve complex signaling between different neuronal systems, as well as the dramatic pulsations and involuntary spasming of muscle groups, not only of the genitals, but also throughout the entire bodymind. Physiochemical changes include not only alterations in the levels of hormones, and neurotransmitters, including the cortical release of endorphins and other biochemicals into the bloodstream. These contribute to the "altered states of consciousness" that scientific research has shown to be an essential characteristic of full-bodied orgasming.

So we can describe orgasming medically as a "spiking" in about a dozen or so observable physical variables. These include such phenomena as the vasocongestive engorgement of genitals and nipples, blood pressure, heart rate, skin temperature, skin coloration, electrodermal activity, respiratory rate and intensity, pupil dilation, muscular contractions throughout the body, releasing of various hormones, neurotransmitters and endorphins, as well as altered states of consciousness. However, it would be a serious mistake to imagine that this is what orgasming is "really" about—or that these phenomena are of primary initiatory significance.

3) Powerfully inherent to the processes of orgasming are rippling or rocketing movements of what we are calling the subtle energies of the bodymind. We have referred to these energies as "subtle" because they are liminal—being both hyperphysical and hypophysical—and not because they lack power. Rather, they are of primary significance, and of great power.

Indeed, we have referred to them as the lifeforce itself—which is called *prāna* or *kundalini* in tantric teachings. These erotic energies are typically not directly observable, are not readily measurable (except sometimes in their inferred effects), and are not tightly concordant with the anatomical and functional structures and systems of the body as described by allopathic medical science.

Such energies are less understood in western systems of medicine—perhaps other than psychoanalysis—than in eastern sciences and, as is well known, the latter are often disparagingly referred to as "mystical" by western science. However, as we have discussed in the previous chapter, almost every known culture in human history has had some way of alluding to these subtle energy systems. Thus,

> *Orgasming is a movement of subtle energies,*
> *rippling, pulsating, undulating, quivering, rolling,*
> *vibrating through our entire bodymind, or some portion of it.*
> *Orgasming is any spontaneous, opening*
> *and expansive movement of erotic energies.*
> *If we are open to our orgasmic potential,*
> *we cannot mislead ourselves into thinking that we*
> *"have an orgasm," rather we give ourselves over to the*
> *momentum of our orgasmic energies.*

Sensual or sexual engagement invites our erotic energies into their dancing. Touching, whether by a warm breeze, by our self or by our partners, stirs the subtle energies of the bodymind from the entire skin surface and from our "roots" in the soles of our feet, through the rectum, perineum, and genitals, as well as from other special "portals" such as our mouth, eyes, ears, and hands.

As touching moves into orgasming, the bodymind opens up to rippling—or rocketing—undulations of these subtle energies often from their pelvic "roots" up through the stomach, heart, throat, and through the crown of our heads.

As is now quite well known, in tantra, these marker locations are often called "chakras." To aid our discussion of orgasming, it is helpful to know that chakras are like wheels or vortices of energy, and that the seven major chakras of our bodymind are:

"Sahasrāra"	*Crown* (Top of Head)—*Freedom of Spirit or Ecstasy*
	↑↓
	↑↓
"Ãjnã"	*Third Eye* (Forehead)—*Vision*
	↑↓
	↑↓
"Vishuddha"	*Throat*—*Truth or Speaking-Out*
	↑↓
	↑↓
"Anāhata"	*Heart*—*Caring*
	↑↓
	↑↓
"Manipura"	*Solar Plexus* (Navel)—*Power*
	↑↓
	↑↓
"Svādhishthana"	*Pelvic* (Lower Navel)—*Flow*
	↑↓
	↑↓
"Mulādhāra"	*Root* (Genitals/Perineum/Anus)—*Passion*

There are also chakras in the hands and feet.

Orgasming does not have to move from root to crown, although this is rather typical—and, in tantric teachings, the momentum of *kundalini* energy upwards, quivering and shooting from the root, through the other chakras, and out through the crown, is often emphasized.

Moreover, orgasming does not have to involve all the chakras. For example, sometimes orgasmic movements can proceed from the root to the solar plexus and then, so to speak, become stuck there. Moreover, limited rippling motions of energy—like a shiver, an undulation or pulsation of some erotic energy, along a particular channel of the bodymind—are often experienced. Indeed, orgasming can occur along any of the thousands of *nadis* or channels that run throughout the bodymind.

For example, in Chapter Ten, I mentioned a friend who regularly experiences full-bodied orgasming through a light stroking under her armpits. This is a quite common experience, although in most individuals it does not achieve such a full-bodied effect. With many of us, such a stroking may only evoke a limited orgasmic rippling between our solar plexus and our throat (or we may be almost entirely blocked and non-responsive in this area).

In a discussion such as this, it can be helpful to distinguish between so-called "peak" and "valley" orgasms. The terminology can be misleading, however, since "valley" orgasming, which is often cultivated in tantric spiritual practice, is a prolonged "multi-orgasmic" process that reaches greater heights of power and intensity than the "peaks" that are commonly experienced when individuals report that they have "had an orgasm." That is, the valleys are actually higher than the peaks.

Other ways to discuss this distinction might be to describe the "pre-tantric" peak climax, associated with fucking, versus the tantric orgasming, valley climax or multi-orgasmic climaxing, associated with sacred lovemaking (the way I am wording this is not meant to imply that fucking cannot be very affectionate or "loving").

Although I do not wish to overemphasize this distinction—and do not wish to make it too "black and white"—there are some important issues here that deserve elaboration. So I will use this distinction merely as a way of clarifying these issues.

➢ *"Pre-tantric" Climaxing.* Let me not be misunderstood, peak orgasms are wonderful. They are what most people achieve when they fuck. They last a few moments and are pleasurably delicious. They are usually emotionally beneficial and physically relaxing, and they involve only a transient loss of consciousness—a physiochemically induced "blanking out," which is usually so brief that the individual does not even realize that there has been any disruption to his or her sense of conscious control. For some, such a climactic peak is reachable within minutes. For others, reaching such a climax may require a lot of stimulation, as well as quite a bit of time and effort. In most instances, the stimulation involved is almost entirely genital. Fucking can be a magnificent experience but, once its climax arrives, it is brief from beginning to end.

With men, pre-tantric climaxing is often almost non-orgasmic because, tragically, many men are so fearful of their erotic energy that they come to know only how to ejaculate; they almost never experience full-bodied orgasming. What such men call "orgasm" is mostly a localized spurting mechanism, in which several groups of muscles—notably the bulbospongiosus and ischiocavernosus group—rhythmically contract causing the propulsion of ejaculate out of the urethra. Many men are so frightened of a full-bodied orgasmic released—a "total orgasm" that would sweep through their entire bodymind—that their climactic experience is limited to this ejaculation.

Although this is done unconsciously, such men usually restrict their "orgasm" by quickening and tightening their thoracic breathing, which effectively holds any accumulation of energy down in the pelvis. These men also typically make little or no spontaneous sound during their arousal, and tend to hold their spinal column stiffly—limiting their movement during sex to whatever is necessary for penile stimulation—and usually moving even their hips only minimally. In short, such men clench their flow, power, heart, and throat chakras, in order to keep their "orgasm" localized in their genitals and their pelvic area.

What many men call "orgasm" is in fact merely an ejaculation, a "squirt-squirt" phenomenon of releasing that affects only the limited—genital—zone of their body, and that may well be pleasurable, but is ultimately not very gratifying. Sadly, the fearful chattering mind is so determined to hold onto its illusion and delusion of control over the sexual event that the energies generated through the root chakra never arrive in the heart: "Sex" can easily become tragically divorced from the passions of open-heartedness.

With women, pre-tantric climaxing often requires substantial amounts of stimulation and, when the climax occurs, it is experienced as a brief rocketing spasm that comes up from the genitals through the body to complete itself somewhere around the throat or third-eye chakras. As is well known, many women close themselves off even to the experience of this brief rocketing "peak." Such women are either so traumatized that they have become genitally numbed, or they allow themselves to accumulate energy in their pelvis only to push it down into their hips and legs. Many women are so frightened of a full-bodied orgasmic release—a "total orgasm" that would sweep through their entire bodymind—that their climactic experience is either aborted entirely or limited to this rocketing spasm.

Although this is done unconsciously, such women usually restrict their orgasm by quickening and tightening their breathing, limiting it to short sharp breaths in the thoracic cavity (or periodically holding their breath altogether). This effectively holds any accumulation of energy down in the pelvis. Such women also typically control whatever sounds they make during their arousal, often clenching their jaw, sometimes along with the abdominal musculature surrounding their flow and power chakras—the spinal column is correspondingly stiff, and movement is often effectively limited to a grinding of the pelvis and hips.

With these women, it is as if they hold themselves so tightly—mostly by unconscious manipulation of their breathing, as well as their sound and their movement—that they require huge amounts of stimulation. They often are sure that they need a particular type of very hard and intense stimulation, whether of the vulva or the vagina (or, with some women, the anus). For example, their orgasm appears to depend on an almost violent stimulation around the clitoral glans, or to depend on their manipulation of a mechanical device like a vibrator.

Such women need this heavy stimulation to continue until the accumulation of energy in the root chakra is so great that it bursts through their clenched and contracted flow, root, heart and throat chakras, like a sudden electric shock. This "electric shock" is brief, but often intensely pleasurable, bringing with it only a brief interruption in their illusory or deluded sense of conscious control, and often evoking an eruption of previously suppressed or repressed emotion—whether joyful, sad, tearful, or merely soft and exhausted. These women often think of themselves as unafraid of orgasming (indeed, in their minds, they want to "have an orgasm"), but their unconsciously-held blockages in the potential flow of energy ensures that their orgasm is limited, pleasurable but of short-duration, and unlikely to sweep them away.

When our egotism tries to control our sensual and sexual energies—when, for example, it tries to get us to be goal-oriented about "getting to ejaculation" or "having an orgasm"—we can be sure that the full spiritual experience of our erotic potential is being thwarted. The thrills of sexification are being substituted for the profundity of our fullest and most ecstatic sexual experiencing. With both men and women, whenever we tell ourselves that we are going to "have an orgasm"—by manipulating the stimulation our genitals receive, as well as the fantasies that are entertained in our consciousness—what we are really doing is ensuring that we do not surrender ourselves to the fullness of our orgasmic potential.

➤ *Tantric Orgasming.* So what is "the fullness of our orgasmic potential"? The brief peaking climaxes that I have just described as "pre-tantric" are like a bargain struck between our fearful chattering mind and the call of our orgasmic pleasuring.

The "bargain" is as follows. A climax will be reached, but only in a limited way, such that our judgmental egotism can believe in its cherished illusion and delusion that it is sovereign in its governance of our body and mind.

Such a bargain is struck because our egotism cannot withstand tantric orgasming, in which the emotional blockages and somatic obstructions that have been constructed by our judgmental mind are swept away in the flowing intensity of our pleasuring. The fullness of our orgasmic potential blows away our egotism's hollow boast that it is an executive agency successfully in charge of our body and our mind.

"Tantra" is a Sanskrit word meaning to weave and reweave the energies of our lifeforce. Tantric practice, as I introduced it in Chapters Fifteen and Nineteen, is devoted to freeing the sexual-spiritual energies of our embodiment, the lifeforce of our *prāna*. The practices of *prānayāma* teach us how to invite the mobility of these energies and how to cultivate our awareness of their movements.

Freeing—that is, weaving and reweaving, or aligning and realigning—our sexual-spiritual energies has two aspects. It implies both a momentum of deconditioning in which our blockages or obstructions are deconstructed or dissolved, and a momentum in which we access or invite the free-flow of our erotic energies and cultivate our awareness of the movement of these energies.

Inviting the free-flow of our erotic energies is sometimes called the "feminine" or *Shakti* aspect of this practice, whereas the cultivation of awareness of these energies is called the "masculine" or *Shiva* aspect.

The dissolution of our egotism and the cultivation of spiritual awareness—which, as I indicated previously, is a mode of experiencing life that is radically different from the construction of discriminative judgments—are meditative practices.

> *In tantric practice, as we release our discriminative judgmentalism, and as our suppressive and repressive egotism recedes, we discover that the "feminine" Shakti and the "masculine" Shiva both dwell within the potential of every human bodymind.*

Living in meditation, we increasingly let go our attachment to identities, positions, and stories, and we find within each of us potentials for experience of which we were previously unaware. Instead of attaching our selves to narratological illusions and delusions—for example, that we are "this" but not "that"—we come instead to align our selves with the Beloved that is within us, our Compassionate Witness. We free our selves from the repetition compulsion that governs our chattering mind's incessant productivity—we free our selves from our egotism's fearful preoccupations with past and future. In meditation, we fall out of judgmentalism, and into the deathful presence of our being-in-the-world along with the dissolution of our egotism. We fall into the Sacred Unity of Love.

Tantra makes our sensual and sexual activity meditative. This meditation may simply involve breathing, or dancing or pleasuring our selves with touch, or vibrating our entire bodymind into our orgasmic bliss. With tantric practice—whether solo or partnered—our "feminine" dances with our "masculine," and vice versa. Whatever has been suppressed or repressed within us becomes embraced and invited into the dancing of our erotic energies. All these engagements with our erotic nature are to be performed meditatively—that is, with spiritual discernment and awareness.

Sacred sex, or even more simply the visualization of sacred sex, is an incredible tantric practice that moves our erotic energies. Indeed, the orgasmic rippling of these subtle energies is the most powerful way to worship, to realign our bodymind with the spirituality of all that is and is not, as well as to evaporate our egotistic attachment to our selves.

Tantric orgasming is described as a "valley" orgasm although actually it is a prolonged, powerful peak experience that is multi-orgasmic. It is an experience in which our erotic energies—*prāna* or *kundalini*—potentially flow up from our root chakra, through our flow, power, heart, throat, and third-eye chakras, to blossom and be released to the universe through our crown.

This path of the kundalini, from root to crown—which western pagans sometimes call "star-tide"—is accessible to most people's awareness, by breathing, by sensual and sexual stimulation, or by visualizations. It is an orgasmic directionality that promotes creativity and sensitivity—not least because it aligns and unites our genitals, our passion or capacity for flow, our power, our heart, our voice and our insightful awareness. It also leads to magnificent, blossoming intensifications of our orgasmic experiencing—our capacity to live in joy, bliss and ecstasy.

Sometimes in tantric practice, the movement of prāna in the reverse direction, down from the crown to the root chakra—which western pagans sometimes call "earth-tide"—is invited by breathing or visualization. Some people find this direction slightly more challenging to access in their awareness. Yet it promotes our sense of serenity—our capacity to live in compassion, appreciation and grace. It is an orgasmic movement of energy—so to speak, from heaven to earth, rather than earth to heaven—but it is not the direction that most of us know as "orgasm," so we will not address it further in this discussion.

Working and playing with our orgasming in tantric practice learning to become aware of the movement of our erotic energies—*prāna* or *kundalini*—upwards from the genitals to the crown, and so to become fluidly multi-orgasmic is a powerful method of spiritual and emotional healing. As we enter this "workplay," we encounter obstructions in various of our chakras. These blocks or obstructions correspond to the traumatization of our erotic potential. They are locations at which the chattering mind of our judgmental egotism is fearfully holding on tight, and managing to block or stifle the kinesis of our erotic energies, the free-flow of our lifeforce or *prāna*. They are locations at which we have become contracted, closed down and controlled—rather than spontaneous, open, expansive and free.

Since there are almost as many ways that individuals tend to resist their orgasmic potential as there are individuals, I am hesitant to make generalizations. However, through my work as a sex therapist and tantric facilitator, as well as in my personal life, I have frequently had the privilege of working and playing with orgasmic responsiveness or non-responsiveness. I have watched what occurs when energies are stirred in the pelvis, and I have listened to many accounts of this experience. So perhaps it will be helpful if I mention three quite common patterns, which I have observed directly, or heard described, in hundreds of individuals.

- Energies are stirred in the root chakra and move up to the power chakra, where they are effectively strangulated. This means, so to speak, that the heart chakra is kept relatively "out of play." Often energy also has to be pushed down into the legs where it also becomes stuck. This pattern is frequently found in men; sadly, it is as if, for many men, the genitals are no longer connected with the heart.
- Energies are stirred in the root chakra and move up to the heart chakra, as if bypassing the power chakra, which then remains relatively "out of play." However, the energies become jammed at the throat chakra. Often they also have to be pushed down into the legs. This pattern is frequently found in women; sadly, it is as if, for many women, they cannot take responsibility for their power and their voice.

- Energies are stirred in the root chakra and move relatively freely through the torso, only to be stifled somewhere between the throat and the third-eye chakras. These individuals frequently report congestion in their cortex, even headaches, before or after they have "had an orgasm."

> *Becoming aware of blocks and obstructions*
> *in the free-flow of our erotic energies*
> *—becoming aware of our emotional defenses*
> *and our somatic constrictions—*
> *and then practicing breathing into them,*
> *is itself healing.*
> *Awareness frees us,*
> *and releases orgasmic movement*
> *where it was previously closed, contained or curtailed.*

For most individuals, the liberation of our orgasmic potential takes practice, and practice, and practice. Practice is, after all, what our spiritual path comprises.

By now it is evident, that the liberating of our orgasmic potential, the shift from "pre-tantric" to tantric orgasming, always involves some combination of five vital factors:

- ❖ *Focusing our awareness on the vibrations within us,*
- ❖ *Breathing (and all the essential practices of prānayāma),*
- ❖ *Moving or dancing,*
- ❖ *Sounding out our vibrations,*
- ❖ *Visualization of the movement of our energies.*

In addition to these general methods, the tantric practice of meditation has traditionally also used:

— *Mantra,* the recitation of special sounds, which are endowed with energetic power;

— *Mudrā,* the adoption of bodily postures or gestures, which, like the *āsanas* of hatha yoga, promote movements of energy and the awareness of these movements;
— *Mandala,* the contemplation of pictorial presentations of cosmic forces and deities, which evoke energetic transformations or transmutations.

In tantra, as in sex therapy, when we workplay on enhancing our orgasmic capacity, we usually begin practicing solo and later transition to partnered sharing. As we become aware of blocks in the flow of our erotic energies—that is, either of obstructions that are usually located at various chakras, or of mental resistances such as distractibility, intrusive judgments, and so on—we bring our awareness to rest on these phenomena. We breathe into the obstructions, and we also breathe to release our attachment to any intrusive thoughts, goal-oriented formulations or judgments.

Letting-go of goals is an especially significant aspect of spiritual practice—including goals to become spiritually adept or enlightened, and goals to experience orgasmic joy, bliss and ecstasy.

Goals are a sneaky means by which our egotism attempts to take over our spiritual practice for its own purposes. By contrast, the mobilization of our sexual-spiritual energies requires an "attitude" of open invitation—a mode of mindful awareness that is contrary to the interests of our chattering mind.

Sexual-spiritual practice requires an attitude that focuses, in a relaxed way, on process, pleasure, and playfulness. Tantric practice is a matter of letting our selves fall into the universe's supreme dance.

As we encounter obstacles, hindrances, resistances, blocks and obstructions, we breathe into them, moving our body as fluidly and flexible as possible—by dancing, or by bringing our selves into some other kind of movement, that opens and expands the areas related to the chakra in which the blockage appears to be occurring. We sound out whatever vibrations occur in relation to the movement of our erotic energies and the chakras in which they may be closed, contained or curtailed. And finally, we visualize the flow of energy within and through our embodiment.

Some tantric teachings offer more complex modes of visualization that free us spiritually without directly involving the chakras, but since these methods are not directly concerned with our orgasmic potential, at least in the usual sense of this term, we will not discuss them further.

Instead, we need to note five features of tantric practice and the workplay that shifts us into tantric orgasming.

1) *Tantric practice embraces "good" and "bad."* The tantric "attitude"—for lack of a better way to express this—is not to oppose the blocks we find within our selves, but rather to embrace and dissolve them. Tantra shows us that to fight against our resistances is simply to establish a more powerful and more cunning mode of resistance. Tantra practices *ahimsa*—the way of Love—embracing the "bad" as well as the "good," and appreciating both aspects as inherent to the divine play of the universe's energies.

However, to embrace our own resistances does not mean that we continue to be attached to them, but rather to trust that our resistances will evaporate—just as eventually the entire edifice of our egotism will dissolve—as our breathing into them invites their dissolution.

> *Tantric practice says "Yes!"*
> *to every "No" that is encountered within us,*
> *and in this way transmutes the "No" of resistance*
> *into a celebration of the "Yes!" to life itself.*

Tantric practice frees us from the constraints of our egotism's attachment to its own judgmentalism. In this sense, tantric teaching acceptingly makes no distinction between "good" and "bad," but celebrates all that *is*—and, in this celebration, that breathes the lifeforce into all things, a profound healing becomes manifest.

2) *Tantric practice embraces the deathfulness of life itself.* The ultimate reason why we allow our selves only the pleasures of a limited, "pre-tantric," orgasmic experience is because fuller tantric orgasming blows away the edifice of our egotism, erasing the boundaries between "me" and the entire universe of life itself. This is what is meant when we refer to the "altered states of consciousness" that accompany orgasming, and to the transcendent experiences of joy, bliss and ecstasy. These experiences imply the "loss" of our egotistic consciousness, of which our chattering mind is terrified. From the standpoint of our egotism, orgasm confronts us with the abyss.

> *Tantric practice appreciates the deathfulness*
> *that inheres to the liveliness of life itself,*
> *and in this way embraces the emptiness of all that is and is not,*
> *the pure light of Love that suffuses the universe.*

Orgasming casts us into this void, the emptiness of all that is and is not. It is a surrendering to the Sacred Unity of Love, and in this experience we come mystically to know the inherency of deathfulness in life itself—the way in which our erotic energy both is and is not, and neither is nor is not.

3) *Tantric practice enlightens consciousness.* I have already emphasized the radical distinction between spiritual awareness and the productions of our judgmental mind—the radical difference between the spiritual discernment of awareness and the discriminations of judgmentalism. In this respect, it is interesting to note how tantric practice approaches the productions of this mind that are most about our sexuality—namely, our fantasies.

Tantra finds fantasy always to have a double-edge. On the one side, fantasies excite us and can bring us closer to the arousal of energies that is involved in orgasming. Individuals who have "peak" orgasms, for example, can often bring themselves from a plateau state of arousal into an orgasmic release by thinking about a favorite fantasy. On the other side, this use of fantasies during sexual play ensures that the orgasm experienced will be brief and limited. It will be a "pre-tantric" peak experience, and not the fuller orgasming of which our erotic potential is capable.

That is, fantasies are a mechanism by which our chattering mind can make concessions to our erotic desire, even while attempting to rein in the fullness of our sensual and sexual expression.

In the erotic methods of tantra, these productions of our egotism gradually drop away, our consciousness becomes clearer, and our awareness rests on the subtleties of vibrational movements within our bodymind.

Often, this focus of our awareness of energy movements is initially approached by allowing our attention to rest, with equanimity, on the momentum of our breathing, and then to scan our embodiment for other streams of energy that may be rippling and pulsing as our desire intensifies.

In moving from "pre-tantric" to tantric orgasming, individuals regularly find that they need less and less stimulation to achieve greater and greater orgasmic pleasure. For example, I have known several women, who had been "vibrator dependent" for their peak climaxing, but who, within a matter of a few months of tantric practice, became multi-orgasmic when their lover simply breathed gently on their vulva. Tantra clears consciousness so that we may become aware and responsive to just the slightest breath.

Tantric practice clears our consciousness by quieting our chattering mind, and in this way opens our entire bodymind to the pure light of Love.

Tantric practice is enlightening—it awakens us to Holy Spirit that courses, quakes and quivers, within, through and all around our bodymind. Through tantric practice, our consciousness becomes authentic, the chattering of our judgmental egotism subsides, and our mind becomes clear, silent, and luminous—expressing all the glories of this universe.

4) *Tantric practice celebrates divine presence.* As becomes clear, tantra knows Holy Spirit to be the divinity of the erotic energies that pulsate and undulate through the conduit of our embodiment. Our sexuality and our spirituality are one-and-the-same, and "God" is presence. The pasts and futures—or "past-futures"—that are inscribed in our representational mind, and that preoccupy our judgmental chatter, are entirely impertinent. The Sacred Unity of Love is entirely here-and-now. Abolishing discriminative judgmentalism, tantric practice delights in inviting not only the divine feminine to express herself in every woman, but also the divine masculine, and it also delights in inviting not only the divine masculine to express himself in every man, but also the divine feminine.

> *Tantric practice releases us from the past and the future,*
> *through cultivating our awareness of the here-and-now,*
> *and in this way finds that all the energies of our humanity*
> *are in each one of us.*

As suppression and repression is relinquished, the presence of all energies is found in every being, and all energies—including feminine and masculine—are to be revered as expressions of divine presence.

5) *Tantric practice heals our alienated being-in-the-world.* Through tantric practice we access our divinity, and we heal the alienation of our erotic energies from our sense of who

we really are. The workplay with our erotic energy that is involved in all tantric methods is capable of mystically transmuting the hostility that is inherent in all our blocks, obstructions, resistances, defenses and hindrances, into the free-flow of Love. Tantra is sexual healing! Its methods demonstrate that pleasure heals, that passions can always be turned into a power for healing, and that orgasming reverses the traumatizations that we have suffered.

> *Tantric practice reunites us with our divinity,*
> *by familiarizing us with our Beloved,*
> *the Compassionate Witness that is within,*
> *and in this way heals us, freeing us*
> *from our compulsions, our addictions, and our suffering.*

With tantric orgasming, excitement transmutes into joy, arousal transmutes into bliss, and consciousness shifts out of egotism's control and into its spiritual opening, expansiveness and ecstasy. Orgasming dissolves the walls that our chattering mind constructs between self and other, as waves of subtle energies flow more freely not only within the bodymind but also from the universe through the bodymind. This is why we understand tantric orgasming to be the vibrational alignment of heaven and earth, a regrounding or regenerating of our spirit, and the quintessential timespace of health, healing, and happiness.

Finally, lest this discussion has seemed too idealizing or abstract, I will mention some of my own experiences on the tantric path. My orgasming—like my meditative practice in general—varies from day to day.

My orgasming has changed noticeably with my aging, and as I have gone further on my sexual-spiritual path. Sometimes it has involved warm rippling sensations through my body, sometimes there has been a rocketing intensity with quaking spastic movements along my spine and through my limbs.

These spastic movements correspond to bursts of subtle energies moving along the body's axis. They trigger altered conditions of consciousness, and are called *kriyas* in the ancient tantric teachings. Sometimes with orgasming I feel a wonderful tingling sensation in the palms of my hands, the soles of my feet, and areas in between—a streaming of movement between and through these extremities, manifesting the connectedness of "me" and all that is around. I understand this to be my experiencing of a magnificent extrusion and intrusion of energies through these portals.

Sometimes, a lifting or opening sensation is experienced at the crown of my head, and this is similar to the lightening of consciousness achieved in some other types of meditation practice. Sometimes with orgasming I have "lost consciousness" and passed out entirely. This occurred more when I was younger and my psychological immaturity was such that I had difficulty tolerating, and maintaining awareness through, the shifting of consciousness out of my egotism's control. Always with orgasming there is this shifting of consciousness, the surrendering of egotism's illusions and delusions of control, and the blissful experiencing of a suffusive timespace with a celestial sense of floating, merging, dancing unrestrainedly in the universe.

Today, I often orgasm very completely throughout my bodymind. But this is, I believe, the result of a significant and lengthy journey of spiritual development. Like most men, I used to think that orgasming meant ejaculating. Now I know that orgasming is much more than the procedure of "squeezing off" an ejaculation—however delightful and relieving the latter procedure may be. And orgasming is also much more than the excitement of a "quick fuck"—however much a delicious celebration of life that such an event may be. Indeed, orgasming often occurs without ejaculation, and can occur without erection, through touching of non-genital areas of my skin surface.

Sexual Health and Erotic Freedom

The journey of expanding and intensifying my orgasmic potential has involved at least a threefold set of developments:

- The spiritual process of allowing my chattering mind to still itself, or to hold itself in abeyance. I have personally found the regular practice of what is called *vipassanā* meditation enormously helpful in inviting my Compassionate Witness into my life, and detaching my self from the productions of my chattering mind.
- The spiritual process of training myself to become able to set-aside ejaculation and to let-go of my goal-oriented thoughts about the processes of pleasure. Sensual and sexual activity, whether solo or shared, has become an endless playful process of pleasuring, rather than an event laden with expectations about its endpoint.
- The spiritual process of becoming aware, without judgment, of the vibrations of my entire bodymind. I have personally found the regular practice of dancing wildly, of allowing myself to sound out whatever noises come to me, and of the methods of *prānayāma,* or "conscious breathing," enormously helpful in allowing myself to "get out of my head" and into my heart, my genitals, and my entire bodymind.

Everyone's tantric path is different. It could not be otherwise. Tantra is not a doctrine and whatever combination of methods and practices suits one individual may not suit another. It is a path on which, as much as erotic sharing may be a major aspect of its methods and practices, one ultimately dances alone, connected to the supreme flow of the universe which is that of the truthfulness of Love. This is, what I call, the *bodyprayerpath.*

I am profoundly grateful for all these processes. Almost thirty-five years ago I was down-and-out, and suffering from chronic and severe depression. Today, I feel myself to be one of the happiest of men. I am neither powerful nor wealthy, but I know about that Love, which is not bound to the oppressive attachments of conventional relationship, but which is the Sacred Unity that embraces all of us.

While I am grateful for my path, I do not want to idealize myself or depict myself as exceptional. Whatever progress I may have made, in the course of my journey along this tantric path, it still feels as though it disappears with some regularity. On some days, I feel spiritually, sexually and orgasmically, nothing and nowhere. On these days, I try not to allow my egotism to evaluate this as a "setback," to condemn myself, or to convince me that the path is anything other than the most precious aspect of my life. I remind myself that I wish only to live in compassion, appreciation, and grace, and that truthfully the universe is abundant in its potential to live life in Love.

At the height of tantric experience, tantric practice allows us mystically to know the way the energies within our bodymind actually move through us, rather than being generated by us, and are integral to the universe's flow of energies.

Self-pleasuring opens us to the spirituality of the universe, and shared-pleasuring involves not only a merging of energies with our partners but also the permeation of all participants with the universe's blissful timespace.

With tantric practice,
we come to know mystically
that our spiritual-sexual energies are transpersonal,
in that they run within and through us,
connecting us to the entire universe,
and upsetting our egotistic sense of autonomy and grandeur
in all our identities, positions, and stories.

For this reason, although orgasming is blissful, it is frightening to our chattering mind because if requires egotism's surrender. We experience how self-pleasuring is never merely personal, and how shared-pleasuring is never merely interpersonal. Orgasming, as the pinnacle of our erotic experience, is the floating, merging, dancing of our spiritual energies—a mysterious breathing of the entire bodymind.

Orgasming moves us into that rapturous timespace in which our erotic nature expresses *"I-am-That!"* or *"That-Thou-Art!"* In Sanskrit this is *Tat Tvam Asi*—and it means that I am not my egotism, and there is no "other." Rather, I am a pulse or vibration of the diaphragm of the entire universe.

21

The Divinity of Human Sexuality

Our traditional belief systems about spirituality usually require us to celebrate life not in the here-and-now, but rather in the there-and-then.

The traditional belief systems that have dominated the history of western culture encourage us, in various ways, to barter our experience of the present for the promise of a future. This caters to our egotism's ambition to believe not only that it is "Right, Proper, True and Effective," but that it is also real and permanent.

Yet all phenomena are impermanent. The future is actually non-existent, as is the past, and human cognition can only recognize and construct the future in terms of its *re*-presentation of the past.

It is an anathema to these belief systems that the presencing of the present might be all that *is,* and that "God" dwells in the here-and-now of our experience.

Our traditional belief systems about sexuality usually require us not to celebrate our erotic energies, but rather to treat them as a dangerous power that has to be controlled, placed under house-arrest and rehabilitated. Moralizing ideologies insist that our sensual and sexual nature is inherently unhealthy and the cause of much of the world's ailments. Our socialization and acculturation ensure our traumatization.

We become disconnected from our sourcing in erotic energies. Alienated from this sensual and sexual wellspring, we get to choose only between phobic and obsessive modes of compulsivity. Our egotism insists that we forego our potential for erotic ecstasy, and settle for only the limited thrills of sexification. We become sensually frustrated and sexually conflicted. We have effectively learned that our erotic potential needs to be oppressed, suppressed and repressed, for the safety of the human community. But the truth is quite the reverse.

Isn't it about time that we relinquished our allegiance to these traditional beliefs about spirituality and sexuality? That we ceased to reproduce the moralizing ideologies promulgated by the establishments of church and state? Isn't it about time that we set ourselves free? Isn't it about time that we embraced the divinity of human sexuality, and set our divine selves free?

Our spirituality inheres to our erotic potential.
Our erotic energies are Holy Spirit,
flowing within, through and all around us.

In our western culture, traditional belief systems—our attachment to them and our readiness to impose them upon our children—are precisely what have prevented us from understanding that human spirituality inheres to our erotic potential, that our erotic energies are Holy Spirit that pulsates and undulates within, through and all around the conduit of our embodiment.

Prevalent, but mistaken, belief systems have prohibited us from listening to "God" as presence in the here-and-now of our erotic energies. Instead, they uphold the ideology of domination, possession and conquest, and require us to perform obeisance to a judgmental "God"—an authoritarian deity who is somewhere "out there," promising us a future in the "there-and-then" if we obey *his* desires.

On the plane of "earthly" affairs, our egotism treats itself as if it were this "God." It implements its ambition to control and exploit whatever is "other"—whether oppressed minorities, the planet, or our own alienated sensuality and sexuality. Traditional belief systems—the religious establishment—are precisely what have coerced us away from spiritual experiencing the celebration of life, imprisoning us instead in morbid and sexually oppressive articles of faith.

In this society, traditional belief systems—and again, our attachment to them, and our readiness to impose them upon our children—are precisely what have prevented us from understanding that human sexuality need not be treated with fear and ignorance. It is true that our erotic potential is, in a certain sense, "dangerous"—dangerous at a communal level to the ongoing empowerment of religious and political establishments, and dangerous at a personal level to the ongoing empowerment of our egotism, with its determination to perpetuate our suffering. But traditional belief systems are what have prohibited us from understanding that it is actually our sensual frustrations and our sexual conflicts that are at the root of the human tragedy of unnecessary suffering. They have prohibited us from exploring our erotic energies so that we might discover that these energies are to be trusted, rather than feared. Truthfully, however, the following is the case:

*Our erotic energies are to be trusted
because they follow a naturally ethical course
aligning themselves with the spiritual vibration of the universe,
and they are to be trusted because they are the
healing power within our lives.*

We live alienated from the experience of this natural ethicality, precisely because we suppress and repress our erotic potential. And so we live alienated from the knowledge that the ethicality of our sexual-spirituality is radically different from the one-thousand-and-one anti-sexual rules and regulations to which our socialization and acculturation have subjected us. Traditional belief systems about our erotic potential are precisely what have perpetuated this alienation from our sourcing in its sexual-spiritual energies.

Through the exploration of our sensual and sexual nature,
we find that "God" is presence,
that godliness is everywhere and in everything,
and that divinity inheres to these erotic energies,
which constitute the essence of our being-in-the-world.

Perhaps the most fundamental way in which our socialization and acculturation betrays us—not only subjecting us to the oppression of our erotic inclinations, but also causing us to internalize anti-sexual rules and regulations in the suppression and repression of our erotic impulses—is that it makes so many of us ardent believers in the axiom that erotic freedom imperils sexual health. This is a lie. It is a ubiquitous delusion based on our failure to understand our erotic potential, and accordingly our failure to understand the principles of sexual health. I believe that these chapters have amply demonstrated that

Erotic freedom is essential,
not only for our sexual health and healing,
but also for our spiritual health, healing, and happiness.

In this beginning of the 21st Century, the human community is desperately crying out for emotional and spiritual health. But this will never come through a revival of belief systems, moralizing ideologies, and articles of faith. For, as we have seen, these inevitably lead, sooner or later, to fundamentalism and fascism—which is, indeed, what we are facing today.

> *Humanity's emotional and spiritual health will only come from liberating our sensual and sexual potential.*

In the context of human desperation, I think we need to be mindful of the following three precepts:

➢ We are well advised to be wary of any "spiritual perspective" that promotes revised articles of faith, a revival of moralizing ideologies, or revelations of "new" beliefs, all of which are tricks by which human egotism seeks to reassert its anti-sexual agenda.

➢ We are well advised to be wary of any "spiritual vision" that panders to our chattering mind's readiness to be enticed and seduced by superstitions, magical happenings, and promises of supernatural events, rather than grounding itself on the experiential and existential realities of our erotic nature. There are miracles in abundance within the bodymind of every one of us, with its exuberance of erotic energies—so it is a trick of our chattering mind to distract our attention away from the realities of our sensual and sexual prayerfulness.

➢ We are well advised to be wary of any "spiritual practice" that is divorced from the sensual and sexual playfulness of our erotic potential.

> *A "spiritual practice" that dishonors our genitals,*
> *rather than celebrating them,*
> *is not authentic,*
> *for the glories of our genitals are the altar for spiritual practice.*

Any "practice" that disavows the energies coming from our root chakra—pretending that only the energies that enter us from above are to be honored—is profoundly mistaken. Only if we are applauded for taking off our clothes and dancing naked, literally and figuratively, empty and alone in front of the glories of this universe, will we know that we are with a community of genuinely spiritual practitioners.

Emotional and spiritual health requires the liberation of our erotic potential. And yet, as I have argued here:

> America today is the most sexually hypocritical and paradoxical society that has ever existed in human history—for it is the most striking example of a culture choking on its own sexification. As we have discussed, in a sexified society, anti-sexual forces feed off the very sexiness to which they are allegedly opposed, and the sexiness of those who fancy themselves on the cutting-edge of cultural change is often little more than a posturing reaction to the anti-sexual faction. With the sexification of a culture, both sexiness and anti-sexiness deter and distract us from deepening our appreciation of the power of our sexual-spiritual energies.

It must be emphasized again that

Without erotic freedom, sexual health is a myth.
Freedom is a necessary condition
if our sexuality is to be expressed safely, sanely and consensually.

Moreover, without erotic freedom, spiritual practice is a sham. Today, we all cry out for emotional and spiritual healing. Today, as much and perhaps more than ever, we need the emancipation of our erotic potential for spiritual reasons. And yet,

Our egotism or chattering mind chatters fearfully in an incessant effort both to exploit the power of libidinal energy, and to control it, channelize it, obstruct it, build over it, immobilize it, or "de-sexualize" and "de-spiritualize" it—as if by the incessant and compulsive repetition of identities, positions and stories that suppress and repress the energy that runs exuberantly within and through us, our egotistic mind could assure itself of the validity and permanence of its own existence.

In this social and cultural context, we need to take a stand for our erotic potential. We need to stand for the truth that

Erotic freedom is essential
for sexual health and for spiritual wellbeing.
We need to bear witness to the truthfulness of this,
and to do so we will need to bear witness
to the divinity of human sexuality.

Bearing witness to the truthfulness of the divinity of our erotic energies, and the need to free them for the sake of our sexual health, our emotional healing, and spiritual journey through this life, is a risky venture—in relation to which, I have seven suggestions.

➢ We must celebrate life, and we must celebrate especially sacred *touching* as reverence for the interconnectedness of all things, and we must celebrate especially the glories of our genitals as the altar for any authentically spiritual practice. We must celebrate our sensual and sexual being-in-the-world abundantly, exuberantly, and without restraint.

➤ We must start by releasing our selves from the suppressive and repressive processes that generate our shame and guilt, our anxiety and conflict, over our erotic nature. This is a workplay of personal growth, and it is also a spiritual adventure. It is aided by our awareness that every sensual and sexual expression in which we participate is a sacred act of worship. Sex is prayerful, and our spiritual practice is the way of the "bodyprayerpath." For our emotional and spiritual healing, we need to "go wild" on this path—to invite our selves to breathe freely, to move freely, to dance freely, to sound out our energy freely, and to vibrate freely into our orgasming.

➤ We must live by the spiritual "Law" that authentic erotic expression is always safe, sane and consensual, and to do this we must commit to live by the "five beautiful intentions," which are to revere all life, to respect the belongingness of things, to celebrate the sanctity of our passions, to express our truthfulness, and to honor the temple of our bodymind.

➤ We must articulate our insights, not only that the pleasures and thrills of sexification are an impoverished and compulsive substitute for the fullness of our sensual and sexual potential, but also that, beyond all the fear and ignorance of our erotic desires—whether compulsively phobic or compulsively obsessive—authentic sensual and sexual expression is a naturally ethical and freely flowing manifestation of our divinity.

➤ We must take a stand, on the social and cultural level, against the oppression of any and all forms of human sexual expression. We must do this because we recognize that we are living in a world, in which religious and political institutions represent powerful anti-sexual forces (that promulgate moralizing ideologies, oppressive beliefs, and persecutory tactics). And we must do this with devotion, because, at an alarming rate, the world is becoming increasingly fundamentalist and fascistic.

➢ We must also act to facilitate and nurture the erotic freedom, sexual health and spiritual wellbeing of all others, and especially of our children.

➢ Finally, we must celebrate life in the spiritual awareness of our divine selves as a conduit for Holy Spirit—recognizing that only through the freeing of our erotic potential can we move not only into compassion, appreciation, and grace, but also into our birthright of joy, bliss, ecstasy. We must enlighten ourselves—dancing naked, empty and alone in the universe—and thus fall into the truthfulness of that supreme flow of the universe, which is the Sacred Unity of Love.

ACKNOWLEDGEMENTS AND APPRECIATIONS

Although written during my term of office as President of the *American Association of Sex Educators, Counselors, and Therapists*, I need to be very clear that I am solely responsible for the opinions expressed in this book, and that I make no claim that my views represent the opinions of anyone else.

This is also true as I express my appreciation to individuals in the field of sexuality and sexual health, for whose contributions to me personally (directly or indirectly through their writings), and to the world in general, I am, in my heart, deeply grateful. That said, I want to thank (in alphabetical order):

> Margot Anand, Juliet Anderson, Patti Britton, Vern Bullough, Mantak Chia, Lia Michele Clarkson, Stan Dale, Alain Daniélou, Joy Davidson, Nik Douglas, Bob Francoeur, Edgar Gregersen, Marty Klein, Peggy Kleinplatz, Alphonso Lingis, Deena Metzger, Jeff Montgomery, Daniel Odier, Candida Royale, Howie Ruppel, Bill Stayton, David Steinberg, Kenneth Ray Stubbs, Beverly Whipple.

Additionally, my gratitude goes to Barrie Ruth Straus and Mary Garofalakis for their editorial suggestions.

I would also like to thank the many teachers I have had on my spiritual path, whose names need not be mentioned here.

And finally, I would like to think that this book is dedicated to my dear son, to my precious stepdaughters, to their generation, and to tantric practitioners everywhere.

ABOUT THE AUTHOR

Barnaby B. Barratt plays and works as a certified psychoanalyst, sexuality educator, sex therapist, and tantric facilitator. Initially educated in England, he earned doctoral degrees in Psychology and Social Relations from Harvard University, and in Clinical and Educational Sexology from the Institute for Advanced Study of Human Sexuality. Barnaby completed postdoctoral research at the University of Michigan's Neuropsychiatric Institute; held the position of Professor of Family Medicine, Psychiatry and Behavioral Neurosciences at Wayne State University (Detroit) for several years; and was elected to the Presidency of the American Association of Sex Educators, Counselors and Therapists. The author of *The Way of the BodyPrayerPath* (Xlibris, 2004) and other books—as well as numerous scientific, professional and journalistic publications—Barnaby is a Fellow of the American Psychological Association, a diplomate of the American Academy of Psychoanalytic Psychology, a life member of the American Philosophical Association, and an ordained minister for his tantric practice; he is also a member of Amnesty International and the American Civil Liberties Union. Barnaby is available for private consultations, as well as lectures, workshops and seminars. He may be contacted through *www.BodyPrayerPath.org*.